Globalisation and Advertising in Emerging Economies

Brazil, Russia, India and China are four of the largest and most dynamic contemporary emerging economies in the world. Strong economic growth in each of these economies has been accompanied by the expansion of the advertising and consumer goods sectors. Using a series of country studies this book explores the dynamics of global capitalism from the perspective of global advertising.

The book highlights the ongoing expansion of advertising and consumerism against the wider socio-economic, political, environmental sustainability and cultural contexts. It provides fresh insights about contemporary global priorities, and argues that advertising plays a key role linking culture and the economy. By presenting individual case studies of advertising campaigns, it offers examples of the globalisation of specific brands. Environmental implications of the expansion of advertising and its role in stimulating consumerism are explored in the context of the four emerging economies. The book compares and contrasts the individual country profiles, and makes an assessment of the validity of the argument regarding their projected importance and the likelihood of their future dominance of the global economy.

Lynne Ciochetto is an Associate Professor at the Institute of Communication Design, Massey University, New Zealand. Her research interests include sociology, anthropology, development studies, environmental sustainability and graphic design.

Routledge studies in international business and the world economy

Globalisation and Advertising in Emerging Economies

Brazil, Russia, India and China

Lynne Ciochetto

Routledge
Taylor & Francis Group

LONDON AND NEW YORK

First published 2011
by Routledge
2 Park Square, Milton Park, Abingdon, Oxon OX14 4RN

Simultaneously published in the USA and Canada
by Routledge
711 Third Avenue, New York, NY 10017

Routledge is an imprint of the Taylor & Francis Group, an informa business

British Library Cataloguing in Publication Data
A catalogue record for this book is available from the British Library

Library of Congress Cataloging in Publication Data
Ciochetto, Lynne.
Globalisation and advertising in emerging economies: Brazil, Russia,
India, and China/Lynne Ciochetto.
    p. cm. – (Routledge studies in international business and the world
    economy; 51)
    Includes bibliographical references and index.
    1. Capitalism. 2. Advertising–Economic aspects. 3. Globalization–
    Economic aspects. I. Title.
    HB501.C56 2011
    337.09172′4–dc23
                                                                    2011026129

ISBN: 978-0-415-56200-3 (hbk)
ISBN: 978-0-203-14486-2 (ebk)

Typeset in Times New Roman
by Wearset Ltd, Boldon, Tyne and Wear

Contents

Tables

Abbreviations

BCG	Boston Consulting Group
BRICs	Brazil, Russia, India and China (collective term)
CEO	chief executive officer
ESOMAR	European Society for Opinion and Market Research
FMCG	fast-moving consumer goods
GDP	gross domestic product
GFN	Global Footprint Network
GNP	gross national product
HLL	Hindustan Lever Limited (pre-2007)
HUL	Hindustan Unilever (post-2007)
IMF	International Monetary Fund
IPCC	International Panel on Climate Change
MSM	Microsoft's Portal for SMS
NGO	non-governmental organisation
PPP	purchasing power parity
SMS	short messaging service
SOE	State-owned enterprise
UNSD	United Nations Statistics Division
USLC	United States Library of Congress
WARC	World Advertising Research Council
WOMM	word of mouth marketing
WTO	World Trade Organisation

Acknowledgements

I wish to thank Massey University, and in particular Pro Vice Chancellor Sally Morgan for her support. I am most grateful for the time to write the book granted by the university's Leave & Ancillary Appointments Committee, and for the funding to visit the BRIC countries. It was also beneficial to attend a number of conferences where I explored themes later brought together in this book. Other people who have been of enormous help and support at Massey are Ken Elliot, who saved me countless times from computer meltdowns, Paul Orsman of the Massey Library staff, who helped kick-start each project with sourcing material, and colleagues who proofed earlier conference papers. Lastly I am truly grateful for the superb work Anna Rogers has done editing and polishing the final text.

I also want to thank the advertising practitioners who were so generous with their time and information: Prem Narayan, Deputy President for Planning, and Rajan S. Krishnan, President Strategic Planning at Ogilvy & Mather India, Art Director Guime Davidson at W/Brasil and Walter Longo, VP Strategic Planning and Innovation, Y&R Brazil. Others who supplied important background information were journalist Preeti Chaturvedi, and Kavita Rayirath, who worked at O&M India between 2000 and 2009.

1 Introduction

'What used to be considered the developing countries of the Third World are quickly becoming the emerging economies of the next world.'
(Noreen O'Leary, 'The Rise of the BRIC', *Adweek*, 2008)

In 2000 the rise of the BRIC economies – Brazil, Russia, India and China – was merely an interesting phenomenon, but a decade later the balance of world power has changed. (The term BRIC was first used by James O'Neill, head of the research group at Goldman Sachs in 2001.) This book will explore the changes in the dynamics of global advertising as they have played out in these four countries, which have captured a lot of media attention in the last decade. India and China have become the growth powerhouses of the world, even weathering the western financial crisis; the importance of Russia and Brazil lies in their natural resources. O'Neill's 2001 prediction that the BRICs would join the dominant economies in 2050 has since been revised. It is now considered that they could be equivalent in size to the G7 by 2032 (O'Neill and Stupnytska, 2009). This book looks at the implications of this projected growth and economic expansion in terms of global advertising, consumer goods markets and the environmental effects of vastly increased levels of consumption.

The BRIC economies are now seen to be the dynamos of future growth for the consumer goods industries of the industrialised nations. Advertising is the lifeblood of such industries, making links between the economy and culture and thus stimulating product consumption. In recent decades advertising has followed the consumer industries into emerging markets. It both stimulates product demand and acts as a force for cultural change through the associations it makes between key values and products. Advertising has evolved in mature markets and expanded into emerging markets, responding to the quite different challenges they present. By fracturing markets, constantly changing media and technologies make advertising increasingly complex. The world has changed dramatically in the last decade and will do so again in the next, but the multinational giants, the world's largest producers of consumer goods, are still the largest advertisers, and they are principally in the fast-moving consumer goods (FMCG) sector. The largest global advertising agency complexes, where ownership is still highly concentrated, have also remained fairly constant.

Background

The BRIC economies are bringing a vast number of potential consumers into the market economy, most of them for the first time. Population projections for 2050 estimate the size of the BRIC nations to grow to 3.2 billion, but the most important figure for economists, advertisers and the environment is the projected expansion of the middle classes.

The middle classes have been defined by a range of criteria, including patterns of consumption, disposable income levels, lifestyle, behaviour and values (Ravallion, 2009). Most relevant here are income levels, particularly disposable income levels, since they relate to patterns of consumption. Using the criterion of income levels above $3,000 per year to define the middle classes in the BRICs, O'Neill predicted in 2008 that, in the next ten years, they would increase by 400 per cent. In 2007 Wilson and Dragusanu (2008), also of Goldman Sachs, defined the middle classes as having an income of $6,000–$10,000, adjusted for purchasing power parity (PPP). In India the size of that group has grown from 1 per cent (ten million) in 2000 to 5 per cent (56.2 million) in 2007. China made the transition earlier: in 1990 this group was 1 per cent (11 million) but by 2007 had grown to 35 per cent (458 million). This rapidly expanding consumer group is a magnet for international marketers. Ravallion (2009) from the World Bank sees it as useful to differentiate the 'developing world middle classes' ($2–$13 per day, 2005 figures), from the 'developed world middle classes' (living on

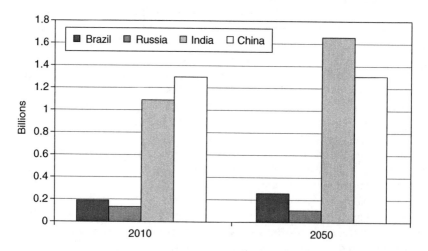

Figure 1.1 BRICs populations 2010 and 2050 (Sources: United States Bureau of the Census International Database (2011a,b,c,d); (2011a) Brazil. Online. Available at www.census.gov/ipc/www/idb/country.php (accessed 21 March 2011); (2011b) Russia. Online. Available at www.census.gov/ipc/www/idb/country.php (accessed 21 March 2011); (2011c) India. Online. Available at www.census.gov/ipc/www/idb/country.php (accessed 21 March 2011); (2011d) China. Online. Available at www.census.gov/ipc/www/idb/country.php (accessed 21 March 2011).

more than $13 per day, the US poverty line in 2005). In one of history's great achievements, India and China have managed to lift millions out of poverty in the last 20–30 years. This change will have enormous global economic and environmental impacts.

The evolution of the global economy

'A country must maintain and improve growth conditions in order to achieve its potential.'

(James O'Neill, 'The Brics and Beyond', 2007)

Since 1945 many Third World economies and markets have made the transition from 'undeveloped' to 'developing' to 'emerging'. One of the fundamental assumptions of contemporary capitalism is that 'growth' rates are an indicator of national economic health: the higher the growth rates, the healthier the economy. Growth has driven globalisation, which has gathered momentum since the 1980s. American and British companies first started expanding internationally in the nineteenth century when mass production expanded the number of products available, and they began to be exported. The advertising industry was born out of the need to sell the vast quantities of new products pouring from the newly established factories. Soap and pharmaceutical manufacturers were among the first to export products internationally, and were soon joined by the tobacco and oil companies. Advances in mass production – in the form of the production line pioneered by Henry Ford in 1913 – increased the speed and quantity of goods produced in the 1920s. The automobile ushered in an era of oil dependence and the twentieth century has since been defined by its increased reliance on oil for energy and the myriad of other oil by-products.

The 1920s marked the first era of large-scale road building in the United States, and consolidated the age of the automobile. The American economy flourished after the Second World War when the industrial machine of the war economy was redeployed into consumer goods production. Other western industrialised economies also developed rapidly in the next decades. As standards of living improved consumption expanded dramatically; American society underwent a major transformation in the 1950s and 1960s as people's basic needs for food, clothing, housing, services and employment were met, along with the fundamental services of water, power and sanitation. By the 1960s, and the end of post-war reconstruction in Europe and Japan, standards of living had also risen in these countries. As economies expanded businesses grew in strength and began to expand internationally, though most of their attention focused on the markets of western industrialised countries.

During the same period many colonies achieved independence and in the following 'development decades' new governments stimulated their economies so they could 'catch up' with the living standards of the industrialised west. Both western economies and the developing countries embraced neo-liberal modernisation models based on simplistic assumptions that industrialisation was the key to development. With 'growth' seen as the goal, and industrialisation the means to that goal, many countries borrowed heavily to embark on industrialisation, a process that they protected behind tariffs. There was no recognition that many of the factors that had supported nineteenth century industrialisation were missing from developing nations in the twentieth century: finance, materials and profits from colonies, technology and an expanding middle class consumer base. There was a wave of import-substitution industrialisation in developing economies but small internal markets quickly became saturated. Countries then focused on production for export. They borrowed heavily from such international organisations as the World Bank and the International Monetary Fund (IMF), or from private banks, for industrial development and the building of infrastructure. As Perkins claimed in *Confessions of an Economic Hit Man* (2006), private consultants often encouraged high levels of borrowing, and inflated projected gains, in the full knowledge that countries would get into debt.

During the 1980s the internationalisation of western business accelerated, facilitated by improved communication technology and digital commerce, which made international business transactions and operations much easier. Western markets were deregulated during the Reagan and Thatcher era of neo-liberalist free market economics. Mergers and acquisitions in the international corporate sector resulted in extremely large corporations that actually reduced 'free market' competition. Many consumer goods-producing companies were transformed into what A.C. Nielsen called 'megabrand complexes' (2003), epitomised by the likes of Unilever, Procter & Gamble, Nestlé and Coca-Cola.

During the 1980s and 1990s many emerging or developing economies experienced financial problems: unable to repay debt, they faced crises similar to that experienced by the global economy in 2008–09. Financial assistance from the IMF and World Bank was made conditional on the implementation of structural readjustment policies, economic deregulation of the economy and the removal of tariffs and trade restrictions. Of the BRIC economies, Brazil, Russia and India were affected. The Indian government liberalised its economy in 1991 and Brazil did the same during the 1990s. Russia also got into economic strife in the 1980s, suffering from the cumulative effects of decades of the command economy. A 'shock therapy' structural adjustment programme implemented in the 1990s, with the assistance of the World Bank, was so drastic that it crippled the economy for more than a decade and living standards declined (MacFarquhar, 2007).

In industrialised countries during the 1980s wages were continuing to rise and markets were starting to flatten. To lower production costs, companies began moving their production facilities to 'developing' (i.e. poorer) countries to take advantage of cheaper wages, less stringent regulations and lax environmental laws. These nations were keen to benefit from the jobs and money such companies could provide and in many cases there was a 'race to the bottom' as contractors competed for orders. The companies could threaten to take their business to other countries if the business environment was not 'friendly'. As a result developing countries often made major tax concessions, which still continue in what are known as 'special economic zones'. Taking a different path, the 'Asian Tigers', led by Japan and including Taiwan, Singapore and Korea, were rapidly transformed into industrialised societies with much higher standards of living, using more of the savings of their frugal citizens for industrialisation.

Workers who became part of this internationalisation of labour, and the outsourcing of global branded production, were particularly hard-hit, often earning less than a minimum living wage (Hertz, 2001; Klein, 2000; Korten, 1995). Basketball star Michael Jordan was paid more by Nike in one year than the total paid to the Indonesian workers who produced the shoes he advertised (Korten, 1995). In countries like China workers continue to be overworked and underpaid. Child slavery persists in India (BBC World News, 23 May 2010) and a number of other countries that supply cheap goods to industrialised markets. In many product categories, such as clothing and electronic goods, prices actually declined in western markets during the 1990s. Because incomes did not decline, purchasers began to buy more products and mass consumerism accelerated, facilitated by greater use of consumer credit and credit cards.

As multinational companies have grown over the last three decades so has their share of the world economy (Buckman, 2004). As markets in emerging economies liberalised during the 1990s both foreign and local business benefited. Industrial development expanded, along with foreign investment, and benefits flowed out into the economy, stimulating economic growth (Stiglitz, 2002). Economic growth brought jobs, rising standards of living for some sectors of the population and an expansion of the middle classes. There were changes in many sectors, including the increased consumption of consumer products, energy and food. As more multinational corporations entered the developing countries they saw the potential of selling – especially personal products, soft drinks and household products (detergents) – to these new consumers, and the opening of eastern bloc countries in the 1990s meant more participants in the global marketplace. The potential markets are enormous: India and China alone make up nearly 40 per cent of the world's population.

The globalisation of the economy in the 1990s and 2000s

Since the 1980s international businesses have expanded both territorially and in magnitude, with mergers and acquisitions creating significantly larger entities. The head offices of these corporations tend to be in North America, Europe or East Asia, but their spread is global. This expansion has resulted in increasing domination over national economies, a process Buckman (2004) describes as the development of the 'global trade supermarket'. Nearly 70 per cent of world trade is currently controlled by the largest 500 corporations, and about a third is conducted between different arms of the same company. Of the world's top 150 economic entities in 2009, 59 per cent were corporations. Many of the largest companies have revenues greater than the gross domestic product of most states. In 2009 the revenues of Wal-Mart Stores, the largest corporation, exceeded the GDPs of 174 countries, including Sweden, Saudi Arabia and Venezuela, and employed more than two million people, more than the entire population of Qatar. If it was a country, Wal-Mart would rank 22nd largest in the world (Keys and Malnight, 2010).

The financial sector plays an increasingly important part in the contemporary global economy. In December 2006 total international banking assets were equivalent in value to around $29 trillion, roughly 63 per cent of world GDP (Fergusson, 2008). The financial crisis of 2008–09, which came about because of 'deregulation' in the American and European financial sector, showed clearly how lack of regulation encourages speculation and criminal behaviour. One of the largest culprits was Goldman Sachs, which was fined by the US Government, though the amount was negligible compared with the profits they had made (BBC World News, 17 July 2010). The economic crisis did not have a significant impact on the growth of India and China, the two major economies with large internal markets, which were proved correct in deregulating slowly and cautiously. The crisis could well mark the end of western economic dominance and a turning point for the global economy ('Recession boosts status of emerging markets', Bloomberg, 2010). China's ownership of American debt increased significantly in the 2000s. The 'shock therapy' liberalisation process in Russia, the only industrialised BRIC country, vindicates Monbiot's proposition (2009) that 'business without regulation is scarcely different from organised crime'. Lack of regulation meant that organised crime *did* take over the Russian economy. In the west lack of regulation has caused similar economic damage, though governments there seem unable to treat the perpetrators as criminals.

The 'age of thrift' and 'the new normal' versus 'consuming your way out of recession'

The 2008 financial crisis coincided with an increasing awareness of climate change and sustainability issues. Businesses are having to adapt to the 'new normal' where consumers are 'spending less, saving more and "shopping smarter"' (Wal-Mart, 2009). Economists and politicians promoting consumption as a way out of recession are looking at 'emerging markets'. The major American automobile corporations in particular are focusing on China, where most have set up production facilities. As McKinsey has noted, many major companies are starting to treat China as their 'home market' ('China receiving unique approach from brands', *Newsweek*, 2010). The Chinese and Indian Governments have also become painfully aware that their internal markets offer the safest key to future growth and economic stability because they are less affected by external economic factors. Loss of export markets cost jobs for Chinese workers. Now the Chinese Government wants the traditionally frugal Chinese people to consume more. In 2004, in the 11th five-year plan, it committed to raising the living standards of the poor and reinforced this pledge in the 12th five-year plan (*The Economist*, October 2010). Greater consumption by the vast populations of India and China will have major environmental implications for the planet.

Global advertising

'Advertising revenue is a good indicator of the state of global business.'
(BBC World News, March 2010)

The big players in global advertising are the world's largest consumer goods companies. The most advertised products tend to be repeat-purchase consumer goods or FMCGs, often with the highest profit margin. Companies can spend up to 25 per cent of their revenues on advertising (BBC World News, March 2010). The financial strength of the company, the product category and the disposable income levels of the target population all influence expenditure levels in different markets.

According to Martin Sorrell, 'Advertising is all about finding out what the consumer wants and giving it to them.' There is a certain amount of truth in this statement, along with his other claim, that 'you don't sell a consumer a bad product twice' (ibid.). However there are many other variables at work and advertising does play an important role in shaping what consumers want (Belk and Zhou, 1987; Pollay, 1986). In emerging markets like India the first task of consumer goods companies when they arrived in the 1920s was to educate consumers about new products or to transfer their buying from traditional unbranded bulk products to branded products. Procter & Gamble is currently facing a similar issue with marketing its Pampers nappies (diapers), a new and relatively expensive product, in emerging economies (*New York Times*, 16 December 2009).

The built-in obsolescence of the contemporary capitalist system requires the constant emergence of new products. The role of advertising is to stimulate desire for those products and translate this into purchases. Such products are launched with a great deal of hype and marketing: look at the launch of the new Apple iPhone in June 2010. But bringing out new products has become increasingly difficult. According to Adams (2010), more than 65 per cent of new products fail even when they are launched by multinational companies. Coca-Cola had to discontinue an energy drink it launched in India in the early 2000s. When the company considered the market was ready it introduced another energy drink, Burn, in 2009 (*Economic Times*, 16 December 2009). Large companies may not be immune to failure but they can afford to wait a considerable time before turning a profit. Coca-Cola's advertising expenditure was $2.4 billion in 2009, making the company the world's sixth largest advertiser (The Coca-Cola Company cited on www.adbrands.net/us.cocacola_us. htm, 16 January 2011).

Though the largest companies in the world are not the largest advertisers, the estimated expenditure of leading global advertisers in 2009 was still larger than the GDP of many countries. Procter & Gamble has been the world's largest advertiser for most of the last decade. More than the total advertising expenditure in Russia of $9 billion (GroupM, 2010). The American company Ford is larger than the GDP of New Zealand (Keys and

Malnight, 2011). Large global advertisers play a key role in national economies. This role includes a large range of support industries and companies,
among them the major market research companies that evolved out of marketers' desire have more accurate information about consumers. Many of
these research companies are linked with the major advertising agency complexes: Mindshare (WPP), GroupM (WPP), ZenithOptimedia (Publicis
Groupe) and Magna (Interpublic). Despite the amount of research done, the

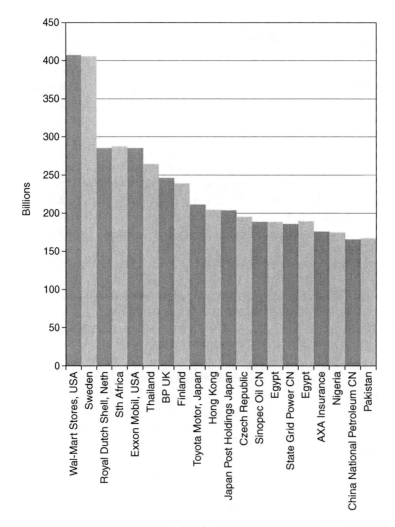

Figure 1.2 Leading global companies in comparison to GDP of nations 2009 (Source: Keys,
T. and Malnight, T. W. (14 January 2011) *Corporate Clout: The Influence of the
World's Largest 100 Economic Entities*. Online. Available www.globaltrends.
com/features/shapers-and-influencers/66-corporate-clout-the-influence-of-the-
worlds-largest-100-economic-entities (accessed 15 March 2011).

success or failure of advertising strategies is still unpredictable but the cumulative effect of advertising is certainly successful in stimulating consumption (Assadourian, 2010).

In the last decade market research has become more sophisticated, with many research companies now conducting cross-cultural studies of consumers to take account of emerging markets like India (for example GfK Roper, McKinsey Company, Goldman Sachs, Millward Brown, TGI). Researchers are particularly interested in patterns of media use, purchasing preferences and online behaviour. The attraction and uptake of new technology is closely linked to changing values, including the almost universal appeal of modernity.

When foreign companies moved into new markets they first brought with them a 'west is best' attitude but soon had to change their approach and become aware of local cultural values when marketing their products. Local companies have the advantage of being familiar and of knowing their customers' tastes (Beinhocker *et al*., 2007). Their products are usually cheaper than foreign branded products. Apart from electronic products and new technologies, which seem to have widespread appeal based on what they deliver, other products tap into cultural values to create brand value in a highly competitive market. Brand values can be loosely applied as they have no essential relationship to the product feature. After all, soap can be sold as inexpensive, pure, sweet-smelling, modern, popular and promoting cleanliness, which in turn can be related to social acceptance, economic success, sexuality or health (Pollay and Gallagher, 1990).

Understanding cultural values is a crucial dimension of advertising and marketing. People do not buy products they do not want or have no use for and they need to value products before they will buy them. One of the ways that advertising appeals to consumers is by associating products with key cultural values. In this process certain values are reinforced and others diminished (Pollay, 1986; Pollay and Gallagher, 1990). Some values are shared by all cultures: valuing children, honouring parents, good health, economic stability and work (Zaitseva, 2008). Advertising cannot help but reinforce some of these values but in other ways it can distort traditional culture by promoting consumerism.

The globalisation of the media and advertising

The globalisation of the 1980s brought about fracturing of both the media and the advertising market over the next decade. Gone forever was the easily accessible single mass market watching the family television set together in the evenings. New media options changed the media profile and stimulated major changes in communication and behaviour. The advertising industry also changed significantly. Although newspaper advertising revenues remained strong throughout the twentieth century, by the 1990s television's share of the world advertising market was increasing annually. By 2003 global newspaper advertising accounted for 30.8 per cent of world advertising expenditure, television for 38.8 per cent (World Association of Newspapers, 2004). Currently online advertising is being accorded 'walk on water' status but let us not forget the 'end of print' in the 1990s. The effectiveness of online advertising and returns on investment have yet to be proven (World Advertising Research Council (WARC), 2009). It is likely that, once the hype dies down, online advertising will be incorporated into a slightly modified media landscape.

Though television became the dominant media for advertising in western industrialised societies after the 1960s, print remained the main vehicle for advertising in the developing world, where high levels of poverty meant very low television ownership levels. These began to increase as disposable income levels rose; when people are poor they spend more than half their income on food. Television ownership began to expand in emerging economies in the 1980s and the trend accelerated in the 1990s. Satellite television further facilitated the expansion of media options, though in some countries its popularity increased only after content was localised, and by the end of the 1990s most advertising on multinational channels was localised, however artificial that localisation may have been (Thomas, 2006). MTV, for example, was not successful with young Indian people until it broadcast local content (Cullity, 2004), reinforcing de Mooij's opinion (2003) that a global teenage community is one of 'the myths of global marketing'. During the 1990s television advertising became more important in many emerging economies. Global advertising expenditure went up dramatically because of the expansion of corporations, the global agency complexes and the proliferation of television channels with the liberalisation of the media in most markets. Satellite and cable television added further channel options, and pay TV helped to segregate the affluent market and made it easier to target. Another significant change during the 1990s was the significant increase in marketing to young people and children.

The profile of the media in the BRIC economies is similar to that in other emerging economies. Television advertising became dominant in the 1990s, except in India, where print still has a slight lead. Increasing domination of transnational corporations over the international economy did not extend to control over the media and in the BRICs control of the media remains in the hands of the government, except in Brazil where ownership is concentrated in one major corporation: TV Globo. The globalisation of the media has stimulated an expansion of advertising which has become the major source of media funding. Programming has delivered consumers to advertisers and content is often dictated by advertisers or censored to meet client demands (Matellart, 1991). Advertising and television programme content reinforce each other and product placements blur the boundaries even more (Fowles, 1996). As the reach of media has expanded and options have proliferated, markets have become more fragmented and advertising has become both more global and more targeted to niche markets.

Though its first applications were mainly for business, personal use of the internet became more widespread in the 1990s. The development of companies like Google and Amazon, which provided searching and filtering services, expanded the information capabilities of the internet and stimulated the growth of online commerce. As user numbers sky-rocketed the commercial uses of the internet expanded beyond shopping as companies tried to think of ways to target internet users: banners, advertising, branded content. The 2004 introduction of Web 2.0 brought in the era of social networking with the establishment of Facebook, Bebo, Myspace and YouTube. The internet became an important means of communication, especially for the young, and further expanded the potential of the internet as a marketing tool.

In the last decade the internet has become an essential part of daily life and a routine vehicle for accessing information. It offers different marketing options and a new marketing model. Alternative search and distribution methods, epitomised by Amazon.com and eBay, mean that cumulative sales from sales of thousands of products available online can outsell limited ranges offered by branded goods, what Anderson calls the 'Long Tail' (2006). Internet purchasing in the BRIC economies, and other emerging markets, lags behind the level of the advanced economies, but this could change very quickly. Internet usage and commerce are growing internationally but in each country the profile of internet use and patterns of internet shopping have been locally modified. A recent cross-cultural study found that internet shopping was not very significant in China, while in Brazil 40 per cent of internet users made purchases online. Internet shoppers tended to be wealthier in all six countries studied (Brashear *et al.*, 2009).

One of the most attractive features about online advertising for marketers is measurability. As corporate budgets get leaner it is easier to quantify. Mandese (2009) sees that currently the culture of advertisers using mass media is 'buying big, highly branded media content and advertising messages', while online search advertising is the polar opposite, based on micro-targeting consumers with the most relevant content and advertising messages.

The smartphone is the latest addition to the advertising mix. The bulk of the population in India and China is still poor with limited levels of internet access, but the smartphone enables those not living in absolute poverty to access the internet. This is the new frontier for the media in emerging economies and uptake levels have been rapid. As the technology gets cheaper smartphone ownership will far outstrip computer ownership, and it seems likely that advertising and marketing on smartphones will follow the same pattern. This may also increase advertising expenditure. Advertisers are coming to realise, however, new media can be expensive, even though it is a cheaper option than large-scale television campaigns. The web may be cheaper than TV, but is much more complex and needs much more support (IAB , 2010).

The globalisation of advertising

Contemporary advertising has its roots in the nineteenth century when consumer goods companies first began using advertising to sell products. Products accompanied imperialism and colonialism, particularly throughout the British Empire, which dominated the world. Among the first international products were soap and patent medicines. Patent medicines were among the most advertised products in the 1880s and 1890s. When Coca-Cola was launched in 1886 it was just one of hundreds of similar patent medicines on the market; the marketers of such products were some of the first to 'sell image rather than product' (Prendergast, 1993). Asa Chandler, the man who changed the fortunes of the company, sold Coca-Cola with a blend of religion, capitalism and patriotism, managing its evolution from patent medicine to soft drink by promoting it aggressively (ibid.).

The international expansion of advertising agencies began in the 1920s when some of the largest companies spread throughout the world and their advertising agencies followed. Among the first to do so was the American agency J. Walter Thompson, which worked for General Motors. The Depression of the 1930s, followed by the Second World War, kept the expansion in check, but again Coca-Cola was an exception. During the war the company's promise to make Coca-Cola available to US troops wherever they were stationed gave an enormous boost to its international expansion and turned it into a 'national' drink (ibid.).

International advertising has expanded dramatically in the last 60 years from an estimated \$39 billion in the 1950s (Pieterse, 2004). Because the war was not fought on its territories, the American economy was the first to expand after 1945 as its war industries were quickly redeployed to the production of consumer goods. The enormous number of products that came onto the market needed to be sold and this expansion provided a great boost to American advertising. The 1950s and 1960s were golden years for American advertising, centred in New York's Madison Avenue; the period has been captured vividly in the television series *Mad Men* (2007). The growth of television offered fresh opportunities for advertisers, especially in the United States where television was always commercially funded. By combining sound, images and entertainment, television proved a compelling medium for advertising, bringing it into the living room. In the next decades advertising expenditure expanded in most of the industrialised nations as their economies grew steadily, along with living standards, disposable incomes and consumer purchasing power. There was little interest in selling goods in 'developing' countries because their markets were so much smaller but, as we have seen, during the 1980s corporations began to move their production to developing countries to reduce their labour costs. This was an era of corporate mergers and acquisitions and many corporations became large complexes of brands. Two key approaches to branding were defined by Wang (2008): the 'house of brands' or the 'branded house'. Procter & Gamble takes the former approach: its many brands have their own identities distinct from the parent company. In the branded house option, taken by the likes of Apple, Toyota, LG and the oil companies, the overall umbrella company name drives the product identification, especially in the more expensive and consumer-durable categories, like electronics.

During the 1980s and 1990s these large multinational corporations increased their share of the global economy and dominance of the consumer markets in many countries. The top global advertisers tend to be a narrow list dominated by FMCG companies such as Procter & Gamble, Nestlé, Coca-Cola, Estée Lauder and Unilever (*Advertising Age*, 'Top Global Advertisers 1999', cited in Belch and Belch, 2004). The top global revenue-earning companies are *not* the top advertisers, but tend to be in the oil and auto sectors. Some of the FMCG companies had been selling their products internationally for decades but now many more also started to explore growth opportunities in the international market because economic changes and liberalisation had stimulated economic growth and the middle classes were beginning to expand (Stiglitz, 2002).

The opening of the BRIC economies, especially Russia and China, appeared to offer marketers fabulous opportunities and there was a massive expansion of foreign investment. Advertising expenditure also grew rapidly. Foreign advertising agencies quickly came to dominate these markets and by 2000 there were few independent local agencies in the top ten agencies in any of the BRICs. Their share of world advertising also increased: by 2005 they accounted for 8 per cent of global advertising but 30 per cent of world growth in advertising (ZenithOptimedia, 2005).

In the last decades of the twentieth century the concept of the single mass market became obsolete and new media options multiplied the possibilities for advertisers. International markets, too, diversified. The contemporary supermarket epitomises this trend. In India in 2009 the American retail company Wal-Mart entered into a joint venture with Bharti Enterprises to open a cash-and-carry chain called Best Price Modern Wholesale, where 10,000 products were on offer (*Wall Street Journal*, 29 May 2009). Though relatively small compared with western markets, where the average supermarket contains about 40,000 different products, this marked a huge change in Indian retailing, where only a few contemporary products were branded and well known, and most shopping is still done in markets and small owner-operated shops.

By 2008 global advertising expenditure reached an estimated $643 billion. Since then the financial crisis has dented growth but the slowdown in the west has been partially compensated for by growth in India and China where advertising expenditure has grown more than 10 per cent per year (Assadourian, 2010). Advertising expenditure is starting to expand as the international economy recovers. The increased market share and profits of foreign companies in emerging markets are clear proof that advertising is successful. In 2009 Unilever India (HUL) increased its advertising expenditure by 66 per cent (to $1.3 billion, Rs6.3 billion) after its profits started to decline. Profits then grew to Rs6.5 billion, slightly more than the amount spent on advertising (HUL, 2010), which suggests that advertising does stimulate demand and product sales.

Agencies

The concentration of the international advertising agency sector is comparable to the dominance of a few corporations in certain product categories. In 2004, 12 agency networks belonged to six major owner groups and controlled approximately $164.9 billion, nearly 75 per cent of all media spending (Powel, 2005). That grouping had scarcely changed in 2009 (*Advertising Age*, 2011). Within the umbrella company agencies keep their own autonomy and individuality, to avoid conflicts of interest between competing clients in the parent group. All the major advertising agencies increased their presence as the BRIC economies liberalised in the 1990s. The big agency complexes also tended to set up their own market research companies. ZenithOptimedia are part of Publicis Groupe, while WPP includes Mindshare and GroupM. Strategies became closely tied to market research and much more focused on niche market groups. By the late 1990s most international advertisers had moved beyond using standardised imported campaigns and were customising campaigns to local markets and using local or regional references (Belch and Belch, 2004).

Advertising agency culture

The internal working dynamics of the major advertising agencies also has an impact on the types of advertising campaigns developed and the strategies used in emerging markets. The head offices of the top global agencies are located in the capitals of industrialised countries. Nixon's overview of the evolution of London agencies in the 1990s reveals an agency culture that is very male-dominated, driven by ruthless competitiveness and the demands of insecure career paths where success is measured by advertising awards. There is enormous pressure to be creative, new and different and to make an impact in a highly saturated marketplace (Nixon, 2003; Byrne, 2005). The desire to gain attention often results in the default standby that 'sex sells' and the frontiers of acceptability are constantly being challenged. Head office agencies also have a tendency towards a 'west is best' attitude, which has led to some spectacular campaign failures in the last two decades when campaigns were exported to foreign markets. Advertising strategies appeal to hearts and minds across many cultures by tapping into cultural values, whether these be universal or culturally specific.

Strategies

In recent decades there have been some dramatic changes in advertising strategies, largely in response to opportunities offered by new technologies and expanding markets in emerging economies. The first big change of the twentieth century was the advent of radio in the 1920s, which launched the sponsored soap opera in the US. Another innovation was the use of psychological persuasion to sell products; playing on insecurities, with the product providing the solution. Though radio continues to be important in many markets such as India, in the 1950s television quickly superseded radio in the industrialised countries.

Product profiles have also evolved. By the 1980s, as markets in industrialised countries started becoming saturated, producers responded to flattening growth figures by diversifying and subdividing product categories. The simple nineteenth century cake of soap has been differentiated into many different subcategories of products: body-washes, shampoos for different hair types, conditioners, cleansers. Skincare now includes moisturisers, day creams, night creams, face creams with sunscreen, and anti-ageing creams. Within some categories products have became more similar, a good example being recent trends in automobile body shapes.

As Doctoroff (2005) has said, 'Branding turns a hard sell into a soft kiss'. With the increasing similarity of products, branding became a key mechanism for differentiation within categories. This attempts to associate products with key cultural values, by appealing to emotions. The ultimate goal is to create an 'emotional relationship' with the brand (product). Branding involves the creation of a product personality, then building up brand loyalty based on product ownership and identification with certain values. Successful branding establishes for a product an elaborate set of emotions and meanings, values and lifestyle associations. Nike was an enormously successful branding pioneer. Its competitor Reebok had captured the aerobics market in the 1980s but Nike's 'Just do it' campaign, created by local Oregon agency Wieden & Kennedy, reversed that situation. The slogan was promoted by massive television advertising campaigns that linked the product with aspirational values, and featured basketball star Michael Jordan.

One of the fundamental requirements of branding is enormous expenditure: 'It takes years and a lot of money to build brand recognition and image' (Rita Clifton, CEO Interbrand, on BBC World News, July 2010). Only the larger corporations could afford this and they successfully used branding to increase market share. Coca-Cola spent $1.1 billion in China over 20 years. It arrived in China in 1979 but did not make a profit until 1990 (Weisert, 2001). In 2010 Kraft estimated that to be successful in China it was necessary to spend at least 10 per cent of your budget on advertising ('China holds promise for Kraft', *Financial Times*, 2009). In 2007 the fastest growing advertising sectors were: fast food (brand value growth 22 per cent), luxury (20 per cent), motor fuel (15 per cent), personal care (15 per cent) and technology (14 per cent) (Millward Brown Optimor, cited in Boyce, 2007). Also of interest is how the brand itself has come to have significant economic value. Intangible assets have become more important than tangible assets and brands account for approximately one third of the value of Fortune 500 companies (ibid.).

Branding also epitomises the cultural role played by advertising. At the macro level it promotes materialism and consumerism, as well as modifying culture by the association of products with key cultural values (Pollay, 1986). Foreign brands have not always been welcomed by local consumers. In the 1990s there were consumer backlashes against foreign brands in China and Russia. One of the responses has been brand camouflaging. Where there is considerable loyalty to local brands multinational companies sometimes camouflage their brands and market them as domestic products. Other strategies involve simply buying up the local brands, as Coca-Cola did with Thums Up in India. Coke has a whole range of products with Chinese names and has often developed soft drinks to suit local tastes. McDonald's has also quite successfully localised in many countries. The reverse is also true: other brands that are made in China, like Budweiser and Heineken, are sold as imported and some products seen as Chinese can be owned by joint ventures such as that between Wahaha and Danone (Wang, 2008). ' "Local" is almost always a construct' in this era of joint ventures, mergers and takeovers (ibid.).

During the 1980s and early 1990s, because these new markets represented only a small proportion of their business, advertising agencies tended to export campaigns developed in the major cities. But strategies developed for industrialised markets did not always work. After a few spectacular failures (e.g. Coca-Cola, Cadbury Schweppes), agencies started to appreciate the cultural differences of local markets, hired local expertise and started to customise campaigns to local audiences. de Mooij has identified seven main types of strategies that are used internationally (2005). Very few campaigns are imported without modification. Cosmetics are a product category that use a lot of global advertising, and commonly use celebrities, endorsements and testimonials in their strategies. Visual images have come to play an important role and seem to be appealing across many diverse cultures. The result is a globalisation of western beauty stereotypes.

Most international advertising expenditure has tended to be on television. As competition intensifies and new media offer different ways of marketing, different strategies have been used. In countries with large rural populations and many cities, multinational advertisers are looking beyond the main hubs, but they are facing increasing competition from local companies which have better knowledge of their consumers. Price is a key factor in selling to poorer people. There have been price wars in the Indian countryside between big brands from Unilever and Procter & Gamble (Dinakar, 2005). One common strategy where disposable incomes are very low is the 'think small' approach: for example, the tiny sachets of shampoo, which would be considered samples in the west, are sold in India for one rupee. The amount in the sachet would not be enough to wash most Indian women's hair, which is worn long.

It is mainly the multinational companies in the FMCG categories that have tackled the rural markets of emerging economies, especially the top advertisers Procter & Gamble, Unilever, Nestlé, Coca-Cola and Pepsi. As countries develop, local brands and companies also increase in size. Doctoroff (2008) has noted that in the future Chinese companies are going to be stiff competition for foreign

Table 1.1 Seven basic advertising forms used worldwide

Announcement
Association transfer
Lesson
Drama
Entertainment
Imagination
Special effects

Source: de Mooij, M. *Global Marketing and Advertising*, Thousand Oaks, CA: Sage. 2005.

companies. One successful local strategy, used by soft drinks manufacturer Wahaha, is based on a Maoist military tactic called spider warfare and uses a complex tier of distributors to target the towns, favouring the distribution channels over the retailers (Wang, 2008).

The global expansion of advertising takes commitment, research, the right personnel, an understanding of local culture and a massive budget. Despite the many obstacles, advertising has succeeded in selling increasing numbers of products to consumers in emerging markets. But what are the environmental implications of the expansion of advertising and consumption in the BRIC economies?

The environmental impact of expanding consumerism

The expansion of advertising in emerging economies stimulates the expansion of consumerism and increases the environmental impact of these populations. Already the high-income nations have outstripped their national ecological reserves and in 2007 they were consuming at the unsustainable level of an average six hectares per person (Global Footprint Network, 2011). In the 1980s the same problems began to develop in the emerging economies as the developed countries relocated their industries. Some industrialised countries even export their waste to these countries, especially electronic waste, despite this practice being outlawed by the Basel Convention (Tickle, 2010).

It is the continued expansion of the middle classes in emerging economies and the growing consumption levels of their poorer populations that will have the most significant environmental implications on the planet in the twenty-first century. The expanded consumption of the 'bottom billion' deserves to have priority but it is the consumption of the middle classes that is likely to take precedence. Consumption has never been related to fairness and equity. In 2010 the world population was estimated at 6.8 billion, with the BRIC countries accounting for 2.84 billion of that figure (43 per cent of the total): Brazil had 196.3 million, Russia 142 million, India 1.1 billion and China 1.4 billion (United States Census Bureau, 2010). It is the projected growth in consumption of the middle classes in India and China that will have the greatest impact. These are currently estimated to be 5 per cent, 55 million, in India (Wilson and Dragusanu, 2008) and 15 per cent in China, 195 million (Doctoroff, 2008).

Expanding consumption increases industrial production, packaging, energy and resource use, waste and pollution. Higher disposable income also means more car ownership, which raises levels of carbon emissions. Other effects include overconsumption, stimulated by the planned obsolescence that is part of the capitalist system, and rising obesity levels resulting from the greater consumption of high-calorie but nutritionally poor fast foods and soft drinks. Rising standards of living increase the demand for dairy products, meat, wheat and rice, which in turn puts pressure on food prices and energy requirements.

The vast potential growth in India and China will be in their internal markets, which provide both insulation from international market fluctuations and a vast resource of unmet needs, ranging from the most basic survival needs to the escalating desires of the increasingly affluent. How China and India undergo the socio-economic transformation of their societies in the next decades will affect the planet and global commodity markets, and multinational corporations and their advertising agencies will play a key role. Some companies are taking a leadership role in corporate social responsibility (CSR) and showing that profit can be combined with making a positive difference. These companies will be the winners in the new era of sustainable capitalism that will be needed if environmental calamity is to be avoided.

Conclusion

> 'Those that do not plan for the future may soon find the future is a problem.'
> (Chinese proverb)

Brazil, Russia, India and China have few characteristics in common, but they do share growing economies. All four are likely to join the western industrialised countries as the dominant economies in the next 25 years. In terms of such key variables as resources, population, consumer profiles and standards of living each has a different profile. Apart from sharing high growth figures, with the exception of Russia where growth rates have slipped in recent years, the BRIC economies are incredibly diverse, and cover a spectrum of political, socio-economic, cultural, geographic and climate profiles.

Because China and India have large populations with low standards of living, their economic growth and how it is managed has major implications for the whole planet in terms of scarcity of resources, especially food, the production of carbon emissions and the acceleration of climate change. The global population is already consuming resources at one and a half times the planet's ability to replenish them. The earth cannot sustain this level of consumption for much longer. The 400 per cent increase in the size of the middle classes in the BRIC economies in the next decade that O'Neill predicted in 2008 is quickly turning into a reality.

Enlightened corporate leadership and planning for sustainable development will drive the next decades. Those who embrace this reality will be the leaders in the new economy, and advertising has a key role to play in this process. It can be a powerful force for implementing necessary social and economic change.

2   Brazil

'It is no longer true that "Brazil is the land of the future and always will be".'
Rosenwald, P. Pointed advice for direct marketers in Brazil.
Advertising Age International (1998)

Introduction

'Brazil is the most western and most mature of the BRIC economies.'
Noreen O'Leary, 'The Rise of the BRIC', *Adweek* (2008)

Brazil, the world's fifth largest country in terms of both population and land area, has always been integrated into the global capitalist economy, unlike Russia and China, which were outside that system for much of the twentieth century. The growth of the Brazilian advertising industry has been constrained by economic and political instability and high levels of poverty. Though a relatively small economic sector, Brazilian advertising was flourishing (creatively speaking) long before it became more closely integrated with global advertising in the 1990s, when foreign companies and advertising agencies increased their prominence. Most of the top local agencies went into joint ventures with foreign agencies. Advertising expenditure expanded then contracted in the late 1990s with the devaluation of the real and high levels of inflation. A blend of influences has resulted in creative and dynamic advertisements, and Brazilian agencies and campaigns have won international awards in the last three decades.

Since 2000 Brazil has undergone a social and economic transformation, characterised by strong economic growth and rising standards of living. The economy has already begun to recover after the international economic downturn of 2008–2009, and Brazil has become an emerging global power. In 2008 Brazil was the sixth largest advertising market in the world (Jones, 2009) and it is the second largest advertising market of the BRICs. Seven out of the top ten advertisers are foreign multinationals and the fact that the list includes a number of auto companies reflects the disposable income levels of an established middle class and the maturity of the market. Levels of social inequality in Brazil are among the worst in the world, but in the last decades social programmes have raised the living standards of the poor, bringing more consumers into the market.

Brazilian advertising expenditure should expand rapidly in the next few years, and become increasingly complex as the growth of online and mobile advertising further fracture the market.

Background: political and economic context

Brazil has a much shorter recorded history than the other BRIC nations: it was 'discovered' by Europeans in 1500 when they were seeking an alternative route to India (*The Economist*, 2009d). When the Portuguese arrived on the South American continent an estimated 1,000 indigenous Indian tribes were scattered over the area that is currently Brazil. The colonists who followed the early explorers and spread inland from the coastal regions made a considerable impact on the environment during the next centuries, soon depleting the coastal forests and establishing *latifundias* (large sugar cane estates). Brazil's earliest 'agribusiness' was sugar cane production, which resulted in the country's first export boom in the seventeenth century. Sugar was produced under an imported feudal system characterised by a small landed elite with a vast number of indigenous slaves who were harshly treated and deprived of their traditional way of life. Plantations caused social and environmental devastation: forests were decimated, waters were polluted and monoculture depleted the soils. When the local labour supply was exhausted Brazil became the largest importer of African slaves into the Americas; an estimated 10–15 million people between 1601 and 1888 when slavery was abolished in Brazil. These figures represented 40 per cent of the entire slave trade (Araujo, 2001, cited at the Museum of Natural History Rio de Janeiro, 2009). The descendants of these slaves make up about 7 per cent of Brazil's present population (CIA, 2011a).

For four centuries Brazil supplied primary products to Portugal; first sugar, wood and metals and later cotton, coffee and cacao. A mining boom in the nineteenth century brought waves of immigrants from other countries in Europe, which increased the cultural diversity. In 1822 the son of the Portuguese king claimed independence from Portugal and crowned himself Emperor of Brazil. This empire lasted until 1889, when Brazil became a republic. A small group of the landed elite that engineered this change then assumed power, and during the twentieth century, like many other South American countries, Brazil was ruled by a small Eurocentric elite with the assistance of the military while the majority of the population continued to live in poverty. French fashions and magazines defined the dress and the beauty ideals of Brazilian upper class women. Magazines, some newspapers and consumer goods were imported from Europe. Brazil has always been part of the international economy and foreign companies came to Brazil in the nineteenth century, with another wave arriving in the 1920s, including General Motors, Nestlé and Esso (Standard Oil/Mobil); Unilever came in the 1930s. It was Nestlé that developed the first instant coffee in Brazil, in cooperation with the Brazilian Coffee Institute, and launched it in 1938 as Nescafé. The top global advertiser, American company Procter & Gamble, was a relatively late arrival in the 1980s and has still not made it to the list of top ten advertisers.

Development in Brazil has always been led by the state and one of the priorities of twentieth century leaders was to modernise the country. In the 1930s President Getúlio Vargas embarked on the first programme of import substitution industrialisation and when President Juscelino Kubtischek was in power (1956–61) multinationals were encouraged into Brazil. Political leadership was fragile throughout the century with leaders lacking any substantial power base. There was a wave of foreign investment in the 1950s when India and China were closed to investment. Many car companies such as Fiat, Volkswagen and General Motors moved to Brazil at this time. In 1964 a US (CIA) backed coup reinstated the military (*New Internationalist*, 2007), whose leaders embraced the development fervour that was sweeping the post-colonial world. In the late 1960s and early 1970s the military governments embarked on a massive programme of state-driven industrialisation. They were heavily reliant on borrowed foreign money and the 1970s were marked by excessive public debt (Purushothaman and Wilson, 2003). The first wave of Brazilian industrialisation created an economic boom between 1967 and 1973 known as the 'Brazilian Miracle'. The state encouraged the establishment of the motor industry, the expansion of agricultural production into the Amazon Basin and the Cerrado grasslands, and, in response to oil crises of the 1970s, the development of an ethanol industry using soya beans. The first road was built through the forest to the Amazon River to export agricultural products from the interior and north-west. This initiated a major onslaught on the lands of the Amazon. Timber was among the first of the products to be exploited. After land was cleared, big farms were established or landless peasants took over the land, and the destruction of the rainforest increased.

Brazil's national debt had grown to $100 billion by the 1980s, and was one of the largest in the world (*New Internationalist*, 2007). In 1982 the government had to suspend foreign debt repayments for the first time. There was a bloodless transition to democratic rule in the late 1980s. Brazil's financial troubles continued and loan repayments were suspended again in 1989. A new president embraced a neo-liberal economic programme of privatisation of state enterprises and reduction of tariffs on foreign imports. Restrictions and import taxes on foreign companies and the import of foreign goods were lifted, and foreign goods flooded into Brazil (O'Barr, 2008). Since 1990 the boom in agribusiness has been the greatest factor stimulating economic growth (McMann, 2008). In 1994 Prime Minister Fernando Cardoso introduced the Plan Real, which began to stabilise the economy and control inflation. Excessive reliance on foreign money and high domestic public debt continued throughout the 1990s (Purushothaman and Wilson, 2003) and in 1998 the IMF had to come to the rescue when the Brazilian economy was hit by the collapse of the Asian stock markets (BBC World News, 2008).

Between 1994 and 2008 economic growth averaged 3.1 per cent (*The Economist*, 2009a). Advertising spending in Brazil has tended to reflect wider economic trends. When the market opened to foreign imports in the 1990s, these goods increased the competition, which also improved the quality of local goods (Valente, DDB cited by O'Leary, 2008). When foreign companies poured into Brazil in the 1990s, encouraged by economic stability and declining inflation, advertising expenditure increased. In the late 1990s the telecommunications industry in Brazil expanded after it was deregulated. Many car manufacturers were building factories and by 1998 1.6 million cars were being sold annually. Television sales were 30 million between 1994 and 1998 and television ownership levels increased from 70 to 85 per cent (Wentz, 1998). The devaluation of the currency in 1998 resulted in a contraction of the economy and a reduction in advertising spending.

There has been steady growth in the Brazilian economy through much of the last decade. According to environmentalist Tim Flannery, since 2000 the world has gone from a position of food surplus to one of deficit (NZ on Air, interview with Finlay Macdonald, 16 October 2010) and Brazil has benefited from the increased international demand for its primary products. It now plays an important role in the global economy as a supplier of resources. Brazil is the world's largest exporter of coffee, sugar, chickens, beef and orange juice. Its commercial forests provide much of the world's wood pulp. Recent growth has been stimulated by significant investment into the commodity sector since 2000 (*The Economist*, 2009d). Its economy is still dependent on external markets and is vulnerable in times of recession and during periods of fluctuation in external demand, which occurred between 2008 and 2009.

In 2002 a new left-wing president, Luiz Lula da Silva, popularly known as Lula, won the election. His platform promised to boost growth and narrow the gap between rich and poor (BBC World News, October 2010). Since 2003 macro-economic stability has increased and external debt has been reduced. Growth averaged 2.7 per cent between 2003 and 2006 (Leme, 2007). After that Brazil's economy started to grow more vigorously – to an estimated 6.15 per cent in 2007. After September 2008 the economy was hit by the economic downturn and the decline in external demand for its commodities. Growth reduced to 5.1 per cent in 2008, then declined further in 2009 to minus 0.2 per cent. Brazil was one of the first countries to start recovering from the global crisis and by the second quarter of 2009 growth was again positive. In 2010 growth was predicted to rise to 7.5 per cent (CIA, 2011a). Brazil still has problems that could affect its future development if not addressed: too much bureaucracy, an ineffective legal system, high levels of corruption, and a large black economy estimated at 6.9 per cent of GDP in Brazil (compared to just one per cent in India and 2.4 per cent in China). A black economy, which tends to diminish as societies grow more affluent (*The Economist*, 2009a), lowers the tax intake and creates a large workforce that is relatively unprotected and insecure.

Brazil has become increasingly integrated in the global economy since the 1990s, when liberalisation was imposed as part of the IMF's structural adjustment policies. More foreign companies came to Brazil and the import of foreign products increased. Some of the big foreign companies had previously dealt with these regulations by establishing production facilities in Brazil. In 2001 James O'Neill of Goldman Sachs was one of the first to see Brazil's future potential when he correctly predicted that it would be one of the world's dominant economies by 2050.

The socio-economic background: highest levels of inequality in the BRICs

As we have seen, after the legal end of slavery in 1888 the feudal pattern of inequality persisted and by the end of the nineteenth century inequalities in Brazil were based on racial differences and the rural and urban divide. A small elite of the urban middle class, the coffee growers and the military dominated the country. There was some expansion of the middle classes after the late 1960s but by the 1980s more than 50 per cent of the 130 million population were living below the poverty line. During the 1990s the severe inequalities continued, with an estimated four million people living in virtual slavery. In 1992 the Pastoral Commission found 15,000 people living as slaves and incidences are still being reported. In the cities large numbers of homeless children were being systematically killed. Levels of social discontent were also high. The destruction of the Amazonian rainforest has also had an impact on the indigenous peoples, who were being murdered and suffering violence at the hands of miners and the police (*New Internationalist*, 2007). Even today land ownership continues to be held by a small minority, and the majority of the rural population are landless: 90 per cent of all arable land is owned by 20 per cent of the population, while 40 per cent of the population owns barely 1 per cent of land fit for agriculture (ibid.). In 2008 Brazil still had one of the highest levels of income inequality in the world (United Nations Development Programme: Human Development Report, 2010). In 2007 the lowest 10 per cent of the population earned 1.1 per cent of national income while the highest 10 per cent earned 43 per cent of it (CIA, 2011a).

Inequality in Brazil is closely correlated to race and most black people fall into the poorest socio-economic groups. There are three main racial groups in Brazil: the indigenous inhabitants, the descendants of African slaves brought to work the plantations, and the descendants of European settlers. Brazilian popular culture tends to reflect a mixture of European and African influences and the resulting vibrancy is epitomised by the annual carnival held in many Brazilian towns and cities, though Rio's is the most famous. Black people may only be seven per cent of the population but the African heritage has a strong influence on both culture and music. As a social group, however, black people continue to suffer discrimination and dispossession and they tend to be invisible in the media and noticeably absent in *telenovelas* (television serial novels) and advertising (Rial, 2001). As happens in Asia, Brazilian television and advertising reflect a historical cultural bias towards what is white and European. When black people appear in *telenovelas* they are usually servants (ibid.).

Brazil has always had very high levels of poverty and these levels are still high: 26 per cent of the population or 48 million people in 2008 (CIA, 2011a). In the last decade, however, poverty levels have been declining significantly for the first time in Brazil's history. The far-reaching *Bolsa Familia* (Family Allowance) programme, introduced in 2004, has extended social welfare to about 21.9 million people (International Labour Office Social Security Department, 2009). These improvements have stimulated the growth of the mass consumer market. In 2009 *The Economist* (2009a) estimated the size of the middle classes (Group C) in Brazil to have increased from 42 per cent in 2004 to 52 per cent in 2008 as a result of Brazil's progress in addressing social inequality. The lower classes have also benefited from a 100 per cent increase in the minimum wage. According to O'Leary (2008), the consumption levels of 20–30 million people increased between 2005 and 2008. Brazil has a relatively young urban population: in 2010 27 per cent of the population was under 15 and 6.4 per cent over 65. In 2008, 86 per cent of the population was urban (CIA, 2011a). A large group of young people is coming into the market as general living standards are rising. The consumer goods markets are on the verge of a massive expansion that will be paralleled by an expansion in advertising expenditure. Reduced poverty has brought a whole new sector into the market (Adese, 2006).

History of Brazilian advertising

Though Brazil experienced decades of military dictatorship, it was not closed off from the outside world in the same way as China and Russia. The consumer classes were a very small proportion of the total population, as they were in India. Like other countries in the Americas, Brazil was more exposed to American than to British influences, and this was reflected in a dynamic local advertising sector as early as the 1960s. As a result of decades of economic instability, advertising expenditure remained fairly static until the liberalisation of the economy in the 1990s. Brazilian advertising has flourished since 2000, expanding to an estimated value of $14.2 billion in 2010. Per capita expenditure has reached $74 (GroupM, 2010). In the last 15 years Brazilian advertising has grown dramatically. In 1995 it was the 34th largest market in the world; in 2008 it was the sixth (Jones, 2009).

Though international companies first arrived in the nineteenth century, the first major expansion was in the 1920s. In 1929 the first foreign advertising agency to come to Brazil was J. Walter Thompson (JWT), which was part of the international expansion of General Motors. Other American agencies soon followed. Ford also arrived in the 1920s, bringing along its advertising agency, N.W. Ayer & Son (O'Barr, 2008). McCann Erickson arrived in the 1930s, following its client Standard Oil/Esso (O'Leary, 2008; O'Barr, 2008); later in the 1950s it became the global agency for Coca-Cola. Further expansion of the Brazilian economy and advertising was halted by the Depression and the Second World War.

Contemporary Brazilian advertising has its roots in the 1960s and according to O'Barr (2008) there were two significant pioneer influences. One was the American agency model introduced to Brazil by Alex Periscinoto, co-founder of Almap. After working for JWT in New York, he returned to Brazil and set up his own agency. Using a sound financial business base, this integrated creative teams, strategies, market research, client focus and creativity. Quite a different style of agency, DPZ, was set up by three Europeans. This brought together aesthetic influences from the European tradition: elegance, style, emphasis on photography and strong imagery (ibid.). These two trends stimulated a wave of creativity in Brazilian advertising campaigns. In subsequent years some of the creative directors who worked in these agencies left to establish their own agencies. According to Washington Olivetto, one of the major figures in contemporary Brazilian advertising, Argentinean advertising was better than its Brazilian counterpart in the 1960s, but then some key creatives moved to Brazil from Argentina and Brazilian advertising improved (Tungate, 2007).

By the 1970s a distinctive style of advertising had emerged. It was colloquial rather than formal and 'very engaging, humorous and "very Brazilian"' (Marcello Serpa of Almap/BBDO, quoted in O'Barr, 2008). Washington Olivetto became a star at DPZ in his teens. In 1987 he left to set up W/Brasil, which is one of the most famous independent Brazilian agencies. By the end of the 1980s Brazilian-owned agencies were outperforming the subsidiaries of American agencies (Mattelart, 1991). Economic uncertainty and high inflation in Brazil at the end of the 1980s was reflected in low levels of advertising expenditure.

During the 1990s regulations on the import of foreign products were relaxed as inflation stabilised. As disposable income levels started to expand people began to purchase consumer goods. Foreign companies descended on Brazil, selling both cheaper FMCGs and luxury items (O'Barr, 2008). Advertising expenditure reached $5.8 billion by 1996, which was 44 per cent of total spending in Latin America but ranked it only 43rd in the world. Per capita advertising spending was $37 ('Adspend in the Americas – a tale of 2 regions', *International Journal of Advertising*, 1998). There was a dramatic expansion in advertising and by 1998 Brazil's advertising market was worth $8.6 billion, elevating it to the sixth largest market in the world. According to Wentz (1998) it was one of the top five markets in the world for a wide range of consumer products. Just four years of economic stability had a significant impact on the Brazilian advertising sector (O'Barr, 2008). The close relationship between advertising expenditure and wider economic trends was highlighted at the end of the 1990s when a devaluation prompted fears of a recession: advertising expenditure dropped dramatically in 1998 and 1999. There was still growth in some sectors, including telecoms, household cleansers, food and personal hygiene. The privatisation of the state-owned phone and mobile companies prompted a flurry of advertising for phone companies. The beverage, finance, car and textile sectors decreased or remained steady, while consumer electronics and real estate were the worst performers (Penteado, 1999).

In the 1990s the profile of top advertisers started to change as regulations loosened and more foreign companies, and global agency networks, came to Brazil (O'Barr, 2008). By 1993 six of the top agencies by billings were foreign (Tharpe, no date). Between 1993 and 1995 the top agency was McCann Erickson Brazil.

Table 2.1 Brazil leading agencies 1995 (all based in São Paulo)

1 McCann–Erickson Brasil
2 Duailibi, Petit, Zaragoza, Propaganda
3 JWT Publicidade
4 Fischer Justus Communicacoes
5 Y&R do Brasil
6 ALMAP/BBDO
7 W/Brasil Publicidade
8 Salles/DMB&B Publicidade
9 MPM Ammiratti Puris Lintas Communicacoes
10 Standard, O & M

Source: Tharpe, M. *Advertising agencies in Brazil* (no date). Online. Available www.bgsu.edu/departments/tcom/faculty/ha/brazil.htm (accessed January 2010).

During the 1990s there was a lot of change in the advertising agency sector, and many mergers and joint ventures were set up with the big multinational agencies. Alexandre Gama, the CEO of Y&R São Paulo, has explained the reason behind these mergers: 'There's a feeling that if you're not in an international partnership with someone, you'll fail … You can be a partner and they can give you resources. We're seduced by this combination.' (quoted in Wentz, 1998). Marcelli Serpa of Almap, one of Brazil's oldest advertising agencies, merged with the agency BBDO to create Almap/BBDO. Another creative director, Nizan Guanaes, worked at W/Brasil before leaving to set up DM9 in 1989 with Duda Mendonça. Guanaes came up with Fernando Cardoso's successful election campaign in 1994. He sold the majority stake in DM9 to DDB Needham Worldwide in June 1997, which resulted in the formation of DM9 DDB; then opened the successful independent agency Africa in 2002 (O'Barr, 2008). Brazilian agencies (or branches of multinational agencies) continued to have a high profile internationally. Almap/BBDO was the third most awarded agency at Cannes in 1998, and DM9 DDB was even more successful. Both agencies are now part of the Omnicom group. Eduardo Fischer and Roberto Justus were another independent team who formed a partnership with Bates. Fischer departed and in 2004 Bates got taken over by Y&R, with Roberto Justus becoming CEO (author interview with Walter Longo, VP Strategic Planning and Innovation, 2009).

After 2000 the growth in economic confidence and stability was reflected in the dramatic expansion of advertising, with advertising expenditure growing from $6.7 billion in 2003 to $12.6 billion in 2008. Growth in expenditure slowed a little in 2009, when there was reduced demand for Brazilian exports, but began to grow again in 2010, rising to an estimated advertising expenditure of $15 billion in 2010 and estimated expenditure of $16.5 billion in 2011 (GroupM, 2010).

In the last decade there has been even more concentration within the agency sector. During the 2000s Y&R soon became the largest agency in Brazil and South America. It built up a strong profile, with a small number of clients, including Casas Bahia, Brazil's largest advertiser for the last decade. Casas Bahia, a furniture and services retailer, is such a big client they have their own Y&R in-house team. Y&R has moved beyond being an advertising agency and is focusing on a multi-strategy approach looking at businesses as total entities. It has reduced its client base to 13 key clients. Y&R is unusual in its flamboyant approach to self-marketing. Two of the key principals, Roberto Justus and Walter Longo, also run the celebrity television programme, *The Apprentice Brazil*, which has been screening since 2004, as a combination of branded entertainment and product placement. The companies that make up the Y&R client list provide the sites for the competition and the judges. As many as 110,000 applicants compete to win a place on the show, which has had up to 9.6 million viewers (author interview with Walter Longo, 2009). By 2008 most of the agencies in Brazil were part of joint ventures with the large global agency complexes, and only 2 per cent were independent (Goodson, 2007).

Companies that dominate national markets in emerging economies are usually those that find some way of selling to the mass market. Casas Bahia reinforces its dominant position in the marketplace by extending credit to the poor. It offers a range of services: customer networks, bonuses and incentives. It also requires instalments to be paid in the store, which encourages further purchases (Young, 2006). Brazilian companies make up about one third of the top ten advertisers. Of the big FMCG companies, Unilever, is consistently a major advertiser, as it is in India, and it is unusual not to see top global advertiser Procter & Gamble on the list. Growth in consumption levels in Brazil has been stimulated recently by the expansion of consumer credit by 28 per cent between 2006 and 2009 (*The Economist*, 2009b).

The state sector is another important source of advertising in Brazil, as it is in India. Petrobras, the state-owned petroleum company set up in 1953 by President Vargas, has had a significant share of the economy, though it has not been a monopoly since 1997. It also plays an important role in the cultural sponsorship of projects favoured by the state. When I visited in 2009, Petrobras was a heavy advertiser of its social service initiatives on television at prime-time (during the *telenovelas*). Political advertising also plays an important role in Brazil and advertising campaigns are crucial to Brazilian elections because the major candidates are allocated large amounts of media time based on the numbers of elected officials. DM9 DDB handled the successful election campaigns of Cardoso in 1994 and 1998. DM9 DDB (Nizan Guanaes) carried out the campaign for presidential candidate Jose Serra while Duda Mendonça developed the campaign for Lula, promoting him as the candidate of 'peace and love', which helped to get him elected in 2002 (Penteado, 2002).

The exuberance and love of life that are symbolic of Brazilian culture seem to carry over into the advertising sector. Brazilian people tend to be positive about advertising, except for political advertising, which they distrust. A recent survey found that people use advertising to help them make product choices. They also find advertising entertaining ('Brazilian consumers see value of advertising', *Ad News*, 2010). It is therefore not surprising that levels of consumer advocacy are

Table 2.2 Brazil top ten advertisers 2009 (expenditure in BRL millions)

1 Casas Bahia	3059
2 Unilever Brasil	942
3 Ambev	915
4 Caixa (Gfc)	847
5 Hyundai Caoa	745
6 Fiat	738
7 Bradesco	735
8 Hypermarcas	682
9 TIM Brasil	578
10 Ford	557

Source: GroupM (Autumn 2010). This Year, Next Year: Worldwide Marketing and Media Forecasts.

low and that Brazilian people have little interest in such environmental issues as recycling (Salles, 2006). People also are fairly positive about branding. Unilever has been in Brazil for more than 75 years, and two of its major brands, Omo and Dove, are considered Brazilian (O'Leary, 2008), just as Lux and Lipton Tea are viewed as Indian companies in India. The profile of the top ten brands in Brazil reflects a mixture of foreign and local brands. The beer market, one of the biggest advertising sectors, is dominated by the Brazilian company Ambev, a subsidiary of Anheuser-Busch InBev. When I visited in 2009 the most common billboard advertisement was for its Skol beer. Although there are a million beer outlets, one for every 199 people according to *The Economist* (2009a), Brazil does not seem to have Russia's alcohol problems.

The auto industry is also an important advertising sector, and most of the big international companies have been producing and selling cars in Brazil for many decades. It is a relatively mature market and has comparatively high per capita car ownership levels compared with India and China. General Motors, Ford and Fiat have been among the top ten advertisers in Brazil in the last decade, in 2003 and 2004 (Young, 2006) and later in 2009 (GroupM, 2010). The Japanese and Korean companies started to arrive in the 1990s and brands like Toyota are also keen to expand into the Brazilian market. A study of branding in Latin America in the late 1990s found that the performance aspects of cars were less important than the emotional benefits of brands: prestige, acceptance by friends and the endorsement of automobile experts (Carramenha *et al.*, 1999). As income levels have increased in the last decade, so have auto sales. By 2010 Brazilian car ownership levels were predicted to reach 33 million or 17 per cent (O'Neill and Stupnytska, 2009), the second highest percentage in the BRIC economies.

Brazilians are known for their preoccupation with looking good, which translates into a healthy market for cosmetics. According to Terzi (2009), urbanisation in Brazil is translating into an expansion of women working in offices, 'a ripe target for grooming and beauty brands'. Grooming is associated with personal and social success and a recent trend has been a 'premiumisation of beauty', trading up from mass brands to prestige products. With increasing life expectancy, the anti-ageing product market is also likely to expand. In her study of beauty brands Terzi found that local brands such as Natura were positioning themselves in terms of Brazil's biodiversity, inspired by the traditional use of indigenous plant ingredients, sustainably produced. The Ekos products are biodegradable and packaged in recycled glass. 'Authenticity is essential for new brands pursuing culture as a point of difference, and to stand out they must embrace and communicate with authority a true cultural proposition' (ibid.). Though Brazil is the third largest cosmetic market in the world, door-to-door purchasing is more common than buying at retail outlets, according to a BBC report (BBC World News, May 2010). Cosmetics advertising is the mainstay of the global women's magazines. In a cross-cultural study of advertising in *Cosmopolitan* in 2002–03, which included Brazil, Clinique was the dominant cosmetics brand in all editions. In the Brazilian edition L'Oréal had modified its global byline 'Because you're worth it' to 'Number one in the world for anti-aging' (Nelson and Paek, 2005).

The Brazilian telecommunications sector has been expanding ever since it was privatised in 1999. In that year it had some of the highest advertising expenditure. The advent of the mobile phone in recent years has given the sector another significant boost. In 2009 Bradesco and Vivo (Telefonica) were among the top ten advertisers (Table 2.2) and in 2009 I saw their billboards everywhere. The telecommunications industry had a high profile in all the BRIC countries when I visited in 2008, 2009 and 2010.

Agency culture

In London and New York, advertising agencies seem to be dominated by young men (mostly under 40), who work long hours and often socialise together as well. There is a 'laddish' and sometimes brutal culture in which women are given a hard time. This male arrogance and self-conceit is often accompanied by ethnocentric or simply ignorant attitudes towards advertising markets in other parts of the world. In the 1990s there were some spectacular failures in 'emerging markets' when campaigns were imported from 'head office'.

I was interested to discover if advertising agency culture was any different in Brazil. In 2009 I asked Guime Davidson of W/Brasil and Walter Longo of Y&R São Paulo. Davidson's experience was at W/Brasil where the principal, Washington Olivetto, sets the standards. According to Davidson, 'Olivetto would not allow such behaviour'. He encourages the people in the agency to work reasonable hours, believing that to be creative you need a balanced life. Davidson did admit that few women worked in advertising as creative directors – less than 5 per cent in his opinion. He also considered that the advertising sector had been overhyped in the media and far more people wanted to enter the profession than there were jobs. When I asked about training and education, he replied that people came into advertising from many sectors. He felt that you can train people to have good ideas. He considered that there had been a loss of creativity in Brazilian advertising in recent years, but that it would return as Brazilian advertising is heavily influenced by the *telenovela* with its dynamic combination of acting and quick dialogue. Davidson did not rate Cannes, or in fact any awards, highly. All the many awards at W/Brasil were jumbled together in a glass case.

Walter Longo was proud that Y&R had been singled out as one of the top workplaces for women in Brazil. He too felt there had been a loss of creativity in Brazilian advertising. I felt that he had perhaps provided some of the explanation when he talked about the Y&R business model: the company does not sell just advertising but offers a whole business and brand package. Perhaps creativity becomes diluted when agencies broaden their brief. Despite the opinions of both Davidson and Longo that there had been a loss of creativity, a consumer survey conducted in 2008 revealed that people felt advertising was more in tune with their needs ('Brazilian consumers see value of advertising', *Ad News*, 2010).

The media profile

The media profile of advertising in Brazil has been fairly stable for decades because of the dominance of television advertising. Traditional media seem to be healthy and new media are adding to the media mix. In Latin America, print advertising revenues are still growing, increasing 11.4 per cent in the five years before 2004 (World Association of Newspapers, 2004). The changes in the media profile in Brazil share some similarities with developing countries where literacy levels are low. When markets are small the main vehicle is print and as incomes rise there is an increase in television advertising. Brazil has high levels of television ownership and a comparatively concentrated television market because of the consistent popularity of certain programmes, like soap operas. Print advertising was the largest category in the mid-1990s, then declined from 51 per cent in 1996 to 42 per cent in 2005, while television advertising increased from 48 per cent to 54.6 per cent over the same period. The radio and outdoor markets amounted to only 3 and 1 per cent of the market respectively (Young, 2006.) WAN-IFRA (2010), by contrast, put print advertising as 25 per cent of total advertising spending in 2005, declining only slightly to 24 per cent in 2010 (2010). The number of radio stations in Brazil has been estimated at 3,600 and they still attract a sizeable audience, according to Neto of Dianet ('Branded radio takes off in Brazil', *Financial Times*, 2009). Outdoor advertising is a very small percentage of spending. Guime Davidson of W/Brasil was unfazed by the ban on billboards in Sao Paulo since 2005, and even thought it was a good thing. Figures were not available for online advertising in 2005 but were estimated as 3 per cent (Young, 2006). The three main locations for advertising in Brazil, according to O'Barr (2008), are product placement in the *telenovelas*, sports sponsorship and the annual carnivals.

When television was introduced in 1950–51 Brazil followed the American model of private ownership, which has led to a similar bias in favour of the interests of owners and big business. The concentration of economic and political power in Brazil is also reflected in the structure of the media, where most of the power has been concentrated in one company, TV Globo (Rede Globo), which has dominated the sector since the 1970s. Initially it was supported by the military government (ibid.). TV Globo, owned by Roberto Marinho until his death in 2003, is the third largest commercial television network in the world, watched by an estimated 120 million people a day. It has 122 affiliated networks throughout Brazil and is the largest network in South America. Programmes are also exported throughout the world (McMann, 2008). Currently there are more than 100 TV channels operating, most of them privately owned, but media ownership is still highly concentrated (CIA, 2011a). In 1993 the British Channel 4 made a documentary, *Beyond Citizen Kane*, about the power and influence of the TV Globo network in Brazil, comparing the power and influence of its owner to that of the fictional character. The owner's political support of Fernando Collor in the 1990 presidential campaign was instrumental in the election win (McMann, 2008) and he used his influence to sabotage Lula's campaign in 1989 (Noble, *et al.*, 2002) but supported him in 2002 when he was victorious.

Subscriber television has not taken off in Brazil as it has in other counties (O'Leary, 2008), probably because of the popularity of existing public programming. The Brazilian people are addicted to the nightly *telenovelas* shown on TV Globo in prime-time. They dominate the television audience for two hours and have had the major market share of prime-time television advertising since the 1960s (O'Barr, 2008). Advertisements during these *telenovelas* cost $200,000 for 30 seconds and are the most expensive slots on television (author interview with Walter Longo, 2009). The media market is also concentrated, dominated by two owners: Editora Abril, which has 70 per cent of the magazine market, and Rede Globo, which controls 70 per cent of advertising expenditure. By law, agencies are required to pay 15 per cent commission. According to O'Leary (2008), TV Globo's domination of television and production means the industry lacks creativity and experimentation.

New frontiers, new media

As in most other countries over the last ten years the internet has become an essential part of contemporary social life in Brazil. New media have also been expanding rapidly in recent years. Personal computer ownership grew 120 per cent between 2002 and 2007, reaching 29 million in 2007. An estimated 16 per cent of the population had internet access in 2006 (Young, 2006) and in 2009 this increased to 38 per cent (76 million internet users), the highest percentage of internet use among the BRICs (CIA, 2011a). Brazil has the world's largest percentage of social media users, and social networking expanded 31 per cent between 2008 and 2009 (Precourt, 2009). Brazil is the largest online market in Latin America. A recent cross-cultural study of patterns of internet shopping found that in Brazil 40 per cent of internet users made purchases online because they liked the convenience. They were heavy users of internet and email. These purchasers tended to be more impulsive and innovative; they had more favourable attitudes to direct marketing and advertising; they were wealthier, risk averse and had more price concerns. There was an age difference between shoppers and non-shoppers on the internet but they were not really any more brand conscious than non-internet shoppers (Brashear *et al.*, 2009). In a 2010 study of 20 online advertising campaigns by Eyeblaster and Microsoft, the focus of interest was in 'dwell times' (the overall length of exposure to ads) and 'dwell rates' (how many people interacted). They found that consumers in South America were the most 'engaged with online advertising'. Advertisements including video pushed up 'dwell rates' and communications that genuinely connected with consumers led to increased traffic to official sites. They also assessed which internet portal generated the best conversion rates, and discovered that instant text messaging was the most successful: it had a response rate of 13 per cent and people stayed at the site on average for eight minutes. Media rich advertisements were more successful than banner ads. The researchers explained the differences between regions as relating to the maturity of the markets ('Web ads have biggest impact in South America', *Eyeblaster*, 2010). The Boston Consultancy Group (BCG) has estimated that by 2015 the number of internet users in Brazil will rise from 68 million to 155 million and the level of penetration will be 74 per cent. Brazilians spend 56 minutes online per day, but the BCG predicts this time will increase to two hours per day in 2015. SMS (short messaging service) is popular in Brazil (61 per cent) but the percentage of people who use search engines is highest in Brazil while the percentage of users who are shopping online (e-commerce) is below 20 per cent ('"Next billion" web users based in new markets', BCG, 2010).

Brazilian people have also recently embraced the mobile phone and uptake has been rapid. In 2007 ownership levels were at 133 million phones, more than 70 per cent of the population, though the figure did not account for people having multiple phones (Meirelles, 2009). In 2009 that number had reached 87 per cent – 174 million out of a population of 198 million (CIA, 2011a) – also the highest level in the BRICs. Brazil also has the largest number of MSN (Microsoft) Messenger users in the world (O'Leary, 2008): 1.2 million Brazilians access the web via mobile web. The BCG estimates that the percentage of mobile phone ownership in Brazil will rise from 86 to 113 per cent – with people having multiple SIM cards (BCG, 2010).

The growth in advertising on mobile phones has accompanied the expansion of the numbers of smartphone users and the usability of the technology. The mass uptake of smartphones is predicted to change consumer behaviour ('Smartphones change consumer habits', Accenture, 2010). As the advertising options are similar to the internet, they will expand and possibly cut into the digital advertising sector figures. The impact will not be as big as predicted, however, while ownership levels are restricted to the middle classes. This sector will expand only when the mass market (the poor) start using smartphones and leapfrog the computer ownership stage of accessing the internet. That may not be too far in the future (BCG, 2010).

Cultural values

Since the 1990s, as marketers became more interested in Brazil, there has been more consumer research into the profile of the Brazilian population. The 1997–2006 GfK Roper Cross-Cultural Consumer Study found that Brazilians share a range of general values with the whole Latin American region, including believing in: 'protecting family, honesty, authenticity, learning, freedom, self reliance and enjoying life'. The study, which excluded the lowest 25 per cent of income earners (Salles, 2006), found that 35 per cent of Latin Americans attended church at least once a week, and felt more confident about the future because of their faith. They spent more time with children and grandchildren – 20 hours per week as opposed to the worldwide average of 14 hours. Brazilians were distinguished by their orientation towards aesthetics, beauty, looking good and individuality. Brazilians also love American and European things, according to Peter Rosenwald of Abril Group (1998), and are not good at saving (*The Economist*, 2009a), which is understandable given the recent decades of high inflation. Brazilians also like brands and have very favourable attitudes to advertising. According to a study carried out by Y&R Brands, 30 per cent of Brazilians buy 80 per cent of the products advertised (O'Leary, 2008). Brazilians obviously like spending and consumer behaviour is changing with rising living standards and greater disposable income. One indicator of this change has been the increased use of credit cards since 1999. Brazil still lags behind India and China, however, in terms of PC ownership (ibid.).

Gender

The expansion of the middle classes has led to more Brazilian women working outside the home, so their participation in the paid workforce is quite recent, as it is in India. A cross-cultural study of attitudes towards, and definitions of, femininity found that women in Brazil aspire to having rich and multi-dimensional lives, and that femininity plays a part, though today the benchmark is not 'natural beauty but naturally made up' (Vascotto, 2004). Brazilian advertising campaigns include a preoccupation with appearance, the body beautiful and sexuality (O'Barr, 2008), which is perhaps a result of the potent mix of cosmetic marketing and the cultural emphasis on appearance. Brazil has become one of the top cosmetics markets in the world. In the 2004 Dove Global Study on Women, Beauty and Well-being, Brazil had the highest number of women who had considered cosmetic surgery and 7 per cent of Brazilian women had undergone surgery (Etcoff *et al.*, 2004). The premium on youth and beauty means the market is expanding for one of the world's most rapidly growing cosmetic product categories: anti-ageing and anti-wrinkle creams. According to Hamilton and Denniss (2005), high rates of Botox use and cosmetic surgery reflect increasing female (and male) insecurity about appearance.

Race

One of the unstated characteristics of the dominant Brazilian culture is its underlying racism, which is reinforced by advertising. An advertising executive was reported by Rial as saying that it was difficult to import American advertisements into Brazil in the 1980s because the number of black people that featured would not be acceptable to the Brazilian audience. The empowerment of black people in the United States has not been paralleled in Brazil (2001).

Strategies

'Brazilians are skilled communicators and their ads reflect the dynamism of the Brazilian people.'

(William O'Barr, Advertising and Society Review, 2008)

Brazilian advertisements are characterised by humour, strong visual imagery, sexuality and semi-naked bodies. As we have seen, Brazilian advertisements have been winning international awards since the 1970s (O'Barr, 2008; Matellart, 1991), and some very clever and humorous campaigns have a cult following. Brazil boasts the longest running ad campaign in the world – more than 800 different 30-second ads in the last 32 years – for the cleaning product Bombril (O'Barr, 2008). Created by iconic local agency W/Brasil, the advertisements are based on the idea that men do not do housework. Actor Carlos Moreno, who has been doing the advertisements since 1978 and has become a celebrity in his own right, impersonates a whole range of characters, including famous people and politicians. When the ad campaign was dropped briefly there was a public outcry and it was reinstated (author interview with Guime Davidson, 2009).

O'Barr (2008) has claimed that when foreign companies came to Brazil they wanted campaigns they could use throughout Latin America, where the main language is Spanish rather than the Portuguese spoken in Brazil. In order to export campaigns there was a downplaying of language and more emphasis on the visual. However, Walter Longo (in an interview with the author), disputed this and said the Brazilian market was by far the largest in Latin America, and that advertisements were not made with a view to exporting them to other countries.

Brazilian advertising is known for celebrating 'the body beautiful and sexuality' and O'Barr has links to advertisements that would not be permitted on television in the United States (Boy Candies, advertisement by W/Brasil). There are, however, some regulations on sexual content in advertising. In December 2003 Brazil's advertising regulatory body, the National Advertising Council, banned the use of erotic content in all alcohol advertising, including animated characters, in an attempt to reduce alcohol consumption among minors (National Law Center for Inter-American Free Trade, 2003). Nelson and Paek's study (2005) of advertisements in *Cosmopolitan* in 2002 found that nudity levels in Brazil were high, though most were associated with ads for cosmetics and fashion. Their later cross-cultural comparison of television advertising in seven countries showed generally less nudity in television advertisements in all countries. Brazilian television advertisements had more nudity in some categories but the largest Brazilian category, by far, was people fully clad, and out of the seven countries Brazil had the second highest number of fully clad people. When there was some degree of nakedness the commonest category in Brazil was 'partially clad' (Nelson and Paek, 2008).

Sport is one of the three main areas where global campaigns can be used (Millward Brown, 2009) and where there are internationally shared values. But Brazil's passion for football (soccer) in particular seems to have led it to develop its own campaigns to accompany such sporting events as the FIFA World Cup, which is contested every four years. The dominance of black Brazilian soccer stars has meant more black people appearing in advertisements, especially in World Cup years. A study comparing how black people featured in television advertisements during the 1994 and 1998 World Cups revealed that 1994 was a year of significant change, with celebrity endorsements by black soccer stars. Many of these stars have blonde girlfriends, and this combination was starting to appear in advertisements as well, though never blonde men with black women. When black women appear in advertisements it is usually in a domestic service role (Rial, 2001).

Creativity

For decades Brazil's creative and award-winning advertising has been produced by independent local agencies staffed by Brazilian people. During the 1990s many of these agencies entered into joint venture arrangements with foreign agencies. At the time it was seen to be a positive move that would allow companies to leverage more financial backing and international expertise, but in 2009 both Walter Longo of Y&R and Guime Davidson of W/Brasil felt that some spark had left Brazilian advertising in recent years.

Another product of creative competition and the premium placed on awards in Brazil has been the phenomenon of the ghost advertisement: campaigns created not to meet a client brief but simply to win awards. They were aired only once, often paid for by the agency. An example from DM9DDB Publicidade for Spicy Catsup won gold at Cannes in 1999 but was shown just once (O'Barr, 2008).

Snapshot studies of advertising 2009

While in Brazil in 2009 I made a quick snapshot survey of outdoor advertising in Rio de Janeiro, Sao Paulo and Salvador. Among the most advertised products were Skol beer ('Skol one litre the most economical way to save') and a social service campaign with a large fist and the text: 'The Federal Medicine Council is fighting for Brazilian doctors and the health of Brazilians'. There were some distinct regional variations. Salvador had a lot of advertisements for entertainment, reflecting the tourism that underpins the city, and many telling people how crime was being dealt with – that 6,600 new police were being employed, for example – or reminding people about controlling noise. Apart from Skol beer the other two main advertising categories were upmarket housing developments and education.

In São Paulo in the south, the ban on outdoor advertising meant that the only outdoor advertising I saw was beside the highway to and from the airport. The emphasis was on consumer electronics – apparently a bulk buy of billboard space – with LG and Samsung prominent (smartphones and a range of other products). There were also a number of automobile advertisements, particularly by Ford, Hyundai and Nissan. The product shot was the most common strategy for electronic goods. There was also advertising for telecommunication services (Bandesco, Claró) and banking and credit services (Banco Real Santando, for example).

There was little advertising on the streets of Rio de Janeiro, except around the highway near the big football stadium. On the way to the city the two most common billboards featured L'Oréal and TIM (Telecom). There was a campaign for McDonald's supporting child cancer. At Copacabana there were ads urging people to keep the beach clean and also many, in freestanding double-sided stands along the edge of the beach, for telecommunications services. There was some advertising in stand-alone displays along the streets of Rio, with the time and temperature displayed underneath. Most appeared to advertise concerts and shows and a few promoting breast-feeding showed a woman breast feeding a baby. There was some advertising for telecommunications companies, including Vivo, Claró and TIM. There was not even much neon on the top of buildings at the end of the main street, Rio Branco. The overall impression, from the three cities visited, was that Brazil had the lowest level of outdoor advertising among the BRICs.

Figure 2.1 Major advertiser Skol beer. The most common outdoor advertisement in Brazil in 2009: 'The Skol one litre is here. The most satisfying way to save.'

Figure 2.2 Social service advertising in Salvador: '6,600 new police officers. The Government is making your life better. Bahia – the land of us all (2009).'

Figure 2.3 Low budget social service advertising. Left: 'When you drink and drive, go home in a taxi not an ambulance'. Right: Education is one of the largest categories of advertising in Brazil (Salvador, 2009).

Figure 2.4 Top foreign advertiser, Ford. Brazil has the highest level of vehicle ownership of all the BRICs (Rio de Janeiro, 2009).

Figure 2.5 Vivo, one of the top local advertisers: 'Talk in Brazil and in more than 190 countries. It's worth being Vivo' – a play on words, 'vivo' also means 'It's worth being alive' (São Paulo, 2009).

3 Russia

'The economic expansion of the last eight years has only restored Russia to its 1990 level of real GDP.'

(Rory MacFarquhar, 'Russia: A smooth political transition', 2007)

Introduction

Russia is a developed industrialised economy with a different economic profile from the others in the BRIC quartet. It has the largest land area in the world, though much of it is uninhabited, and there is still considerable potential for future expansion of the agricultural sector, which has been neglected over the last two difficult decades since the Soviet Union finally collapsed in 1991. Though Russia's industrial capacity is underutilised and in decay, educational standards are good, right through to the tertiary sector, which is important for future development. The economy was essentially bankrupt in 1989 and the first ten years of liberalisation were chaotic. The sudden introduction of capitalism, when there was a powerful political bureaucracy and no political or legal infrastructure, led to rampant corruption. Totalitarianism was replaced with economic control by an unregulated oligarchy of former Communist bureaucrats. The free market really never got a chance. Inflation soared and the economy imploded. In the last decade the combination of rising international commodity prices and Vladimir Putin's leadership has stabilised the economy, but it was restored to 1990 levels only in 2007 (MacFarquhar, 2007). Of all the BRIC countries Russia was the most adversely affected by financial crisis in 2008 and 2009, when its export markets contracted. In 2009 growth was negative minus 7.9 per cent – but in 2010 it had expanded to reach 3.8 per cent.

The fortunes of the Russian advertising sector have paralleled these wider economic changes. There was a burst of expansion in the early 1990s when foreign advertisers first arrived: advertising expenditure reached $2.7 billion in 1997 (Savchenko, 1999). Many foreign companies left during the 1998 financial crisis and though there was an expansion of Russian advertising, it did not replace the foreign contribution. According to Mark Sanor of Ernst & Young total advertising expenditure declined from $1.3 billion in 1998 to $572 million in 1999. After 2001 advertising began to expand and by 2002 expenditure had reached $2 billion ('World Magazine Trends 2004/2005', FIPP/ZenithOptimedia). By 2005 that figure was $4.6 billion and it reached a high of $9 billion in 2008. During the international financial crisis expenditure plummeted to $6.7 billion in 2009 but by 2010 it had reached $7.4 billion and is predicted to reach $8.5 billion in 2011 (GroupM, 2010) but has yet to regain 2008 levels.

Political and economic background

In the Soviet era products were scarce, there were few to choose from, quality was poor and supply was erratic. Consumer products were given low priority under state socialism but the breakdown of Communism unleashed consumer demand, though declining living standards meant people could not afford the newly available products. The retail sector was poorly developed. Shops were entered through dark and barricaded doorways, and there were neither signage nor window displays to indicate what was on sale. Rather than retail stores and supermarkets, street kiosks, often clustered together in key locations, were the main outlet for a whole range of items. Prices varied depending on the price paid for goods by kiosk owners. In the next decade the retail sector was showing signs of change. Because distribution was quite difficult, people would descend on main cities and buy up goods for resale back in their home towns (Wicken, 2006). The retail sector has continued to expand and people have quickly adapted to change. Russians are now very used to a large range of products on their shelves, compared with only one or two options in the Soviet era (Zaitseva, 2008).

In 1989 Russia was already a developed industrialised society and had been one of the two political superpowers of the second half of the twentieth century. It had a legacy of 70 years of Communist rule and a command economy, in comparison with China, which had followed the Communist economic model for only 30 years. After Mikhail Gorbachev began gradually to introduce economic reform, *perestroika*, in the 1980s, an economic crisis prompted a change of direction and a rapid and brutal structural adjustment programme was introduced in the early 1990s. The World Bank and the IMF were instrumental in promoting this approach and the economist Jeffrey Sachs played a leading role. Economists who opposed this approach, including former Senior Vice-President of the World Bank, Joseph Stiglitz (2002), believed further economic decline would result from such stringent structural adjustment policies.

Many of the institutions of politics and power in Russia had evolved out of the feudal system of centralised control, and economic changes were introduced in the absence of any systems of governance or an equitable justice system. There were few checks and balances. The liberalisation of the Russian economy accelerated after 1991 as the Soviet socialist system was dismantled and state assets were privatised. The economically ignorant population sold off their allocated shares very cheaply, while those who had been in power in the Soviet era quickly took over the state-owned enterprises they had formerly run. Former

Communist Party members used their positions to gain access to wealth and benefits. Ownership was soon in the hands of an economic oligarchy, and the Russian mafia, all connected with the military and the former secret service, the KGB. The privatisation of the economy was characterised by rampant corruption, financial speculation and profiteering. In 1997 it was estimated that nearly 73 per cent of the banking sector was under mafia control and the trafficking of nuclear material was a particularly lucrative activity (*The Economist*, February 2007). This process of transition was paralysed in 1998 when the Russian state was again bankrupt and unable to pay its IMF loans (Morris, 2005). The World Bank estimated that the Russian economy had decreased by 7.6 per cent between 1987 and 1997 (World Bank, 2008).

Foreign firms flooded into Russia in the early 1990s, hoping to market goods to 'deprived' Russian consumers. It was not, however, the easiest or cheapest place to do business and many foreign firms found profits were elusive. Levels of consumer demand were not as high as expected because of the rapidly declining standard of living and wider economic uncertainty. Many foreign products could be purchased only with foreign currency or were simply too expensive. Some foreign firms took advantage of high levels of consumer demand to flood the market with poor quality goods, often made in China (Petrov, 2000).

The election of Putin as president in 2000 – he had become acting president a year earlier when Yeltsin resigned – brought about political and economic stability and economic growth rates started to rise. The main source of Russia's economic strength was the exploitation of natural resources and the surge in international commodity prices (MacFarquhar, 2007). Later in the decade the oil and gas industry still accounted for nearly 25 per cent of GDP, much of the state's tax revenue, and 33 per cent of state income (O'Leary, 2008). When Putin was re-elected in 2004 economic growth and poverty reduction were the key goals. To facilitate the expansion of foreign investment, in 2006 it was made easier to convert the rouble to foreign currency, which also stimulated tourism (Grech, 2006). Because it is heavily dependent on exports of oil, gas, steel and aluminium, the Russian economy was one of the hardest hit by the 2008–09 economic crisis when export markets dried up. The government is now keen to broaden the economic base and build up other sectors of the economy. On the Russian president's 2010 visit to the United States he indicated that Russia wanted to set up its own Silicon Valley (BBC World News, June 2010).

A number of problems must be tackled before they retard Russia's future growth. These include a declining workforce, high levels of corruption, the urgent need to upgrade the infrastructure after two decades of neglect (CIA, 2011b) and the pervasiveness of the black economy. Income statistics are not accurate and, more importantly, state tax income is lost through non-reporting. Business and economic activity continues to be developed without law, transparency or honesty (*New Internationalist*, 2007). Another problem identified by international credit rating agency Standard & Poor's is the relative weakness of local companies and their lack of resources, which makes them more liable to takeover by foreign multinationals. Such takeovers have been occurring in the consumer goods sectors, especially food and beverages (Wiggins, 2008). In the early 1990s most cigarette manufacturing in Russia was quickly taken over by foreign companies (Morris, 2005).

Social background

Under the Communist system Russia's social structure was relatively flat and the gap between the income levels of those at the top and bottom of the system was not as wide as in capitalist economies. When the social welfare system was dismantled in the 1990s the poor lost their social safety net of subsidised food, housing, transport and secure employment. For the mass of the population the results were devastating: the numbers living on less than $2 a day increased by 30 per cent. The living conditions of the poor continued to worsen, with women in particular badly affected. The consumer goods industries were also affected as people could not buy products. For most of the population, living standards were worse than they had been under the Soviet system. According to the UN Human Development Index, Russia scores well in terms of human development – food, education, health, housing, employment (United Nations Development Programme, 2011) – but poverty levels are high compared with other industrialised nations. Poverty levels averaged around 30 per cent for most of the 1990s but declined after 2000, down to 19.6 per cent in 2002, according to the World Bank (2010). These figures were higher in a 2002 report by Amnesty International (published in 2002), which found that almost one in three Russians were living in poverty, that basic pensions were below survival levels and that more than 60 per cent of pensioners were at risk (cited in *New Internationalist*, 2007). In 2007 the percentage had gone down further, to 13.1 (CIA, 2011b).

Russia is the only BRIC economy to have a declining population, predicted to go down to 109 million by 2050 (US Census, 2011b), owing to a combination of declining birth rates and poor health, mainly that of men. Male life expectancy is 59.7 years (the same as the Dominican Republic) compared with women at 72.1 years. Russia has high abortion and suicide rates but the profile is largely the result of poverty, alcoholism, stress and disease. Russia has the highest per capita consumption of cigarettes in the world (Morris, 2005) and alcohol consumption is also very high. An estimated 60 per cent of accidents are considered to be alcohol related. Alcohol consumption levels dipped in Russia during the 1980s, but since the Soviet era ended social economic uncertainty has contributed to increasing consumption and rates of alcoholism have doubled. Per capita pure alcohol intake doubled during the 1990s, from 3.8 to 8.7 litres in 2003 (Kuznetsova, 2008).

Though social inequalities and poverty grew after 1991 the small percentage of extremely rich people has also expanded. Russia has 53 dollar billionaires, and Moscow 88,000 dollar millionaires (O'Leary 2008). The middle classes were much smaller in Russia than in other industrialised countries. According to Wicken, in 1994 they made up between 10 and 15 per cent of the population, which amounts to between 14.8 and 22 million people (1996). By the late 1990s the middle classes had contracted to 10 per cent of the population; the middle classes in the United States at that time made up 64 per cent of the population (*Moscow Times*, 2000). In the last decade, as the economy stabilised and incomes started to increase, consumption levels have risen and the middle classes have begun to expand.

MacFarquhar estimated that though average wages increased more than eight times between 1999 and 2007, for the average Russian this was simply a return to 1990 levels rather than being 'an economic miracle' (2007). Even the middle classes have struggled with high costs of living and comparatively low incomes and Russia still has low ownership levels of consumer durables compared with western European countries (Grech, 2006). Workers' salaries doubled between 2003 and 2008, and in 2006 consumption grew 27 per cent. In Russia growth and rising living standards tend to be confined to the main cities and the oil cities, so the effects are not as widespread as in, say, China, where improvements are spreading to the third and fourth tier cities (O'Leary, 2008).

A whole generation of Russians has now grown up in the post-Communist era. The population is relatively young and urban with 73 per cent living in cities in 2008. In 2011, 13 per cent of the population was aged over 65 and 15.2 per cent under 15 (CIA, 2011b). The proportion of older people is higher than that in China, where an ageing population is seen to be a problem. Older Russian consumers can remember the austerity and security of the Soviet era, but those under 25 have no such memories and have no difficulty in embracing consumerism (O'Leary, 2008).

Advertising in Russia

There has always been advertising in the Soviet Union and Russia, but its nature has reflected the wider political and economic situation, and there are three clearly defined eras: pre-Second World War, 1945–90 and post-1990. Before the First World War Russian advertising was similar to that of other capitalist countries; dominated by rational descriptive strategies that emphasised internationally common product qualities. After the revolution in 1917 the focus of advertising became political propaganda for the new government. The posters of the time included examples of the flowering of early Russian modernism and abstraction. One, which epitomised the merging of political idealism and modernism, was El Lissitzky's 1919 lithograph, 'Beat the Whites with the Red Wedge', which features in most western design textbooks as an icon of early modernist Russian design. After the ascent of Stalin, the modernist abstract style was dismissed as decadent and replaced by socialist realism. After 1945, under the Soviet command economy, advertising took on a more functional role. Its main purpose was to fulfil socially and politically defined goals, including getting rid of surpluses, which were often of poor quality (Hanson, 1974). The market expanded after the 1960s and by 1980 the Soviet advertising market was estimated to be worth $750 million (Mattelart, 1991).

In many ways the expansion of commercial advertising since 1989 symbolises some of the wider changes in Russian society and economy, and the blossoming of outdoor advertising has changed the landscape of Russian cities.

During the first years of the market economy, until the economic crisis of 1998, advertising expanded rapidly but disjointedly. Rapid changes created major dislocation in society and it was hard for advertisers to identify markets and audiences. Multinational companies and their agencies soon dominated the Russian advertising sector but profits were low because margins were small. Strategies tended to be broad-based and untargeted. When foreign agencies used lifestyle advertising it was often misunderstood and resented by the Russian people. Because there was no tradition of commercial advertising there was no local professional expertise. Since understanding consumers and trying to meet their needs had been alien concepts under the Soviet system, local advertising was comparatively crude and unsophisticated. Businesses had different agendas and little experience of the market. Economic instability caused by rapid liberalisation made the future uncertain and the dangers presented by the mafia encouraged a business focus on short-term gain rather than long-term planning.

Foreign companies saw the post-Soviet Russian market as a great opportunity for expansion. Because of the high investment costs and the need to sustain long-term investment, only the major international corporations, which could withstand the risk of failure and could afford to wait for long-term results, had the financial resources to venture into Russia. Most of the large multinationals in the FMCG sectors came to Russia in the 1990s. Though there had been a long period of consumer deprivation, and demand was high, the market was still quite small because disposable incomes were so low.

In the early 1990s Russia seemed to offer a unique opportunity for foreign advertisers to shape the market. Both local and foreign advertising expenditure expanded until 1997, growing from $250 million in 1993 (Tantsura, 1995) to $655 million in 1995, and reaching $2.7 billion in 1997 (Savchencko, 1999). There was a rapid decline to $1.8 billion in 1998. Foreign advertisers, hardest hit by the devaluation of the rouble, reduced their advertising expenditure or withdrew completely from Russia (ibid.).

The fast-moving consumer goods companies have dominated Russian advertising expenditure in the last two decades. In 1993 the most advertised products were spirits, cigarettes and chocolate bars (Goldman, 1993) but during the 1990s personal products emerged as the dominant sector. As foreign investment flooded into Russia the percentage of foreign advertising spending increased from 33 to 56 per cent. By 1995 nine of the top ten advertisers were foreign companies. Procter & Gamble has been the largest advertiser since the 1990s, while L'Oréal has emerged as the second largest advertiser in the last decade. Procter & Gamble came to Russia in 1991 and since then the Russian arm of the company has been its fastest developing subsidiary. Procter & Gamble sells more than 70 of its brands in Russia, the main ones being Ariel, Tide, Fairy, Blend-a-med, Pampers, Always, Pantene, Head & Shoulders, Wella and Gillette. It has dominant market share in 75 per cent of the categories where it operates, especially detergents, shampoos and diapers (Procter & Gamble corporate website, 2010). Procter & Gamble has also started developing cheaper products, such as Tix detergent, for the lower tier markets (as it has in China). This is what Doctoroff (2005) calls 'downward brand extension'.

Chocolate is an important advertising category in Russia: in 1993 it was one of the three most advertised products. When the Mars Corporation came to Russia in the early 1990s it inundated the market with Snickers advertising, making aggressive use of American images and slogans, and bombarding the public in a manner reminiscent of Soviet political propaganda. Snickers quickly became a leader in the confectionery sector, valued at an estimated $2.5–$3.2 billion. Mars, along with Schweppes, saturated the market with so much advertising they stimulated a consumer backlash. By 1998 people had turned against Snickers and it became an 'icon for the US invasion of Russia'. This 'Russianisation in the chocolate market' resulted in a drop of the foreign share of total sales from 80 per cent in 1992 to 33 per cent in 1998 (Caryl, 1998). Foreign soft drinks have not become as popular in Russia as they have in other countries even though PepsiCo has been in Russia since 1974 with its Tropicana brand. The most popular low-alcohol drink is still a fermented bread-based drink called *kvass*.

The alcohol and cigarette industries in Russia are among the largest advertisers. These are also sectors where there are strong interest groups and lobbies, and on which the government depends for taxes. In 2004, for example, an attempt to ban drinking in public was foiled by the strong alcohol lobby (Osbourn, *BMJ*, 2004). As anti-smoking legislation increased in the industrialised nations in the 1990s the international tobacco industry began to focus more attention on emerging markets like Russia, and during the 1991–93 period Russian imports of foreign tobacco and cigarettes grew exponentially, stimulating local demand. In 1990 Russia was the third largest cigarette market after China and the United States. According to Morris the cigarette market was relatively unregulated in the 1990s and was the largest advertising category. Though there had been a wide range of anti-smoking policies in the Soviet Union, during the transition period cigarette companies took advantage of confusion over the status of Soviet legislation. As part of the liberalisation of the economy foreign companies were allowed to enter into joint ventures or buy up bankrupt Russian companies. Within a short while all cigarette

Table 3.1 Russia leading advertisers 1995

Procter & Gamble
Mars Russia
Mosekspo
Dandy (Dirol, Stimerol)
Unilever and Urinus
Wrigley
Matshushita (Panasonic)
Cadbury (Schweppes)
L'Oréal (Garnier)
Samsung

Source: Wicken G. 'Marketing in Russia' (June 1996). *Admap Magazine*. Online. Available www.warc.com/admap (accessed December 2009).

manufacturing in Russia was in foreign hands. Multinational companies brought some major changes to the sector. By the mid-1990s foreign companies, as well as promoting their global brands, began taking over older brands from the Soviet era, and launched new brands for the Russian market. Iava, the most popular cigarette brand in post-Soviet Russia, had been taken over by BAT (British American Tobacco Company) when it bought the factory in the early 1990s (Morris, 2005). BAT documents, made public through litigation in the US, revealed that the company had created demand for legal and smuggled products, and followed this by investments and forging political connections.

In July 1995 tobacco advertising was banned on television but there continued to be a high level of tobacco advertising on billboards (ibid.). Billboards provided a cheap option for advertisers when times were difficult at the end of the decade (Savchencko, 1999). By the end of 2000 multinational tobacco companies had invested $1.7 billion in Russia. A 2001 attempt to rein in the industry was undermined by powerful industry lobbying (Morris, 2005) and by 2002 tobacco advertising, totalling £26 million, was the major outdoor advertising category in Russia (TNS Gallup poll cited in Morris, 2005). In 2006 tobacco advertising was also banned on billboards (Grech, 2006).

Multinational tobacco company investment remained high after 2000. Investment by cigarette companies in Russia amounted to 4 per cent of foreign direct investment and cigarette production had increased by more than 400 per cent. Since 2000 the tobacco companies have stimulated demand both by developing new products and by increasing their advertising marketing efforts. Since the opening of the economy, new brands, with filters and a lighter taste, have been developed to appeal to new smokers, particularly women, whose cigarette consumption has grown, especially in cities. Comparison surveys in Moscow between 1985 and 1995 indicated that there was an increase in smoking among young people, particularly girls (*Multinational Monitor*, May/June 2005).

Russia has always been famous for its high levels of alcohol consumption. Twenty years ago there were only four types of alcohol available: vodka, wine, beer and local brandy. The national drink was vodka, traditionally drunk on every occasion. It is relatively tasteless, so the consumption motivations are quite different from the west, where choice largely is based on taste (Kuznetsova, 2008). Until television advertising for alcohol (spirits) and cigarettes was banned in 1995, expenditure was high (Savchenko, 1999).

Social patterns of alcohol consumption have changed radically in the last decade. Instead of drinking at home, people are going out more, especially in major cities. Kuznetsova (2008) considers that alcohol consumption has increased since 2001 because incomes are rising, rather than, as in the 1990s, as a response to social and economic deprivation. Vodka is still the most common drink and very cheap: in March 2008 half a litre cost R100, or $4, but could be bought for as little as R70–80. Russia is now one of the fastest growing alcohol markets in the world, especially for whisky, rum, liqueurs and other spirits.

Beer became the fashionable Russian drink in the 1990s: per capita annual intake increased from 24.2 litres in 1994 to 28.4 litres in 1999. As late as 2001 beer was not considered an alcoholic drink and there were no regulations defining the quality or quantity of alcohol content (Savva, 2001). Beer is still regarded as a soft drink by many Russians, and the country's brewers have enjoyed huge success since the collapse of the Soviet Union (Osbourn, 2004). In 2005 regulations on beer were introduced in an attempt to curb alcohol consumption by young people. Strategies that were forbidden included using human, animal or cartoon characters (such as Joe Camel for Camel cigarettes). It was also forbidden to suggest that drinking beer would help social, sporting or personal success, or improve one's physical or mental condition. Beer advertisements were banned on television between 7am and 10pm and in publications that dealt with youth, health or sports, and on billboards within 100 yards of a hospital, school or athletic centre. There had been similar advertising regulation on spirits since 1995 (*Alcohol and Drug Abuse Weekly*, 2004; cited in Shemesh, 2004).

Beer sales account for 19 per cent of the alcohol market ($3.4 billion in 2007). Of the 1400 beer brands in Russia, between 40 and 50 advertise on television. Most of the brands are local and western brands account for only 10 per cent of sales (though 17 per cent of the value). All beer production is in the hands of multinationals (Kuznetsova, 2008). In 2002 the brewing industry was the second largest category in outdoor advertising, spending $9 million, much less than the tobacco sector (TNS Gallup poll, cited in Morris, 2005). The Russian Government, 'no longer willing to be a leading alcohol consumption country', introduced legislation in 2009 to limit the advertising of alcohol in an effort to reduce high levels of alcoholism. With a contracting market beer companies are focusing product development and marketing on targeting women (Euromonitor, 2010). Certainly when I visited in 2008 and 2010 beer advertising, especially foreign brands, was prominent in outdoor advertising in kiosks and freestanding advertisements on the main streets of Moscow and St Petersburg.

Foreign media and advertising agencies came to Russia relatively early. In 1988 Silvio Berlusconi's Pubitalia was one of the first foreign companies to enter Russia. It was allocated a three-year contract for control of the foreign advertising on three Soviet television channels. Foreign advertising agencies soon followed. Y&R was the first to enter Russia, also in 1988. It established a joint venture agency with the Russian agency Sovero. The government has been a key advertiser in Russia since the late 1980s and has close ties with major advertising agencies. In 1993 the government awarded the largest campaign of the next decade, for the 1993 privatisation of state enterprises, to joint venture Y&R/Sovero (Goldman, 1993). In 1989 Saatchi & Saatchi was hired to consult with Gosteleradio, the government committee in charge of Soviet Union radio and television. In 1990 McCann Erickson took 51 per cent ownership in a joint venture with the news agency Novosti (Mattelart, 1991). In the early 1990s major western advertising agencies in Moscow included D'Arcy Masius Benton & Bowles (Mars, Procter & Gamble), Ogilvy & Mather, BBDO (Wrigley, Pepsi, Avon), BSB/Saatchi & Saatchi, McCann Erikson (Coca-Cola) and Young & Rubicam/Sovero (Goldman, 1993). These agencies, except for Ogilvy & Mather, were among the top ten American advertising agencies in 1995 (Biagi, 1996).

There were three types of advertising agency in Russia in the 1990s: foreign agencies, large newly formed Russian advertising agencies and the medium and small Russian agencies. Estimates of the number of agencies in Moscow varied from 1,000 to 2,000 but the total number in Russia was 4,500 (Savchenko, 1999). Moscow has always been the heart of Russian advertising.

Though advertising expenditure was increasing, agency profits were slow in coming. In 1993 most agencies were getting the majority of their revenue not from advertising but from public relations, promotions, direct mail and distribution. Cheap production costs, and presumably billings and media rates, meant that agencies could not make the same profits as in the west. Many of the variables that contributed to instability in the economy also affected the advertising sector. The support system was negligible, the media was ill-defined, and taxes and regulations were confusing. In 1993 a government committee was formed to set up a regulatory framework that would introduce some order into the advertising sector (Goldman, 1993). On an operational level advertising agencies were also held back by such difficulties as the absence of copyright laws or a robust legal system. There was creative theft, where companies put forward pitches and the job was then awarded to a different company, which was then asked to execute its rival's initial concept (Wells, 1996). As we have seen, there was a shortage of local advertising expertise, both for copywriters and art directors (Burgoyne, 1995; Repiev, 1997).

After the 1998 debt crisis and the devaluation of the rouble, many foreign companies left Russia because their businesses were no longer profitable. Others reduced their expenditure. Later in the decade expatriates in advertising agencies 'left en-masse' when the foreign business sector contracted. They were replaced by Russians who had been trained in the same agencies but were paid at local, rather than foreign, salary rates. The Publicis Groupe pulled out of Russia in 1998 after the head of the Moscow office was beaten up by local racketeers trying to sell him 'protection'. A number of other agencies also pulled out at this time (O'Leary, 2008). This presented an opportunity for local producers to push their brands and even President Boris Yeltsin urged consumers to buy Russian goods (MacFarquhar, 2007). 'Russianness' came back into vogue (Caryl, 1998) and by 1998 Russian advertisers made up 30 per cent of all advertising revenues. A reduction in advertising rates meant more local advertisers could afford to advertise (Savchenko, 1999). Russian marketers who had gained their experience working for global brands now used their expertise to promote Russian brands. The level of local expertise developed quickly, especially in the late 1990s. With the downturn many higher priced foreign goods became too expensive for Russians.

Expanding disposable income levels in the 2000s, and the growth of the middle classes, drew the big multinational companies back to Russia, and those that had stayed had consolidated their positions. As Standard & Poor's had predicted, there have been a number of takeovers of Russian companies in recent years by Unilever, PepsiCo, Kellogg's, Kraft, Nestlé, Coca-Cola and Carlsberg (Wiggins, 2008). Notably, most of these were companies that had remained in Russia through the downturn at the end of the 1990s.

As the economy stabilised in the early 2000s Russian advertising revenue grew steadily, increasing 500 per cent from $940 million in 2000 to $5 billion in 2005 (Grech, 2006). Growth in advertising expenditure outstripped economic growth. By 2006 expenditure had reached an estimated $5.9 billion and then increased to $9.07 billion in 2008. A decade after the 1998 crisis, when the market had stabilised and income differentials had consolidated, Russia was again affected by economic crisis. Expenditure fell to an estimated $6.7 billion in 2009 (GroupM, 2010). Russian markets are not predicted to return to pre-crisis levels until 2012, but the long-term prospects for advertising are good, according to Jones (2009b) and by 2011 advertising expenditure is predicted to grow to $8.5 billion (GroupM, 2010). Revenues in Russia were predicted to increase by an average 5.5 per cent in the two years after 2009 ('Chinese, Indian shoppers keep spending', Nielsen, 2009). Adspend levels in Russia increased by 10 per cent during the first half of 2010, when the World Cup increased television advertising sales ('Advertising expenditure levels rise in Russia', Lenta, 2010). Publicis returned to Russia in the 2000s and all the major advertising agency complexes are again represented. WPP, which entered a joint venture with Video International in 2004, is now the largest entity (O'Leary, 2008).

Procter & Gamble is Russia's largest advertiser. By 2004 its expenditure was much higher than other leading advertisers. At $636.6 million it was twice that of L'Oréal ($314.7 million), the second largest advertiser. In 2008 P&G's advertising budget was $301 million, compared with L'Oréal's $190 million and Unilever's $144 million. Most of its expenditure is on television advertising: in 2008 it spent $180 million, 60 per cent of its advertising budget (Jones, 2009).

Market research companies also came to Russia to provide consumer information for advertisers. Geoff Wicken's company BMRB came to Russia to implement the market research package, the Target Group Index (TGI), which was licensed to the Moscow research company COMCON-2. The Russian data released in 1995 was based on a sample size of 26,000 individuals over ten years old, from 12,000 households in 45 different cities. The greatest inroads into the Russian market had been made by FMCGs with strong brand images, which is logical given the low

Table 3.2 Russia leading advertisers 2009

P&G
L'Oréal
Unilever
Henkel
Mars Inc
Reckitt Benckiser
Danone
Nestlé
Wimm-Bill-Dann
MTS

Source: GroupM (2011). Russia's leading advertisers in 2009 by advertising expenditure.

levels of disposable income. As there were no local colas, this category was dominated by global antagonists Pepsi and Coca-Cola. Non-cola soft drinks were dominated by local brands, though foreign brand Fanta was successful. Russian brands dominated the chocolate bar sector, but foreign brands dominated the filled bars sector as there were no Russian equivalents. Though foreign shampoos were popular the market was dominated by cheaper Russian and Bulgarian brands. Both Nescafe Classic and Jacobs had managed to create a market in the instant coffee sector and had over 11 million buyers, while the Procter & Gamble brands Tide and Ariel were used in five million households (Wicken, 2006).

In the last decade PepsiCo has invested more than $3 billion into Russia, including the $1.4 billion takeover of the Lebedyansky Company, one of the largest Russian juice makers, in 2008. PepsiCo's key brands in Russia are Pepsi Cola, Aqua Minerale and Lipton Iced Tea. In 2009 PepsiCo announced plans to invest $1 billion in Russia over the next three years as part of its ongoing strategy of expansion in emerging markets ('Pepsi to invest $1 billion in Russia', PRN Newswire, 2009). In December 2010, for $3.8 billion, PepsiCo acquired 66 per cent of Wimm-Bill-Dann (PepsiCo corporate website, 2010). Established in the early 1990s, this has been one of the most successful local food corporations in Russia. Its national dairy brands have such folksy names as Little House in the Village, Happy Milkman and Kuban Cow (Wiggins, 2008). Before that takeover Nestlé was the largest foreign food and drink advertiser in Russia (AdIndex, cited in Jones, 2009b).

There was a change in the profile of products advertised after 2000 as the economy stabilised and incomes rose. Chocolate was no longer a major product category, and key emerging sectors have been the telecom industry and in the consumer durable market. By 2005 telecom companies (Beeline, MTS and Megafon) were among the leading Russian brands. In 2008 five of the top 20 advertisers were Russian: Beeline, Megafon, MTS, Wimm-Bill-Dann and Eldorado (AdIndex, cited in Jones, 2009). The largest advertising categories at the end of the 2000s are the food, soft drinks, personal products and telecom companies. Procter & Gamble is the largest advertiser, as it is in most countries. When I visited Russia in 2008 MTS and Beeline were the commonest outdoor advertisers on the streets of St Petersburg, Moscow and Novgorod, and Maybelline adverts were conspicuous as well.

Another indication that standards of living are rising is the increased purchasing of motor vehicles. Purchase levels go up when incomes reach about $9,000 (adjusted for PPP) per capita (Wilson and Dragunasu, 2008). In Russia there is also a recently emerged wealthy sector with abundant disposable income. Though the car manufacturers are not among the top ten advertisers, billboards for automobiles were common in key cities in 2008 and 2011 and social service advertising was another prominent category.

The Russian advertising sector seems to be on the road to recovery after declining dramatically in 2009 to $6.3 billion, though it will be some years before it regains the expenditure levels of 2008 ($8.6 billion). The trade association AKAP claimed that advertising expenditure increased by 10 per cent in first half of 2010, and television advertising by seven per cent, boosted by the World

Cup in South Africa. Outdoor advertising increased 13 per cent to R15 billion ($4.8 billion), and all areas experienced growth. Advertising expenditure had reached $7.4 billion in 2010 and is predicted to increase again to $8.5 billion in 2011 (GroupM, 2010).

Media

One of the most significant and symbolic changes brought about by liberalisation has been the introduction of advertising, including foreign advertising, on television. Because the Russian Federation is so vast in size and stretches over 11 time zones, television is the medium with the capacity to reach the greatest audience. In the 1990s it quickly became the dominant advertising medium, especially for foreign advertisers, and this dominance continues to the present day. There are close ties between advertising, the media and the state. In the sector that sells advertising there are only three main companies: Video International, Gazprom Media and CTC Media. Video International, established by one of Putin's advisers, controls 80 per cent of television advertising sales. It has a partnership with WPP (O'Leary, 2008).

There was a high level of advertising allowed on television in the 1990s compared with today. In 1995 the permitted daily quota increased to four-and-a-half hours (Burgoyne, 1995). Since 2000 the number of television channels in Russia has doubled and the cost of advertising increased by 237 per cent between 2005 and 2008 (O'Leary, 2008). The amount of advertising time allowed per hour was reduced from 15 to 12 minutes in 2006, and the daily total had to be less than 15 per cent of daily broadcasting. In 2008 it was further reduced to nine minutes per hour (ibid.).

The media profile of advertising is continuing to change. The proportion of print advertising was consistently 40 per cent throughout the 1990s ('World Magazine Trends 2004/2005', FIPP/ZenithOptimedia). This began to decline in the next decade, reducing to 30 per cent in 2000, 28 per cent in 2005 and down to 16 per cent in 2010. That year television advertising stood at 58 per cent, having increased rapidly from 46.3 per cent in 2005. Outdoor advertising was 11 per cent of the total in 1998 (Savchencko, 1998) and this sector has remained consistently larger than in other BRIC countries though it too is beginning to decline, from 18 per cent in 2005 to 15 per cent in 2010. The Russian media profile has broadened in recent years with the uptake of social media, internet marketing and mobile marketing. The internet is still a small sector of the advertising market, accounting for 1.2 per cent in 2005, four per cent in 2008 and 4.4 per cent in 2010 (Wan-IFRA, 2010: 913). There are comparatively low levels of internet penetration in Russia, which is only 27.1 per cent, slightly higher than China, but much lower than in western industrialised countries (Jones, 2009).

Computer ownership levels have risen throughout the decade. Internet users have expanded from 9.2 million in 2000 (CIA, 2001) to 40.8 million in 2009 (CIA, 2011b). By 2005 online advertising was already the fastest growing medium, having grown 71.4 per cent over 2004. But at $60 million it still only represented

1.2 per cent of advertising spending (Grech, 2006). Internet advertising is increasing quite rapidly, and in 2008 had reached 2.8 per cent, though this is still a small percentage of the total advertising spend. Expenditure was expected to grow with greater broadband penetration (Jones, 2009). Internet advertising experienced the fastest growth, with sales jumping by 33 per cent to $3.5 million in the first half of 2010. Procter & Gamble was the leading online advertiser, spending R220 million or $8.8 million ('Advertising expenditure levels rise in Russia', Lenta, 2010).

Mobile phones are much more affordable than computers and ownership levels in Russia are already very high. In 2009 mobile phone ownership had reached 230 million (CIA, 2011b), up from 2.5 million in 2001 (CIA, 2001). The uptake of smartphones should increase internet access in Russia as it has in other countries. It is only the big companies with large advertising budgets that have the resources and budgets to explore new media options.

Cultural values and attitudes

Russia was a relatively modern industrialised society in 1991. Though there was little choice and product quality was often poor, people were familiar with the products common in capitalist societies. Television ownership levels were also high and people were familiar with western culture. Russian society has changed dramatically in every sector over the last two decades. New opportunities, such as foreign travel and the entry of foreign companies and products, have stimulated consumerism. Though Russia still upholds traditional values such as 'the primacy of family, social acceptance, stability and health', people are also 'ready to pay any price to become wealthy, famous and successful' (Zaitseva, 2008).

In the 1990s the Russian people welcomed the end of the Soviet era, but mistakenly assumed that there would be an automatic transition to the lifestyle of western high-income nations. Instead they experienced economic and political chaos and a decline in standards of living. In this context foreign advertising carried mixed messages. For many people it symbolised the changes that were taking place, but others were resentful when advertising showed them products they could not afford, or could be bought only with hard currency that they did not have. People were also annoyed when products were advertised that were not available for purchase (Wells, 1996).

Consumer attitudes changed during the next decade as conditions started to improve and people got used to the changes. A 2005 ROMIR Monitoring survey found that 25 per cent of Russians felt negative towards advertising and 78 per cent did not trust advertisements, yet 46 per cent said they had brought products based on advertisements they had seen (Grech, 2006). Results from a TGI survey carried out at the same time were similar; 45 per cent of those surveyed liked to find out about new products and services, while 63 per cent said they did not trust advertising (except for children who trusted it and wanted to buy the products shown). People were price conscious and expected to pay more for foreign brands (Wicken, 2006). The CEO of Publicis Groupe, John Farrell, has claimed that Russians are more receptive to advertising and less cynical that American and British consumers. They are also quite market literate, even though Russia does not have a long history of advertising (O'Leary, 2008). In 2008 the CEO of the Russian food corporation Wimm-Bill-Dann, Tony Maher, was quoted as saying that Russian people like brands: 'They are conspicuous consumers. As they get more money they trade up' (Wiggins, 2008). Russians may like brands but this does not mean they are loyal to them. Like the Chinese, they are emerging consumers who enjoy trying many brands. Price is a key factor in whether they will try a product (O'Leary, 2008).

New media also seem to be having an effect on consumer behaviour. A study by Millward Brown found that people who had previously shopped on the internet were more likely to be loyal to brands, though there was quite a variation between countries: the difference in brand loyalty of internet users compared with non-internet users was 10 per cent in Russia, 2 per cent in China and 15 per cent in India. Though there was some variation with product category the average digital consumers were more likely to be 'transmitters', defined as 'knowledgeable category consumers who influence others with their opinions' ('Digital consumers more loyal to brands', Millward Brown, 2009).

After 80 years of Communism there has been a resurgence of the Russian Orthodox Church but the majority of people are not religious. They may value the family but the declining population seems to reflect a lack of optimism about the future and a response to recent social and economic dislocation. Women have always taken part in the workforce, as well as managing the household, so there is not an emerging group of women working for the first time, as there is in Brazil and India. A TGI study also revealed that the Russian people were pessimistic about the future; they were often melancholy (57 per cent) and they were made shy by indecent anecdotes (Wicken, 2006). This does not mean that Russian people do not have a sense of humour or make jokes about sex. One Russian marketing person told me that there was a lot of sexual innuendo and humour in print advertising, though less on television (private communication, Julia Astashkina, 2010).

Low levels of disposable income have limited the rapid expansion of a youth-oriented consumer culture in Russia but it does still exist. By 1999 the youth market (ages 15–19) was already growing and teen spending amounted to $3 billion. In a survey on teen attitudes to brands, 26 per cent of Russian teenagers said there were things they would not wear or use if they were not the 'right' brand. This level was higher than in Brazil or China but lower than in India (Moses, 2000). In the west the expansion of satellite television and greater independence and affluence has stimulated the child consumer market, but there is little written on this in Russia. The expansion of new technology and rising living standards may prompt an expansion of the youth and child sectors in the next decade. As yet computer ownership levels are relatively low compared with high-income nations, and with China, where online activity and advertising are increasing rapidly.

Liberalisation has also led to the growth of a small percentage of very wealthy people, who were also documented in the TGI survey (Wicken, 1996). Rich for the first time, they are often keen to show off their status with luxury brands. According to Dmitry Korobkov, the chairman of ADV Marketing Communications, as the market gets more mature 'luxury products gradually cease to serve as show-off elements only and are more and more used for personal pleasure' (quoted in O'Leary, 2008). Russia has become the world's fourth largest market for luxury goods; which was estimated to be worth $13 billion in 2008, a 200 per cent increase from 2006 (O'Leary, 2008).

Increased car ownership over the last decade is tangible evidence of greater disposable income. When Russia's new car buyers, members of the elite or middle classes, were interviewed by Carsten Ascheberg of the Sigma Institute Germany in 2006 and 2007, they were purchasing better-equipped and more expensive vehicles. The emerging trend was towards more cultural pluralism and cosmopolitanism and the socio-cultural identity of the consumer was becoming more important in purchasing decisions. Ascheberg defined the new lifestyle elites as, first, the new business milieu, second, young status-seekers and, third, the modern elite. Increasingly, these groups wanted to express their individuality in their car purchasing, rather than showing off their wealth and status. The young status-seekers and the modern elite, with a 20 per cent response rate, were most interested in such features as sustainable technology driving systems. The new lifestyle elites also expressed their individuality in their purchases of clothing, fashion and home furnishing and in the choice of the district where they lived or aspired to live (Ascheberg, 2008).

Advertising strategies

When foreign advertisers and their agencies first moved into the Russian marketplace there was a high level of pent-up consumer demand: people wanted whatever was available and affordable. In the early 1990s it was sometimes enough just for advertisers to announce that they had goods to sell (Burgoyne, 1995). Advertising strategies tended to be broad-based because it was difficult identify the markets (*Art Direction*, 1992). Russian agencies were new to commercial advertising and relatively unsophisticated. Some early advertisements simply tried to raise brand profiles with large billboards displaying the company name without selling any specific product or using any particular strategy (Goldman, 1993). Economic instability encouraged local advertisers to focus on short-term gains rather than long-term planning and their position was much weaker than that of the international advertisers, who were planning for the future and building brands, and had the financial backing to support long-term strategies.

From the outset television was the main advertising medium. Kelly (1998) found that television advertising in 1994 was an undifferentiated mix of 'biscuits, banks and cigarettes, footage of tanks, aeroplanes and heavy artillery'. FMCGs were the main products advertised, which went with low levels of disposable income and the entry of all the major multinational companies. As more products became available and foreign businesses set up production facilities, the numbers of foreign products also increased. Many of the multinationals set up joint licensing deals. For example, Meloni, the company that sold Indesit washing machines, provided free samples of Tide detergent from Procter & Gamble (Savchenko, 1999).

As we have seen, image and lifestyle association strategies that were common-place in the west were not always successful or understood in Russia, where people's responses were often ambivalent. According to Goldman, an American intern in a Moscow agency, pragmatic campaigns were often more successful than image-based campaigns. Marketing a razor by saying 'lasts three months, can use with cold water' would be more acceptable than 'look how sleek you can look' (*Art Direction*, 1992). Attitudes to the west and western products were also mixed. Some groups attacked McDonald's restaurants under the impression that they were being sold inferior meat. But when the world's largest McDonald's was opened in Moscow in Pushkin Square in 1990, people queued for hours.

One approach, used by cigarette companies, Mars and Schweppes, was blanket advertising or the saturation approach. Marlboro sponsored tobacco kiosks on street corners, where most shopping was done. The multinational companies also heavily promoted their generic international brands: L&M, Parliament, Chesterfield, Marlboro, Camel, Lucky Strike, Kent. These brands swamped the market and made local and cheaper brands invisible. Generic billboard advertising was used to swamp many markets throughout Europe at this time. By the mid-1990s Moscow was inundated with L&M advertisements (Philip Morris), encouraging people to 'rendezvous with America'. Brands like Camel (R.J. Reynolds) and Marlboro were also common. From anecdotal evidence Morris (2005) deduced that the young were attracted to the new brands but older consumers remained loyal to older brands. According to Morris, the amount of advertising space devoted to 'Marlboro Man' was small compared with other Philip Morris brands, but when I visited both Moscow and St Petersburg in 1997 Marlboro billboards were by far the most common: the streets were saturated with the brand.

By 1997 consumer ambivalence to foreign advertising had morphed into active anti-westernism 'especially at a time when feelings of nationalism and anti-westernism were intensified by the Kosovo war' (Morris, 2005). People had been discouraged by the empty promises of the transition to capitalism and turned away from the deluge of advertising for products like Mars and Snickers. In response foreign advertisers developed strategies more appropriate to the Russian market, switching, for example, from general year-round advertising to seasonal promotions of certain products like aspirin in winter and anti-perspirants in summer (Savchenko, 1999).

Morris's case study of advertising for Iava cigarettes, actually an ex-Soviet brand, reveals the evolution of advertising strategies and themes during the 1990s. In 1997 BAT relaunched the brand with two options, Iava and Iava Gold, in competition with Philip Morris's L&M. Japanese Tobacco Industries also relaunched the Russian brand 'Petr 1' (Peter the Great). The new Iava campaign played with the late 1990s fashion for 'Russianness' and the general backlash against foreign advertising and images. The slogan 'The counter-strike – Iava strikes back' tapped into anti-American feelings and made references to the popular *Star Wars* movies. On one level the strategy evoked nostalgic references to the past era of Soviet superiority (the lower class interpretation), while the middle classes liked the cleverness of the parody, especially as they knew BAT was a multinational company. As the recession of 1998 deepened the Iava advertising expressed 'powerful fantasies and desires about national consciousness and difference'. It was very successful in both timing and branding. Theresa Sabonis-Chafee called this approach 'ironic nostalgia' (Aleksandrov, 2003). Philip Morris eventually dropped the American themes and replaced them with more international references (Morris, 2005).

After 1998 there was a resurgence in Russian advertising for Russian companies, which took the opportunity left by the departure of many multinationals and their agency creatives. There was a definite bias towards using Russian national identity as a central theme, especially for such products as alcohol, tobacco, dairy products and core consumer goods. A wide range of strategies were used including historic heroes, events and figures (like Peter the Great and Nevsky) from both the distant and the more recent past. Some companies used imagery and language from the Soviet socialist-realist period. Theresa Sabonis-Chafee considers that this type of nostalgia functions like fairy tales by tapping into tradition and making implicit comparisons with the realities of contemporary life (cited in Morris, 2005). Attractive to the psychology of social groups desiring compensation, this type of strategy was commonly used to market cheaper brands to lower income groups (Aleksandrov, 2002 cited in Morris, 2005). Sabonis-Chafee has identified three types of popular cultural references to the Soviet past, or 'communist kitsch': utopian-nostalgic, ironic-nostalgic and camp. After the late 1990s the Iava campaigns became more sophisticated, visually branded, and with a continuity of stylistic features such as type, layout and excellent photography. Russian people, particularly bearded men, were used as models and the vocabulary was more relevant to Russia: 'our', 'soul' and 'team' (ibid.).

Morris concluded that Russian advertising is as sophisticated as that in the rest of Europe, and Russians like parody, irony and advertisements that are intertextual and self-referential. He calls this semiotic understanding of pastiches of Soviet, Russian and foreign cultural artefacts 'ironic-utopian nostalgia'. Russians enjoy Russian and foreign cultural artefacts, and appreciate the differences, while consuming global brands made in foreign-owned factories by multinational companies. The rapid changes in the marketing of cigarettes, beer and alcohol indicate that the Russian identity that is being tapped into is evolving. 'What is most Russian about readings of these adverts is perhaps that its positioning is so insistent and at the same time so unstable' (ibid.).

The alcohol market is both highly regulated and growing, despite the regulations. In recent years the restriction of television advertising of alcohol has prompted the industry to explore alternative strategies. In September 2007 Diageo, the world's largest alcohol company, used an online campaign to promote Bailey's Irish Cream across a number of markets, including Russia. Called 'Moments of Pleasure', free samples were offered online, and a range of gifts were given to the first million who signed up. Diageo got 120,000 Russians to sign up. Johnnie Walker whisky was promoted with Formula 1 sponsorship, combined with a 'responsible drinking ambassadorship' programme. Another strategy was to sponsor the training of more than 10,000 Moscow bartenders in 2007 (Kuznetsova, 2008).

Women and girls

In recent years tobacco companies have been targeting Russian women and girls with aggressive and seductive advertising that exploits ideas of independence, emancipation, sex appeal, slimness, glamour and beauty. In Russia, 24 per cent of girls aged between 13 and 15 and 27 per cent of boys in the same age bracket smoke cigarettes (Center for Disease Control and Prevention, cited by Women and Tobacco: Essential Facts, 2010). In 2007, R.J. Reynolds launched a new type of cigarette for women, Camel No. 9, backed by a major advertising campaign. They advertised in fashion magazines like *Vogue*, which had a large youth readership, and presented their slim cigarettes in colourful and fashionable packaging. In 2009, BAT launched Pall Mall Scarlet Aromatic cigarettes in attractive bright cherry and silver packets designed to appeal to young girls. Pall Mall Scarlet Aromatic was exclusively developed for a pilot launch in Russia at a maximum retail price of $1. In 2010, Imperial Tobacco redesigned Davidoff cigarettes with sleek red, white and silver packaging to project a cosmopolitan feel and create 'the ultimate fashion accessory' (Women and Tobacco: Essential Facts, 2010).

Russia is an important cosmetics market and this is one category in which standard globalised campaigns are widely used. When I was in Russia in both 2008 and 2010, some of the most common outdoor advertisements were those for cosmetics, mainly Maybelline mascara (owned by L'Oréal). Using printable vinyl, which makes them easier to produce, some of the advertisements on the sides of construction sites were multiple storeys high. They were part of a global campaign that used a shot of internationally famous American actress Eva Longoria from *Desperate Housewives*.

A survey conducted by MediaComm found that promotions and sponsorship were the most effective advertising strategies for major brands on television – based on the criteria of awareness, purchase intent and sales – compared with image-based or product news strategies (Zaitseva, 2008). Another strategy being used more frequently is product placement. PQ Media predicted that total product placement spending in TV, film, internet, video games, recorded music and other media will grow at double digit rates in Russia between 2011 and 2014 and that Russia will be the fastest-growing market ('European product placement set for double-digit growth', 2010).

Snapshot studies of advertising 1997, 2008 and 2010

In 1997 I made a snapshot study of outdoor advertising in St Petersburg and Moscow to explore if the profile of products advertised reflected many of the wider changes happening in society. There was a significant amount of foreign advertising concentrated in large-scale billboards, freestanding signs on the main streets and small-scale proliferation of company logotypes. Foreign advertising tended to use more photography compared with Russian advertising, which concentrated on illustration or text alone. Russian advertising still had resourcing and budget constraints and little professional expertise. Foreign advertising tended to promote consumer products whereas a higher proportion of Russian adverts promoted cultural events. The product profile of outdoor advertising was dominated by repeat purchase consumables: cigarettes and fast food rather than expensive consumer durables with the exception of kitchen appliances. Another area of growth was mobile phones and new technology. There was no evidence of political or social service advertising. Emphasis on cheaper products and repeat purchase consumable items reflected low levels of disposable income.

In two recent snapshot surveys of outdoor advertising, in 2008 and 2010, I discovered that the profile of outdoor advertising in metropolitan Russia (Moscow and St Petersburg) has changed significantly since the 1990s. More expensive products are being advertised. The most advertised products are telecom providers, mobile phones, cars, make-up and beer. On the outskirts of the cities on the main highways advertisements for heavy-duty industrial products and equipment predominate, while on the outskirts of Moscow there is a lot of advertising for housing developments. Most outdoor advertising has no Russian references apart from the use of the Cyrillic language. The product shot was the most common strategy, except in the personal products and service categories. The most significant difference between 1997 and 2008 was the absence of cigarette advertising on the streets.

In 2008 I saw much higher levels of social service advertising on billboards than I did in 1997. A very prominent outdoor campaign in St Petersburg showed a large photo and a quote from the writer Alexander Grin urging people: 'Be kind to one another. Malice is the source of evil.' There were a number of anti-smoking billboards in St Petersburg ('No smoking – Freedom means not being dependent.') and others urging the protection of children. In Moscow in 2008 and 2010 I saw more generic ads and banners celebrating the past, with coats of arms on them similar to those I saw in 1997. One campaign in Moscow had the slogan: 'If you take drugs you are on your own'.

Figure 3.1 Foreign advertiser: global campaign – L'Oréal Moscow, the second largest advertiser in Russia. Digital printing on vinyl skins enables enormous advertisements on the sides of construction sites (2008).

Figure 3.2 Social service advertising in St Petersburg (2008) 'Be kind to one another. Malice is the source of evil' (Poet Alexandr Grin).

Figure 3.3 Beer is one of the most advertised products in Russia. Product image rather than lifestyle association is the commonest strategy for beer advertising (2008).

Figure 3.4 Provincial political advertising (Yaroslavl, 2008).

Figure 3.5 Leading Russian advertiser, telecom company Beeline, using lifestyle association to target the youth market (Novgorod), 2008.

4 India

'India is firmly on the growth expressway.'
(Tushar Poddar and Eva Yi, 'India's rising growth potential', 2007)

'During the first millennium, merchants referred to India's glittering and dynamic market as "the bird of gold". That bird is preparing to take flight again.'
(Eric Beinhocker, Diana Farrell and Adil Zainulbhai, 'Tracking the growth of India's middle class', 2007)

Introduction

India and China have recently captured global attention because of their high growth rates, especially throughout the recent international economic crisis. The Indian economy is still in 'take-off' mode, however, running about ten years behind China in terms of development and sectors such as advertising. China started liberalising its economy in 1979 but in India this process did not gain momentum until more than a decade later. Unlike China, however, India has not been entirely divorced from the world for part of the twentieth century, so changes brought about by liberalisation have been much less dramatic. Though India is an unwieldy democracy, poverty reduction, economic change and rising levels of consumption are all occurring and have been accompanied by profound social and cultural changes. All these are taking place in the context of the resilience and continuity of centuries-old traditions and value systems.

As a result of liberalisation there has been a surge of economic growth since 1991. Some sectors of India's economy are booming and an increasing number of people are joining the middle classes and embracing consumerism. Both the consumer goods industries and advertising are expanding rapidly. In 2010 advertising expenditure in India was estimated as $5.6 billion (GroupM, 2010) compared with $1.56 billion in 1997 (Grech, 2006). The evolution of advertising in India, as in the other BRIC economies, reflects both global changes in advertising and the unique features of the local context. Advertising has also responded to the changes in the media, especially the advent of the internet and mobile phones.

Background

India has been one of the fastest growing major economies in the world since 2003 (Poddar and Yi, 2007) and the advertising sector has grown with it. The socio-economic context, and deep-rooted cultural traditions of gender, caste and religion, affect India's advertising industry. This background plays an important role in defining consumer priorities, wants and needs, and in the campaigns and strategies that are used to market products. The wider political and economic context has also had a major impact in the legislative sense and in terms of the policies that affect the standards of living of the population. Socialist ideals inspired the government that came to power when India became independent of Britain in 1947. During the following four decades the economy was closely regulated, highly bureaucratic and protected by tariffs and import restrictions. Many of the big international companies have been in India a long time, but some, including IBM and Coca-Cola, departed in 1973 after the Foreign Exchange Regulation Act limited foreign ownership in companies to 40 per cent (Matellart, 1991). This legislation remained in place until 1991. The government was hostile to business until the 1980s when Rajiv Gandhi recognised that the country was still stagnating after 30 years of independence and living standards had not improved. He made attempts to the reform the economy by borrowing money to stimulate economic growth through investment, but this led the country into indebtedness and by 1990 India was almost bankrupt.

The liberalisation then introduced was similar to the structural readjustment policies imposed by the IMF and World Bank when countries default on loans. (The finance minister, and now prime minister, Manmohan Singh had in fact just returned from working at the World Bank.) Legislation loosened regulations and tariffs and encouraged foreign investment by lowering high trade barriers, reducing tariffs (for example from 200 to 15 per cent) and delicensing industry, which stimulated both industrial growth and exports (Poddar and Yi, 2007). Nearly two decades after China and about the same time that Russia opened up to capitalism, the Indian economy began to grow, increasing almost 6 per cent between 1995 and 2005 (Brown, 2006). These changes also enabled India to join the World Trade Organization (WTO) in 1995. As economic growth created jobs, income levels rose and the middle classes began to expand. There were few global products available in India until the late 1990s. With more disposable income the consumption of goods also increased. Foreign companies and their advertising agencies expanded into India and advertising expenditure increased dramatically. The revenues of the top ten advertising agencies doubled between 1990 and 1995.

Because India has 15 official languages, national advertising campaigns are difficult, except for those targeting the educated, English-speaking middle classes. Until 2000 the concept of western retail was almost unknown in India and most shopping was done in markets and small, mostly family-run, retail outlets, of which there are 12 million (Chaturvedi, 2008). The first western

Table 4.1A India leading advertising agencies 1990

		Gross income (US$, millions)
1	Hindustan Thompson Associates	10,901
2	Lintas: India	8,690
3	Mudra Communications	5,585
4	Ogilvy & Mather	4,534
5	Everest Advertising	3,941
6	Ulka Advertising	3,590
7	R.K. Swamy	2,732
8	Clarion Advertising	2,652
9	Contract Advertising	2,321
10	Chaitra Advertising	2,158
		Total 47,104

Table 4.1b India leading advertising agencies 1995

		Gross income (US$, millions)
1	Hindustan Thompson Associates, Bombay	24,846
2	Ammirati Puris Lintas, India, Bombay	16,451
3	Mudra Communications (DDBN)	12,671
4	Ogilvy & Mather, Bombay	11,150
5	Ulka Advertising (JWT), Bombay	8,410
6	Contract Advertising, (JWT), Bombay	6,862
7	Trikaya Grey, Bombay	6,128
8	R.K. Swamy/BBDO Advertising, Madras	5,870
9	MAA Group (Bozell), Bangalore	5,149
10	Rediffusion-Dentsu, Young&Rubicam	4,605
		Total 102,142

Source: Tharpe, M. 'Advertising Agencies in India compiled by Marye Tharpe' (no date). Online. Available www.ou.edu/class/jmc3333/india.htm (accessed 13 May 2011).

retailers to come to India have been the supermarket chains. Since 100 per cent foreign ownership in the retail sector is still illegal, these companies are entering into joint ventures: Carrefour (Reliance) and Tesco (Tata Corporation). Wal-Mart joined with Bharti Enterprises in 2006 and opened the first outlet of its cash and carry chain called Best Price Modern Wholesale in 2009, stocking about 10,000 items ('Wal-Mart to open Indian arm', *Wall Street Journal*, 2009). Because wages are low and poverty levels high, there is a vast pool of servant labour, so many middle class women do not do housework, cook or shop for food. The domestic household market is therefore quite different from that of other countries.

India has become a global supplier of goods and services. Recent rates of economic growth have continued to be high: 9 per cent in 2007, 7.4 per cent in 2008 and 2009. India now ranks as the fifth largest economy in the world (CIA, 2011c). Eighty-five per cent of current growth is now propelled by internal demand (BBC World News, 27 September 2010). Indian firms have also grown and become more efficient as competition increased after 2003 (Poddar and Yi, 2007). Certain specialised sectors have evolved. Higher educational levels in some sub-groups has stimulated the growth in the information technology sector. Foreign call centres are also relocating businesses, taking advantage of India's English-speaking population. India is booming and there is vast potential for further growth, especially among the expanding middle classes, but it is the vast rural market that beckons the leaders in the FMCG sector. Better living standards and changing technology will affect rural communities, though there are some problems that could slow down future development: poorly developed infrastructure and high unemployment levels, which lower the level of tax collection and government revenue. Goldman Sachs considers that environmental issues and low levels of female literacy could further constrict long-term development. Future shortages of educated and skilled people could be a major problem. Most importantly, India needs to deal with poverty and inequality (ibid.), which defines the nature of its market. The black economy is estimated at 1 per cent, which is considered low (*The Economist*, 2009a), though bribery and corruption are widespread, as was highlighted in the lead-up to the 2010 Commonwealth Games.

Social structure

At the time of Independence the Indian socio-economic profile was pyramid shaped, with a small wealthy elite and the remnants of royal principalities at the apex and, at the base, the vast majority of the population, who were very poor. The well-travelled, affluent elite was defined by the National Council for Economic Research in the 1980s as 'the very rich and consuming class' (Euromonitor, July 2001). This group has always been outward looking and used to purchasing products overseas, especially when local product quality was poor. The government's initial focus after Independence was on increasing food supplies and raising the living standards of the masses. One early initiative, supported with foreign assistance, was the 'Green Revolution', which introduced new seed types and technology. Production did improve but there was not much change at the macro level. In fact inequalities and landlessness increased, prompting the first wave of urban migration by the poor. Because poverty levels were high the market for consumer goods continued to be small for decades. From 1960 to the 1980s two-thirds of household income was spent on food (Pashupati and Sengupta, 1996). The socio-economic profile of India only started to change in the 1980s, and then rapidly in the 1990s. As part of this expansion the wealthy elite has grown and India now has more millionaires than the United States (O'Leary, 2008).

No amount of advertising can change behaviour if people do not have the money to purchase goods. In emerging economies like India demand levels are often higher than purchasing ability. In 2002 the size of the 'consumer class' in India was estimated at 121.9 million, 12 per cent of the population (Worldwatch Institute, 2004). The big players in FMCG sectors have been targeting the vast potential market of the rural sector, where even small purchases can cumulatively yield high profits. Many companies have sold products in rural markets for decades but recently they have expanded the number and diversity of their strategies. The growing middle class, a narrower group than 'consumers', is the sector that most interests marketers. Research tends to focus on this group, for example the GfK Roper Worldwide Annual Study looks only at the top 75 per cent of income earners (Salles, 2006). Wilson and Dragusanu consider the growth of the middle classes in India to be about ten years behind that of China (2008). An estimate by the research company McKinsey puts that figure at 55 million (Beinhocker *et al.*, 2007). Advertising expenditure has skyrocketed as producers try to seduce the middle class market.

New niche markets are emerging, including women working in the professional and service sectors. The Indian population also has a very young age profile. In 2010 only 5.2 per cent of the population was over 65 (CIA, 2011c), a vastly different profile from that of China and Russia. There are 200 million people aged 15–24, and the average age in India is 24 (Sinha, 2009), so the youth and child markets are growing in importance. Other features of Indian society make it quite different from the other BRIC economies. Most people live in large multiple-generation extended families. The government needs to meet the basic needs of India's 250 million poor: food, health services, housing and education. Raising the level of tax collection would facilitate this, as would the elimination of corruption and bribery. Poverty elimination will also create more consumers, which would be good for business but also have an impact on the environment: it is the consumption lifestyles of the middle classes that most endanger the planet and pose the greatest threat to sustainability.

Gender roles and sexuality in India are constrained by strong traditional values. This is very much a male-dominated culture with clear gender stereotypes. Because the social welfare system is inadequate, sons have traditionally taken care of the older members in the family. In the past this bias has led to the practice of female infanticide; now new scanning technology means that female foetuses are often aborted. The result is reflected in a gender imbalance, though not at China's level. In the traditional extended family the son's mother runs the household and the daughter-in-law's role is less important. Gender inequality is reflected in the lower levels of female literacy. In the 2001 census only 47 per cent of women were literate compared with 73.4 per cent of men (CIA, 2011c). Gender imbalance is also reflected in attitudes to the working middle class woman: women's work is always seen as less important than men's (Sharma *et al.*, 2008).

Indian society is urbanising rapidly and city dwellers tend to have higher average standards of living. In 1991 India had 27 cities with populations of more than a million and by 2010 it was estimated that number would rise to 43 (*World Gazetteer*, 2010). Though marketers pay a lot of attention to India's cities, this is still a predominantly rural country. In 2008 only 29 per cent of the population was urban and 52 per cent of the population still worked in agriculture (CIA, 2011c). That rural population lived in 627,000 villages and over 300 towns with populations over 100,000 (US Commercial Service, 2008). Poverty continues to be a real problem in the countryside, where underemployment and unemployment are high. Other social crises are the result of corporate industrialisation of agriculture. There have been as many as 200,000 suicides in rural India in recent years as farmers face debt repayments they cannot meet (Renton, *The Independent*, 2011). Rural poverty also contributes to accelerating urbanisation. The huge numbers of poor people have been largely neglected by advertisers except for the giants in the FMCG sectors who have embraced a multi-layered strategy approach, with different strategies for different target audiences throughout the social spectrum.

The history of advertising

India has had an advertising sector since the nineteenth century. The country was a British colony for 200 years and after the Industrial Revolution British products were imported for the small colonial market and the Indian elite. The British brought print advertising to India when they established the first newspapers in the nineteenth century. A strong print-based culture persists today and India has the second largest newspaper circulation in the world. Print has always been India's main advertising medium, though that pre-eminence has been declining since the 1990s and is now almost on a par with television advertising expenditure (WAN-IFRA, 2010). The latest sectors to emerge on the Indian scene are mobile and internet advertising. Mobile phone ownership levels had reached more than 670 million in 2010 (CIA, 2011c). The growth of this sector is likely to overtake internet advertising when smartphones become more widespread, simply because of affordability of access. The major advertisers in India have always been the international FMCG companies, which have tended to focus on television advertising because it had the broadest reach, but they have been quick to branch into new media, as well as targeting the rural poor with extremely localised strategies.

Advertising in India has always been dominated by foreign products: some, like Lux, Surf and Horlicks, are regarded as Indian brands (Sharma *et al.*, 2008). The chief advertiser in India throughout most of the twentieth century, and one of the first foreign companies to set up in India, was Hindustan Lever Ltd, the local branch of British soap manufacturer Lever Brothers (which changed its name to Hindustan Unilever – HUL – in 2007). HUL traces its history in India back to 1888 when Lever Brothers first started importing Sunlight soap (Hindustan Unilever website, 2010). Now HUL's brand profile includes Wheel, Lux, Pears (soaps), Close-up and Pepsodent (toothpastes), Knorr, Swirls and Kissan (foods), and Dove and Pond's (cosmetics). Its dominance is comparable to that of competitor Procter & Gamble in most other countries. Unilever, the parent company, has also been among the top five global advertisers for some decades. In 1939 the company established its own advertising agency Lintas (Lever International Advertising Services) in India. General Motors arrived in India in 1928, bringing its home agency, J. Walter Thompson.

There was little international expansion of business or advertising in the next decades because of the Depression and then the Second World War. After 200 years of colonial rule, the post-Independence government was inward-looking and not business friendly (Poddar and Yi, 2007). Advertising revenues in India in the 1950s were low, estimated at $300,000 (Cutler *et al.*, 1992). Revenues grew slowly in the following decades until the 1990s, reflecting the general inertia in the economic sector and little change in standards of living. Markets for consumer goods were small. Companies were also not allowed to declare advertising as a tax exemption expense, which was a further disincentive. As we have seen, however, the major international companies did have a presence in India. The top advertisers in India between 1976 and 1984 were primarily companies promoting soap, detergents and personal products, a typical profile in developing countries where disposable incomes are small. The market was very concentrated in those sectors. In the 1980s three brands in 17 different product groups had more than 50 per cent of the market share (India Tradepoint, 1995). The top ten advertisers accounted for 40 per cent of all advertising, while the top 50 advertisers accounted for 80 per cent (Sachdeva, 1984). A few brands dominated each of the main product categories. Hindustan Lever, Colgate Palmolive and Procter & Gamble were the main competitors in the soap, detergents and personal products sectors.

Multinational companies expanded into India during the 1980s but the major impetus was in the 1990s as the economy began opening up to foreign business. Economic growth rates have averaged more than 7 per cent since 1997, reaching 9 per cent in 2007 but dropping back to 7.4 per cent in 2008 and 2009. By 2010 growth had increased to 8.3 per cent (CIA, 2010c and 2011c). There was a parallel rapid expansion in advertising: expenditure peaked at a high of 49 per cent growth in 1994–5. By 1999 expenditure had reached $1.78 billion, a 136 per cent increase over the preceding decade. At 3.2 per cent of global share, this percentage was much lower than India's percentage of world population (World Advertising Trends 2001, *International Journal of Advertising*, 2002). Advertising also grew in economic importance, reflected in its share of GDP increasing from 0.28 per cent in 1990 to 0.36 per cent in 2001–02 ('Zenith Media's Ad Forecast foresees growth for television and radio in India', 2002). Advertising spending per capita also increased significantly, from 60 US cents in 1990 (Cutler *et al.*, 1992) to $2.10 in 2000 (Global adspend trends, 2002) and reaching $5 per capita in 2010 (GroupM, 2010).

During the 1990s there was also a significant increase in television advertising, especially after foreign advertising was permitted on the national television channels (Doordarshan). FMCG advertising continued to dominate the product profile. In 1992 it still accounted for 90 per cent of advertising, 45 per cent of that being bath soaps and laundry detergents; the other key categories were soft drinks, garments and textiles, tyres, chocolate, cigarettes and tea (Pashupati and Sengupta, 1996). The product profile did begin to broaden after 1990. By 1996 rising levels of domestic income were reflected in more advertising for vehicles and electronic goods. Since living standards have improved mostly in urban India marketers have been targeting this group, especially via satellite television. In the 1990s the most-advertised products on these channels were spirits, consumer durables and expensive clothes (The Economist Intelligence Unit, 1997).

Foreign agencies have been in India since the 1920s. Some of the earliest foreign agencies to set up were J. Walter Thompson, which evolved into Hindustan Thompson, and Ogilvy & Mather India (now Ogilvy India) which traces its roots back through the Mather connection to 1928. The effects of liberalisation on advertising were dramatic: there are very high levels of foreign ownership and a high level of concentration. In 1992–93, 11 of the top 20 agencies in India were aligned with foreign agencies (Pashupati and Sengupta, 1996) but within seven years that number was up to 15, and 12 of those were American. By the late 1990s foreign joint venture agencies accounted for 75 per cent of the market share and the largest 25 agencies accounted for 75 per cent of billings. In 1999 the maximum ownership by foreign agencies was 76 per cent. By 1999 there were 400 registered advertising agencies in India employing roughly 18,000 people (Srivinas, 1999). This was a much smaller number than in China, which had 80,000 registered agencies for only a slightly higher population.

In the next decade the ongoing concentration of agency ownership was also reflected in revenues. The top five agencies in 2000–01 earned 42 per cent of all revenue (Emerging Markets Economy, August 2002). Hindustan Thompson was the first agency from India to win the Grand Prix at Cannes in 2008 for its 'Lead India' campaign for the *Times of India*. The executives I interviewed at Ogilvy & Mather India in Mumbai in 2010 claimed that the Spike Asian Advertising Awards were regarded as more important than the Cannes awards. An emerging trend since 2006 has been the big agency complexes in New York and London outsourcing advertising production work to India because of its high levels of creativity and expertise. Costs can be as low as one eighth of those in the United States and the time differences make turnaround times fast (Fowler, 2006).

Advertising expenditure in India has continued to expand rapidly since 2000. From $1.9 billion in 2003, it grew to $5.2 billion in 2009, and is estimated to reach $7 billion in 2011 (GroupM, 2010). The recovery from the international economic slowdown seems to have been positive, and print, television and radio revenues all increased by 31 per cent between March 2008 and March 2009 ('Chinese, Indian shoppers keep spending', Nielsen, 2009). Expansion in the Indian market has brought with it the increasing attention of multinational consumer goods companies ('Recession boosts status of emerging markets', Bloomberg, 2010). The main advertisers driving this growth were telecommunications companies, political advertisers, FMCG and consumer durables ('India ad industry to defy downturn', *Economic Times*, 2009).

In December 2000 alcohol and cigarette advertising in print media was banned but I saw cigarette advertising on billboards when I visited central and southern India in the early 2000s. In 2001 a ban on television advertising of alcohol hit the satellite channels, which had relied heavily on this source of income (Seghal, September 2000c). The FMCG giants continued to dominate expenditure throughout the next decade but other sectors such as telecommunications were growing rapidly. The laundry and detergent sector became much more competitive as local manufacturers introduced cheaper alternatives. Hindustan Lever Ltd. (HLL) share of the shampoo market dropped from 69 per cent in 2001 to 49 per cent in 2005. Its profits were further undermined when Procter & Gamble cut the prices of its premium detergents, Tide and Ariel, and HLL was forced to follow suit (Dinakar, 2005). HUL experienced another downturn early in 2009 and growth declined for three quarters in a row over 2009 and 2010. The company responded by increasing its advertising expenditure by 66 per cent to $1.3 billion (Rs61.3 billion) and profits grew to Rs63.25 billion, slightly more than its advertising expenditure ('Hindustan Unilever boost adspend levels', HUL, 2010), which seems to indicate that advertising did stimulate demand and product sales. As consumer markets expand in India, they are also diversifying. The fastest growing categories are cosmetics, mobile phones, electronic goods and automobiles. In the 1990s there were no modern retail outlets in India but in the last decade the retail sector has become much more sophisticated, as have consumers, and the personal product marketers have added anti-ageing products to their product range. Hindustan Unilever was the first to develop skin-whitening cream for the Indian market in the 1970s (Marur, 2007); this has evolved into the largest category of personal products in the country.

The Indian Government has always been a major advertiser. Political advertising is important around election time but government departments also do a lot of advertising. During the 'socialist' 1950s–1970s small newspaper proprietors saw advertising as a virtual subsidy – 'a gift of government'. In the 1970s about 25 per cent of government advertising spending went to these newspapers, and government spending accounted for 20–25 per cent of India's total advertising spend (Jeffrey, 1997). The Indian Army and the Ministry of Tourism are other major advertisers. The latter has a $50 million advertising budget and the 'Incredible India' account has a mandatory annual tendering process where the account is split into five sections and spread among five different agencies. In 2008 India attracted 5.08 million tourists.

The automobile sector is also growing rapidly as the middle classes expand. Currently there are 20 million automobiles in India but these numbers are expected to increase dramatically in the next few years (O'Neill and Stupnytska, 2009). That expansion was helped by Tata launching its $2,200 Nano in 2008. Foreign car manufacturers are starting to see the growing middle classes in emerging economies like India as a solution to current stagnant growth prospects in industrial economies ('Ford sets its sights on India', Ford India, 2010).

Higher income earners are attracting the marketers of luxury brands, including alcohol companies like William Grant, one of the biggest Scotch whisky producers, and Diageo, the world's largest spirits company. Their focus is marketing premium whiskies and brandies to higher income earners. Diageo entered into a joint venture with Indian distillery Radico Khaitan in 2006 ('Drinks brands look to India', *Economic Times*, 2010). The luxury goods market – those earning more than Rs1 million a year in 2000 terms ($21,890, or $117,650 adjusted for PPP) – was estimated by McKinsey to be 0.2 per cent in 2005, but this still amounted to 2.2 million people (Beinhocker *et al.*, 2007).

The telecommunications sector is another area where advertising expenditure is increasing quickly. When I visited Rajasthan in 2005 mobile phones and services targeting young people were among the most common advertisements on billboards. The media profile has further diversified as levels of internet access and ownership of mobile phones have accelerated in recent years. The mobile phone is more affordable than computers and the sector has expanded rapidly. Nokia, which arrived in India in 1995 and in 2003 introduced the first mobile phone customised for the country, has dominated the mobile market. By 2010, however, Nokia was being challenged by new smartphones and starting to lose market share (Venkateswaran and Philip, 2010). The mobile phone has made a huge difference to rural communities, enabling them to leapfrog the landline stage. When smartphones become cheaper the majority of Indians will be able to skip the computer stage and access the internet straight from their phones. Smartphones will also give the rural population cheaper internet access, allowing millions of people to become part of the digital world.

Advertising and the media

Print has always been the dominant advertising media in India. This dominance started to decline in the 1990s, from 68 per cent in 1991 (ZenithOptimedia, 2002) to 58 per cent of advertising in 1999 (Srivinas, 1999). This decline continued after 2000 but print has still not been overtaken by television. In 2005 print media advertising accounted for 47 per cent of advertising, compared with television's 42 per cent. Five years later print was further ahead, with a 48 per cent share compared with television's 40.7 per cent (WAN-IFRA, 2010). Indian newspapers did suffer economic losses during the 2008–09 downturn and in 2009 the government offered newspapers a 'stimulus package' ('Indian newspapers receive further support', Televisionpoint, 2009). India, along with China, has the largest number of newspapers sold in the world and in contrast to declining rates elsewhere levels of newspaper readership continue to increase. The financial newspaper sector is also growing, and more foreign papers are being established. The reason for this growth, especially in the non-English press, is the expansion of the middle classes. The largest advertising category in the newspapers is education (WAN-IFRA, 2010).

Although small, the magazine sector in India is very healthy. Growth in the women's magazine sector reflects the increasing participation of females, especially from the middle class, in the paid workforce. A number of foreign women's magazines, including *Cosmopolitan, Vogue, Marie Claire* and *Good Housekeeping*, have been launched in India in recent years. They target the independent urban women working in the professional and service sectors; 'women in offices' who are concerned about their appearance and grooming, symbols of personal and social success (Sharma *et al.*, 2008). Magazine circulation numbers have grown more rapidly than was expected. Women's magazines are almost entirely funded by advertising, much of it for cosmetics, and tend to reinforce female stereotypes of beauty, especially that of pale skin (skin-whitening creams). According to the editors of *Cosmopolitan*, Indian readers are less conservative about boundary-pushing content than those in many other countries (Timmons, 2008). A 2005 cross-cultural comparison of advertising in *Cosmopolitan* found a higher level of customisation of advertising in the Indian market than in other countries (Nelson and Paek, 2007).

Television advertising has been expanding since the 1990s but has not yet caught up with print. Television ownership levels were low until recently and in the 1990s Gallup polls estimated that only 59 per cent of the Indian population had exposure to television (Euromonitor, 2001). The viewing population was differentiated by income. The poorest viewers watched village communal sets, while the affluent middle classes watched satellite and cable television after its introduction in the 1990s. Rates of television ownership in India continue to be low in comparison with other countries: only 32 per cent of Indian households owned a television in 2006 (World Bank, 2008c). Language differences create a problem for broadcasters as there are 15 official languages in India. Before the mid-1990s levels of television advertising were quite low. Foreign advertising was not allowed on the national channels of the state television network, Doordarshan, until 1994 (Pashupati and Sengupta, 1996). The Indian government continues to control Doordarshan but its monopoly of state-owned broadcasting ended in the early 1990s. During the next decade the television sector became increasingly reliant on advertising for its funding. The arrival of satellite television in the 1990s gave an enormous impetus to the growth of advertising and by the end of the decade there were about 60 private satellite stations in India. Television as a percentage of total advertising expenditure grew from 19 per cent in 1991 to 39 per cent in 2000 (ZenithOptimedia, 2002). Some of the private stations were free-to-air and relied on advertising for all of their revenues (Seghal, 2000a).

The printed media audience is likely to be older, more literate and more affluent. Television caters for the undifferentiated mass market and has tended to be dominated by repeat purchase consumable (FMCG) advertising, especially the global big league: Unilever, Procter & Gamble, Nestlé and Coca-Cola. In 1993

75 per cent of television advertising was accounted for by five major product groups: toiletries and detergents, cold drinks, foodstuffs, cosmetic and health products (Bajpai and Unnikrishnan, 1996). At the end of the 1990s personal products continued to be the largest category. Tobacco and electronics were the fastest growing categories and automobile advertising was starting to expand. According to HLL, the largest advertiser in India for decades, television advertising was the most cost-effective medium in the 1990s. The estimated cost of reaching 1000 people by television was Rs5 (less than ten US cents), compared with Rs100 in print media (A&M Media Reports cited in The Economist Intelligence Unit, 1997).

By 2004 print expenditure was $1.2 billion (Rs5,450 crore; one crore equals ten million rupees), while television advertising was $1.1 billion (Rs4,860 crore) (Adex, cited in *The Hindu Business Line*, 2005). The number of advertisements on television has increased more than 300 per cent from 86,000 shown a week in 2001 to 260,000 (2.6 lakh) in 2005 (*The Hindu Business Line*, 2009). Despite these overall increases in advertising expenditure, the money is not going to Doordarshan. According to TAM Media Research, Doordarshan earns only Rs500 crore ($102 million) in adspend compared with Rs4,500 crore ($918 million) spent on private channels, despite the fact that the state broadcaster gets more viewers and its rates are as much as 50 per cent cheaper. Doordarshan reached 107 million households compared with 85 million households that get satellite and cable television. FMCG advertisers make up the top ten advertisers on each of the Doordarshan channels. The biggest advertisers are HUL (9 per cent of total advertising expenditure on Doordarshan), and ITC (International Tobacco Corporation) at 2 per cent. Personal products companies are big advertisers on Doordarshan because their products are more affordable for the mass market than other products that focus on satellite channels. Doordarshan has a strong presence in rural areas ('Adspend evades Indian broadcast giant', *Business Standard Television Point*, 2009). Because so many languages are spoken in India, radio and outdoor advertising still play an important role, especially in the regions, but as a percentage of overall advertising they are relatively small. Radio's share increased from 1.2 per cent in 2005 to 3.2 per cent in 2010. Outdoor advertising, on the other hand, had declined from 7.6 per cent in 2005 to 4.9 per cent in 2010. Outdoor figures are still much higher than those for the internet (WAN-IFRA, 2010).

The internet arrived in India in the 1990s but because of the high cost of computers purchase levels have been comparatively low. By 2009 the number of internet users was 61 million or 5.5 per cent of the population (CIA, 2011c). Web advertising took off internationally after the introduction of Web 2.0 in 2004 but it is a small sector in India, increasing from 0.86 per cent in 2005 to 2 per cent in 2010 (WAN-IFRA, 2010). When I asked executives at Ogilvy & Mather India (in Mumbai, 18 February 2010) if they considered Martin Sorrell's prediction (CEO of WPP) that internet advertising would expand to 25 per cent of advertising expenditure would apply to India, Prem Narayan, deputy president for planning, shook his head and said: 'This is a poor country. It's not going to happen.' The major multinational companies in the fast food, mobile phone, clothing and sports shoe sectors have been the early users of online marketing because they are targeting middle class youth, still a sizable sector because of India's large population. Online social networking has enabled marketers to target internet users more effectively.

Mobile phone marketing, which is already very competitive, has more potential in India because the smartphone ownership levels are likely to be much higher. Mobile ownership had reached 670 million in 2010 (CIA, 2011c) and India is the world's second largest telecommunications market. According to the Mobile Marketing Association India, mobile advertising expenditure in India in 2010 had reached Rs1.25 billion ($27.9 million). Marketers have begun moving beyond text messaging to develop branded content for mobile phones. One of the key advantages of mobile marketing in a multilingual country like India is its capacity to communicate to audiences in specific languages. It is also a useful tool for targeting remote rural audiences. Mobile marketing also enables customisation of marketing to consumer preferences. In 2009 Hewlett-Packard targeted students with a campaign that featured the message: 'Your notebook tells your story' ('Mobile advertising set to grow in India', Telecom Yatra, 2010).

New media such as mobile phones offer new opportunities for companies both to grow and to provide social services. Nokia, for example, is enabling poor people in rural India to buy phones by instalments. It sells its phones to a microfinance company which then sells them on to rural women. Nokia is also joining with a number of partners, including Maharashtra State Agricultural Marketing Board, Reuters Market Light, Madison Research and Pearson plus government agencies and non government organisations (NGOs), to deliver agricultural, general and educational information to rural areas through its Nokia Life Tools Programme delivered by mobile phone ('Nokia targets India for growth', CIOL News, 2009). A 2010 survey by Nielsen found that Nokia was one of India's most trusted brands ('Nokia, Colgate, most trusted brands in India', *Economic Times*, 2010). The uptake of smartphones has also been relatively rapid; lower income groups are buying clones of more expensive smartphones. Also forging ahead is the development of special applications (apps). One such programme, M4Mumbai, created by Raxit Sheth, informs people when the buses are arriving at their stop, extremely useful when the transport system is chaotic. Online applications for mobile phones are predicted to reach the millions in the near future (BBC World News, 2010).

Values and culture

Before the 1970s Indian society took pride in 'being Indian and buying Indian', and there was an ethos of civic responsibility. After that period the introduction of television, and its accompanying advertising, had an enormous impact on values by tending to present a narrow profile of affluent lifestyles. Only a few studies have critically investigated the values promoted in Indian advertising (Vilanilam, 1989; Baijpai and Unnikrishnan, 1996). Vilanilam, writing in the

1980s, the early days of advertising expansion, considered that television advertising was targeting the elite and ignoring the poor. The main effect was to create a revolution of rising expectations among the rich and the poor (1989). Widespread exposure to television contributed to the growth of materialism and the undermining of traditional values, especially among children. Advertising played on the obsessions of many Indians to 'go foreign, buy foreign and be foreign' (Baijpai and Unnikrishnan, 1996).

India is still a very religious tradition-bound society. Eighty per cent of the population are Hindu, differentiated by rigid and strongly held caste distinctions. There is pervasive discrimination against lower caste people, who are not allowed to move up the social and employment scales. Those at the bottom of the caste system are termed 'untouchables' or *Dalits*. Another 13 per cent of the population is Muslim. There are also 80 million tribal people who live on the periphery of the social system (BBC World News, 2010). Some 500 key families effectively rule India under a semi-feudal political system that is loosely 'democratic', meaning people do vote (Majumder, 2009).

The driving political and cultural values in the decades after Independence were social equity, the elimination of poverty and a strong commitment to family and community, interwoven with the inequality and rigidity built into the Hindu caste system. There is still a strong commitment to the extended family, traditional gender stereotypes and religion. Arranged marriages are a key part of that tradition and even today more than 90 per cent of marriages are arranged. In traditional Indian society women had much lower status than men and this continues to be the case in rural areas and in Muslim communities. The activities of women in rural households are still severely constrained by the mothers-in-law. Since the 1980s such cultural traditions have been undermined by consumer culture as India has become integrated into the global economy and has opened its doors to western corporations, media and products. Advertising of consumer products uses both references to traditional and modern values.

In the first government study of social groups, conducted in the 1980s, the National Council for Economic Research (Euromonitor, November 2001b) identified five levels of spending power: very rich, consuming class, climbers, aspirants and destitute. There has always been a well-travelled, affluent elite in India – the very rich – a small internationally connected group which looks overseas for its purchases, especially when product quality in India was poor. This was the group first targeted by print and then television advertisers. Most people in India are still poor but some of the big multinationals have sold to this sector for a long time.

As we shall see later, some major advertising campaign failures in the 1990s made it clear that foreign marketers did not always understand Indian consumers. In order to market Indian consumers more effectively, research was carried out to identify key local values and beliefs. Gallup was one of the early companies to conduct such research and many studies were completed by American academics exploring the viability of companies using campaigns from the United States in India. Importing standardised advertising, which reduces costs, seemed appropriate in India where English is widely spoken. A number of studies concluded that because the Indian and American middle classes shared many characteristics, imported campaigns would work in India (Chandra *et al.*, 2002; Khairullah and Khairullah, 2002). The Chandra study found strong similarities between the Indian middle classes and the American audience in culture and patterns of consumption. However, Belch and Belch (1990) pointed out as early as 1990, global campaigns were more suited to certain product types (airlines, perfumes, cosmetics) and most international campaigns continue to be customised to the local market.

Since India has no social welfare or health system, people have traditionally been concerned about health and wellbeing. However an Indian FMCG firm, Dabur, has recently found a shift in concern; from disease and ill-health five years ago, to good health and wellness, which is also affecting people's product choices. These changes are related to the rise in the number of younger middle class consumers, a market that is growing in importance. Young consumers are driving cultural change. India has a very young age profile, with 30.5 per cent of the population under 15 in 2010 (CIA, 2010c). A survey carried out by Synovate India looked at 1,743 consumers aged between eight and 24 in New Delhi, Bangalore and Mumbai (which account for 5 per cent of the total population) and found the ability to make informed decisions was highly valued. Their primary sources of information were family and friends (78 per cent) and important secondary sources included television commercials ('Word of mouth most trusted medium in India', Synovate, 2010). The sheer size of India's population, especially the 700 million rural people who have yet to join the middle class, presents a wealth of marketing opportunities and more marketers are beginning to appreciate the possibilities of selling to the this population, as the big FMCG companies have been doing for decades. More recently these companies have also broadened their range of strategies.

Strategies

India's economy was gradually liberalised in a stable political environment in the 1990s, with none of the major social dislocation experienced in China and Russia. The dominance of foreign advertisers and advertising agencies came about rapidly, but most of the leading agencies had been in India for a long time and could build on decades of expertise and familiarity. The main characteristic of advertising in India in the last two decades has been the increasing 'Indianisation' or localisation of content. Other strategies and approaches have evolved in response to changing consumer profiles, products and new technology.

New products and brands

Some of the products introduced were new to the Indian market. HLL had been marketing to the Indian population since the 1920s. One of its first tasks was educating consumers about new products or to buy branded products rather than traditional unbranded bulk products. One achievement has been persuading the Indian public to use toothpaste rather than chewing on *neem* twigs, which was the traditional way of cleaning teeth. Selling lipstick was a similar challenge as Indian culture tended to define beauty in terms of hair, eyes and skin. Feminine hygiene products were not commonly used in India in the 1990s, so Procter & Gamble provided information packs about female health and beauty care when they introduced these products (Smita, 2002). Indian middle class consumers have begun to show trends seen in other international markets. When HUL relaunched its Pond's anti-ageing skin cream range in 2008 it was responding to the changing consumer demographic, from women aged between 35 and 40 to those over 20, and to men as well. The core of the market was women in the 28–30 age range. There was a growth in the overall market in India for preventative skin care through anti-ageing creams. There are three main cosmetic categories in the Indian market – skin lighteners, moisturisers and anti-ageing creams – and Nielsen research revealed that anti-ageing creams, at 2 per cent, was the smallest category but the fastest growing (Sharma, 2008).

Social service advertising

The Indian Government has been an important advertiser since Independence. One of its early campaigns, back in the 1960s, was promoting a mass uptake of condoms to control population growth. That campaign, which was accompanied by brutal behaviour including forced sterilisations, met with little success. A researcher doing fieldwork at Lintas in 1997 compared this earlier approach with the successful 1990s Lintas campaign for Kama Sutra condoms. He considered that the failure in the 1960s was the result of lack of consumer understanding. Issues of gender, sexuality and people's attitudes to children were ignored and people were lectured at and told what to do. The 1990s Kama Sutra campaign exemplified changes in both strategies and understanding target markets. It was aimed at the educated middle classes by appealing to lifestyles and making associations with values and dreams (Mazzarella, 2003). This campaign would not have been effective with the earlier target group.

The Indian Government is also keeping up with changes in technology. Ten per cent of the world's fatal road accidents occur in India and in 2009, in an effort to reduce this number, the government launched a multi-strategy social service campaign. Traditional advertising, including television, billboards and posters were used, but new media were also important: YouTube, Facebook and Twitter ('Indian Government turns to Facebook, Twitter', *Hindustan Times*, 2009). The root of the problem may, however, lie in the licensing system – many people do not know how to drive safely – and all the communication in the world will not solve that problem.

Standardisation

As multinational companies expanded their advertising on television in the 1990s they often imported western campaigns that seemed appropriate simply because India had a large English-speaking population. However, many, including Nike, Coca-Cola, Reebok, Sony, Panasonic and McDonald's, suffered spectacular failures. In 1997 Coca-Cola, soon after it bought out local brand Thums Up, featured an advertisement where a child used a bungy-jump to grab a bottle of the drink. A number of Indian children died trying to imitate the advertisement and the campaign had to be withdrawn ('Coca-Cola India pulls ad after another child dies', *Advertising Age*, 1997). Sometimes foreign campaigns were grossly insensitive to local culture. When Cadbury-Schweppes compared a chocolate to Kashmir – 'Too tempting. Too good to share' – the campaign caused an uproar and had to be taken off the air (*The Economist*, 2002). Agencies began to develop localised strategies where the content was more relevant to Indian culture (Seghal, 2000b).

Branding

The Indian market is dominated by FMCG companies, including the Indian company Dabur, which is the fourth largest such firm in the country. Such companies tend to take the branded house approach, in which they form an umbrella for a range of stand-alone individual brands. Automobile and consumer durables companies, and the iconic Indian brand Tata, also follow this approach (Wang, 2008). There was no consumer backlash against foreign brands in India in the late 1990s, as in China and Russia, because people had long been accustomed to their presence. Some brands, such as Lux, are even considered to be Indian. There has been less pressure to develop brands with Indian names, although where foreign companies have taken over local brands they retain the local title, like Thums Up (Coca-Cola). Because India has been on the periphery of western culture through its colonial history, and continues to be connected with Britain through the large Indian diaspora living there, there is less of a cultural divide between India and the west.

Many regional brands co-exist with national Indian brands, including Dabur and Godrej (which did enter a joint venture with Hershey in 2007), and the multinationals. In the past strictly regional brands have tended to rely for their advertising on local television channels, newspapers, billboards and radio. Because their products were customised to local tastes they had a sizeable market. National advertisers with both national and regional brands use print and outdoor media nationally and locally, as well as digital media. Advertisers need to be aware of fundamental regional differences in language and customs, such as the way *sarees* are worn. In recent decades regional brands have had to respond carefully to changing media opportunities and the competition from bigger players using television campaigns (Chaturvedi, 2008), but they have also been expanding their market share.

Celebrity endorsement

One of the easiest ways in which foreign companies can customise international campaigns to local culture is to use a local celebrity endorser and this is a common strategy. HLL has used it since the 1920s. In 2005 it celebrated 75 years in India with a spoof of its early ads featuring entertainer Shahrukh Khan and some of the former endorsers (O'Barr, 2008). In the 1990s Adidas used international cricketer Sachin Tendulkar, and L'Oréal increased its sales at this time by using Miss India alongside other international models (Fannin, 1999). With the success of Bollywood the levels of celebrity endorsements and product placement in films and television have increased from 25 per cent of television advertisements in 2001 to 62 per cent in 2008. The top endorsers in 2009 included cricketers Mahendra Singh Dhoni and Tendulkar and Bollywood stars Khan, Katrina Kaif and Priyanka Chopra. More than 70 products were endorsed by this group alone: Dhoni was at the top with 26 deals, followed by Khan with 21. Oversaturation can, however, create problems because when celebrities endorse so many products people cannot identify them with any particular brand. Big brands that used celebrity endorsers in 2009 included Coca-Cola, Lux (Unilever) and Dabur. To be successful the strategy needs to be embedded in a strong campaign, according to Coca-Cola and Dabur ('Use of celebrities has mixed results in India', *Economic Times*, 2010).

Product placement and '360-degree brand positioning'

In 2007 India was the world's fourth largest market for product placement in television programmes and movies. Television was the first choice, especially in soap operas, and then cinema ('India will be the fourth largest product placement market', indiatelevision.com, 2007). Product placement is not a new phenomenon: the cigarette companies have been doing it for years. In 2003, a World Health Organisation study found that of the 900 movies produced in Bollywood a year, 76 per cent showed the consumption of tobacco (Bowes, 2003). Cigarette advertising was banned on television in 2004. Product placement strategies have intensified recently. In a recent Bollywood remake of *Stepmom*, Tupperware featured prominently throughout the movie, two-thirds of which was set in a kitchen sponsored by German kitchen maker Poggenpohl. Both companies were sponsors of the film, which also had trailers promoting their products. This is known as '360-degree brand positioning', where the product features in the film, is part of the production and the company is involved with sponsorship, promotion and in-film branding. For this companies can pay anywhere from $666,000 (Rs30 million) to $44.5 million (Rs2 billion) (Raval, 2010).

Targeting women

The major advertisers in India are the cosmetics and personal products companies – HUL, Procter & Gamble and Colgate Palmolive – and women are their key target market. The images presented in advertisements, aimed at selling more products, play an important role in defining contemporary ideals of beauty and femininity. Because these product categories commonly use global branding they play a key role in defining international standards of beauty. However, the biggest cosmetic category in Asia, skin-whitening cream, is certainly not a global product. Campaigns used to market this would not be permitted in the west because of their inbuilt social and racial discrimination. HUL, as Hindustan Lever Ltd, originally developed the product but all the big foreign cosmetic companies now have their own versions. These companies dominate the market. Advertising campaigns tap into traditional value systems that associate pale skin with class and status, combining them with an overlay of westernised beauty: fine features, big lips and long eyelashes. Advertising strategies for skin-whitening creams often use the novella format, in which, by using the product, an ugly duckling is transformed into a beautiful, and then successful, woman. Often the theme of romance is woven into the plot, as in the advertising novella for Pond's Skin Whitening Cream (Shah, 2008). Some of the most striking examples of foreign advertisements for such creams come from the big multinational companies: Procter & Gamble (Olay UV Whitening), L'Oréal (White Perfect) and HUL (Pond's White Beauty, Fair & Lovely). There are a number of examples of these advertisements on YouTube.

Favoured occupations in these campaigns are: working in an advertising agency, the media or as a flight attendant. The marketing blatantly equates pale skin with employment, marriage and social success. Recently the target market has been extended to include men: Fair & Lovely Menz Active by HUL. Models and people with pale skin and fine westernised features dominate both advertising and television programmes. As a result, large sections of the population with darker skin and different facial features become devalued.

Cosmetic marketers have also tried to modify traditional beauty ideals in order to sell western products such as lipstick. In the 1990s HLL embarked on a massive campaign with the slogan 'Who's watching your lips today?' (Smita, 2002). Western beauty stereotypes are also being extended to body type. In the last ten years there has been a noticeable thinning down of models and actors in Bollywood movies and in advertising campaigns. The relentless presentation of unrealistic stereotypes creates anxiety and self-consciousness about image and appearance, and the product then offers the remedy (Hamilton and Denniss, 2005). Rapidly rising rates of cosmetic surgery in India indicate that women are becoming more dissatisfied with their appearance (Frumin, 2008). The personal products market is diversifying further as the Indian middle class market comes

Table 4.2 Indian skin-whitening advertisements on YouTube

Fair & Lovely from Hindustan Unilever. 'The obstacle to obtaining my dream job was my skin' www.youtube.com/watch?v=KIUQ5hbRHXk&feature=player_embedded
Men's Fair & Lovely Menz Active (2006). www.youtube.com/watch?v=3MLZj6lkn7Q
Links from Mouli G. Marur, G. (2007)
www.youtube.com/watch?v=KIUQ5hbRHXk
www.youtube.com/watch?v=mPd7ZZv65R4
www.youtube.com/watch?v=KXVXqPvNGYg
www.youtube.com/watch?v=eqtWUezP8VA
www.youtube.com/watch?v=nWls3U7ZZ1E

---

to share the tastes of the global middle classes. Some of the latest products to be promoted are anti-wrinkle creams, which are a developing market for HUL, L'Oréal and Procter & Gamble.

To western eyes Bollywood movies may seem overtly sexual, but there is little physical contact or actual kissing. Kissing was banned on television in 2001 (Seghal, 2001). In the last decades in the west there has been a continual pushing of the boundaries of intimacy and the promotion of explicit sexual content, but the default strategy of 'sex sells' has definitely not been exported to India. A recent cross-cultural study of nudity in television advertising by Nelson and Paek found low levels of nudity on Indian television (2008).

In contemporary Indian urban centres some of the traditional gender and age roles in the family are being modified, especially as people move away from their families for work and education and live in nuclear families. The role of the extended family and obligations to parents are being modified. The two-generation family, with just parents and children, is more common in advertisements that trade on modernity, and depict contemporary retail settings. The role of women in marriage and the family is changing, as more middle class women go out to work. This trend is much slower in rural India and is reflected in the fact that, in the 2001 census, only 47 per cent of Indian women were literate (CIA, 2011c). Other multinationals have tapped into cultural traditions such as arranged marriages. In one commercial a young girl drives her father to a McDonald's restaurant where he eats his first hamburger, while she agrees to meet the boy he has arranged for her to marry (O'Barr, 2008).

Multi-strategy approach

The Cola Wars, between Coca-Cola and PepsiCo, provide a good example of how strategies have changed and how the big companies, with a suite of products, use a wide range of strategies to target many different audiences. The wars have been fought in India since Coca-Cola returned in 1993, after decades of absence. It invested more than $1 billion over the following decade in its attempt to regain market share, recording its first profit in 2001. Price was one area of acute competition. Both companies covered the rural landscape with billboards and sold 200ml bottles for Rs5, about ten US cents, the cheapest price in any country. Both companies took over local companies in the 1990s. Coca-Cola and Pepsi came under attack in 2003 and 2006 for high levels of pesticide residues which affected sales. Their stiffest challenge has been Indians' preference for fruit juice over soft drinks, and the national preference for tea. The beverage market in India is the third largest in the world, about $1 billion (Ramzy, 2009).

The increasing sophistication of the Indian middle class market is reflected in product launches and strategies. One recent category to emerge is the energy drink sector, which is growing at more than 50 per cent a year. When Coca-Cola first launched an energy drink between 2001 and 2003 it was not a success; but by 2009 the company considered that the market was ready and there was greater demand. When it launched Burn that year, the market already included SoBe, Gatorade

(PepsiCo), Red Bull, Cloud 9 and Power Horse. Coca-Cola's strategy was to target a niche group, especially young 'socially active and adventurous' urban males. Strategies included displaying 'Burn-inspired' cars at venues in Mumbai, New Delhi and Bangalore, as well as sampling, event sponsorship and digital media ('Coke targets Indian energy drinks market', *Economic Times*, 2009).

Online marketing

Coke and Pepsi have also been quick to use online marketing. Both companies have set up branded websites, such as Coca-Cola's www.myenjoyzone.com, in order to build up a band of loyal followers (Smita, 2002). Sunsilk shampoo has also used the internet to reposition itself, wanting to target a new market of 'fun loving girls who are into fashion and hairstyles' rather than 'older *saree*- or suit-wearing women with long hair and post-graduate degrees'. It used such traditional strategies as billboards and television to promote the website: www.gangofgirls.com, where girls can share advice about careers, beauty, family and their daily lives (O'Barr, 2008). One of the largest sectors to use online marketing is matrimonial advertising, modifying the tradition of arranged marriages. Two of the most popular sites are www.shaadi.com (Sethi, 2008) and Orkut, a social networking site owned by Google (www.orkut.com) that also functions as a matrimonial site and a way of finding marriage partners. Internet banners also advertise matrimonial sites.

Social networking

Some of the big brands have been investing heavily and successfully in social networking sites. When Procter & Gamble took over Gillette in 2005, it was the biggest razor brand in India. But most men used double-edged blades or did not shave at all, and 90 per cent of consumers did not purchase disposable razors. Procter & Gamble launched its triple-edged blade on a specially created social networking site. The strategy used the results of commissioned research conducted by Nielsen, which had found clean-shaven men were more likely to be promoted and were more attractive to women, and set up a forum to discuss these ideas. The strategy also stimulated considerable interest in all media: newspapers, television and the internet ('Social media boosts Indian sales for P&G', 2009).

Targeting youth and children

India has more young people under 25 than any other nation ('Young consumers lure big brands in India', Hindustan Times, 2010). Western values such as independence, hedonism and self-expression are more common in advertising to Indian youth than to other sectors. Advertising targets niche groups in certain media, apart from mainstream television which addresses the mass audience, including magazines (Gen X), television channels like MTV in India and Nickelodeon (Nick) and children's channels (Belch and Belch, 2007), and increasingly on the internet. Yum Brands, the owner of Pizza Hut, is planning to treble its restaurants in India by 2015 and is using social networks to engage with young people. It has 12 million followers on Facebook.

Think small

Despite all the attention given to the middle classes, most Indians still live in the rural villages where traditional cultural values are dominant. Despite a sizeable rural middle class, there is a distinct urban/rural divide in standards of living and consumer disposable income levels. Most recent growth has been in the cities and rural populations tend to be poorer. More attention has been paid to the rural sector in the last two decades. The largest and most successful foreign companies in India have achieved their dominant position by marketing to the poor and rural population, which in 2008 totalled 830 million people, or 71 per cent of the whole country (CIA, 2010c). HLL (HUL) and other FMCG companies have responded to the issue of poverty by providing very small single-use packages or sachets, or small bottles in the case of Pepsi and Coca-Cola.

During the 1990s some of the major players in the FMCG market launched a massive assault on the rural sector. HLL embarked on a wide range of marketing projects. Its advertising agency, Ogilvy & Mather, launched Programme Outreach to target rural consumers and significantly expand the company's rural sales force (Kilburn, 2000), and Project *Shakti* (meaning power), which supported rural self-help groups with a range of its products: Lifebuoy soap, Wheel detergent, A1 tea and Nihar Coconut Milk Plus shampoo; Project Nova expanded the company's direct selling network. HLL significantly increased its profits in the 1990s (Euromonitor, 2001). Other strategies used by multinationals to target rural communities included setting up *e-choupals* (cybercafés) in villages, using mobile vans with television screens, games, door-to-door selling, folk dances, placing tiles in village wells and shoe racks in temples, painting the horns of sacred cows and putting up scarecrows in the countryside (Kilburn, 2000).

Snapshot studies of outdoor advertising 2001, 2002, 2005 and 2010

In the last decade I have made four trips to India, in 2001, 2002, 2005 and 2010, during which I collected images of outdoor advertising. Although personal products are the largest advertising category in India, they are noticeably absent from outdoor advertising. I also observed regional differences in outdoor advertising, which reflected contrasting local preoccupations and sometimes timing. When I was in the south, for example, it was election time and there were political posters everywhere. Film posters are another major category in central and southern Indian cities. In 2001 and 2002 Coca-Cola was the largest foreign advertiser in southern and central India; in 2005 Pepsi had that role in Rajasthan and Delhi. Apart from these companies there was little evidence of foreign advertising. In the south, the most commonly advertised products were cement and men's underwear. In central India cigarette advertising seemed to dominate while in Rajasthan in 2005 top place went to agricultural products such as pumps, tractors and mechanical parts. Underwear for men was also commonly advertised, as it was in the south of India a few years earlier. Advertising for cars and trucks was also common. There was a considerable increase in advertising in Rajasthan for mobile phone services in 2005, which reflected a growth in marketing of that sector throughout India. In rural India many of the billboards were quite traditional, with no images and just hand-painted script. In fact, a lot of advertising was hand-painted on the sides of buildings and walls and the roller doors of retail outlets. There was much more use of photography in the cities, especially Chennai, Mumbai and New Delhi, where global products like jeans, cars and airline companies tended to be advertised. Also in New Delhi there were more western women in advertisements, and they were more likely to be partially clad. Indian women never appeared like this.

Figure 4.1 Traditional rural hand-painted advertisement for water pumps on a wall in Rajasthan in 2005. Cheap energy and government subsidies have encouraged wasteful water usage in India.

Figure 4.2 Tata mobile phones targeting the youth market. India's largest company Tata uses the 'branded house' approach, keeping the company name across a broad range of products (2005).

Figure 4.3 State Bank of India advertisement for credit cards. Liberalisation of the banking sector has given rise to new financial products and services. Expanded use of credit cards and credit accompanies rising standards of living and facilitates the expansion of consumerism in India. Banks are now encouraging spending and lending, when previously loans were hard to get (2010).

Figure 4.4 McDonalds Mumbai customising products for local tastes. Advertisement on the left is for 'Chatpata McAloo Tikki Burger (2010).

Figure 4.5 Modern retail services have arrived in India only in the last ten years. The image of new trends in retail also reflects social changes with an image of a nuclear rather than the traditional extended family (2005).

5   China

Thirty years of change in China from 'to get rich is glorious' Deng Xiaoping to 'made in China, designed by the world'. (Advertisement on BBC World News, 2010)

'China suffers from the double ills of authoritarianism and rampant commercialism.'
(Jing Wang, *Brand New China*, 2008)

Introduction

This chapter explores the world's love affair with China, an attraction based on its growth and motivated by profit. In the last decade China has captured global attention in almost every sector, including advertising. It has now been nearly 30 years since the Chinese economy embraced capitalism, or 'market socialism', and commercial advertising was first permitted. The expansion of advertising and consumerism in China differs from most other emerging economies, because this is still a Communist state. China has been one of the few countries to develop its own strong national brands to challenge foreign domination in the consumer goods market. It is also unusual in having high levels of government regulation. This legal and bureaucratic framework has helped to shape the evolution of the consumer goods and advertising sectors in the last three decades. After the opening of the economy, the Chinese quickly developed their own consumer goods industries. The advertising sector has also evolved rapidly, from the types of products sold, to consumer priorities and the marketing strategies employed.

The first foreign companies to enter China were Japanese, soon followed American companies. Advertising agencies followed in the wake of these clients, and their first arrangements were joint ventures with local agencies and state-owned enterprises (SOEs). During the first ten years of commercial advertising in China, levels of disposable income were low and there was a shortage of quality consumer goods because, as in India and Russia, the standard of local goods was poor. Demand for foreign consumer durables was so high that it was hardly necessary to advertise. During the next decade the government initiated and monitored product quality regulations. By the late 1990s the quality of many Chinese products had vastly improved. In the 1990s more foreign companies entered the country and those numbers increased after China signed the WTO Agreement in 2001. During the 1990s the major Chinese consumer goods corporations started to market their products abroad, as well as in China, and began to engage foreign agencies to market those goods. Since 2000 the foreign advertisers have had strong competition from local corporations, and in recent years smaller Chinese companies have also become stronger and used their local knowledge to develop successful local campaigns. The large multinationals are beginning to expand their marketing beyond the major cities of Beijing, Shanghai and Guangzhou. Overseas companies are diversifying their strategies to adjust to the idiosyncrasies and complexities of doing business in China. In the last decade new media, primarily the internet and mobile phones, have changed the media mix in China, and have brought fresh challenges and opportunities in the continually expanding Chinese market.

Socio-economic and political background

'China can no longer really be said to be "emerging".'
(Jim O'Neill, *The Brics and Beyond*, 2007)

'The world will pay more attention to China, especially when most Western countries are mired in the bog of debt problems.'
(Lu Zhengwei, quoted in Joe McDonald, 2010)

The Communist government under Mao Tse-tung failed to achieve its ultimate goal of turning China into a modern state. Only when China engaged with the global capitalist system did it manage to achieve a huge amount in a spectacularly short time, though the social and environmental costs have been high. China had experienced a century of social and political unrest before 1950. After decades of conflict the Communist Party finally managed to overcome the Nationalist Army and establish a Communist state in what was then an overwhelmingly impoverished and rural nation. The Chinese Communists, who had had been supported throughout their struggle by the Russian Communist Party, introduced far-reaching social and economic changes based on the Russian model including land collectivisation and industrial socialisation. However, when Russia was embracing 'de-Stalinisation' in the late 1950s – in other words, a decrease in rule by terror – China was moving in the opposite direction. Relations with Moscow were severed in 1963. Industrialisation and development were the goals of the Chinese Communist Party, but Mao proved to be economically illiterate. His first major economic policy, the Great Leap Forward of 1958, forced peasants to produce steel in their backyards and to focus on industrial production rather than agriculture. The result was widespread famine and the death of millions. After Mao stepped down as head of state in 1962 he remained head of the Communist Party with the support of the army. This enabled him to instigate the Cultural Revolution, which swept the nation from 1965 to 1969 and aimed to purge China of the evils of 'old ideas, customs culture and habits' (Evans and Donald, 1999, cited in O'Barr, 2007). Fortunately for China, when Mao died in 1976 the leadership moved in a new direction and the first steps were taken to liberalise the economy in order to stimulate economic development.

The centrally driven Communist command economy, like that in the Soviet Union, was characterised not by supply and demand but by outputs specified by political directive. After 1979 the government began to introduce market-driven practices, described as 'market socialism' or 'socialist construction'. Accompanying slogans included the now famous 'Get rich by working' and 'To be rich is glorious' (Schell, 1984). China's eastern seaboard was the area first marked for development by the government, and where they established special economic zones. This area saw the most spectacular and rapid growth during the 1980s and 1990s. Other changes included the dismantling of 'the iron rice-bowl', the government's employment and social security system, and many workers in SOEs were laid off over the next two decades. By 1995 unemployment reached 30 million mostly owing to these redundancies. It was estimated that about 8.9 million workers lost their jobs in 1996, and another 11.51 million in 1997 (Cao *et al.*, 1999). The government has continued to subsidise the key SOEs.

Since 1979 the Chinese government has been attempting to modernise and develop the economy and raise living standards. With the opening of the economy, consumer goods production expanded. During the 1980s and 1990s multinational companies were keen to enter the Chinese market, attracted by the potential profits of selling to so many new consumers. When China first permitted foreign investment in the 1980s the Japanese electrical goods manufacturers were among the first companies to enter the market. Consumers, tired of inferior local products, were very receptive to imported high quality foreign goods (Xu, 1990). After the suppression of the pro-democracy movement in Tiananmen Square in 1989, and in protest over China's human rights record, the US Trade and Development Agency suspended new projects in China from 1989 to 2001. But that did not stop American investment in China, which expanded from $2 billion in 1978 to more than $75 billion in 1997 (The United States–China Business Council, 1998). The foreign FMCG companies missed the first wave of entry into China in the 1980s, but began expanding their presence in the 1990s, entering into joint ventures with Chinese companies to make their products within China. They soon became major players in the FMCG market (Hooper, 2000). Responding to this competition, during the 1990s Chinese regional governments made a concerted effort to raise the quality of local products and there were enormous improvements by 1997 (Cui, 1997). In the 1990s China quickly became the 'factory of the world' as companies came to China seeking cheaper labour and a less rigid regulatory environment. China's surplus with the United States went from $10 billion in 1990 to $103 billion in 2002 (Worldwatch Institute, *2004*). After China joined the WTO in 2001 more American companies set up factories producing for the United States market. But economic growth in China has continued to be very uneven. Most production was located near the eastern seaboard and the interior lagged well behind. Inland provinces have only recently started to develop, and this will create a huge demand for both raw materials and products.

China has emerged as a producer of cheap, primarily low-end consumer goods for export to the world. Economic growth in China averaged 9 per cent between 1975 and 2000 (Brown, 2006), and since then has continued to be steady. By 2003 Chinese GDP was growing twice as fast as that of the United States. The US trade deficit with China, which was $124 billion in 2003, continued to increase for the rest of the decade, reaching $226 billion in 2010 (US Census, 2010). Growth rates in China averaged 10 per cent between 2006 and 2010, despite the economic crisis and a downturn in exports (*The Economist*, October 2010). Raising standards of living has become a higher priority since the crisis in western industrial countries during 2008 and 2009, when China's export markets contracted. The Chinese Government, realising it could no longer depend on exporting, began to focus on developing internal markets as a means of stabilising future growth and as protection against external economic influences ('China set for spending boom', Bloomberg, 2010).

As the last decade progressed Jim O'Neill pointed out (2007) that China and the other BRIC economies should no longer be considered 'emerging economies' in the classical sense. The changing balance of power in the international economy intensified during the recent economic crisis. As western economies face another five years of relative hardship, marketers in many product categories are looking to China, and India, for their future growth ('Recession boosts status of emerging markets', Bloomberg, 2010). Many major corporations are starting to treat China as 'their home market', a philosophy summed up by Hubert Hu of Boston Consulting Group as 'Let's invent in the West and ship to China'. China is currently the biggest market for automobiles and television sets, and the second largest market for personal computers. The key growth areas are cars, jewellery and cosmetics ('China receiving unique approach from brands', *Newsweek*, 2010). China is now the second-largest economy in the world, behind the US. In terms of market capitalisation, four of the globe's ten most valuable companies – China Mobile, PetroChina, the Industrial & Commercial Bank of China and the China Construction Bank – are headquartered in China. The prediction from an economist at the Industrial Bank in Shanghai has proven accurate: 'The world will pay more attention to China, especially when most Western countries are mired in the bog of debt problems' (Lu Zhengwei, cited in McDonald, 2010).

Social background

The prerequisite of advertising in China, as everywhere, was the population having the disposable income to buy products. One of China's greatest achievements has been to lift the greatest number of people out of poverty. In the first decades of the Communist state China had a command economy and a comprehensive welfare system, and advertising played a central role only for political propaganda. SOEs provided for all aspects of daily life. Improvements in standards of living, a reduction in poverty levels and social redistribution, core values in Communism, were tackled in the early decades of Communist rule. Only when liberalisation began, which improved living standards and brought more products onto the market, could the population become consumers. In the 1990s advertising was encouraged to stimulate the purchasing of products and economic growth. As the marketplace became more competitive advertising played a more important role.

The flattening of population growth has also been central to China's later development. The one child policy introduced in 1979 was very successful in reducing population growth, though the human costs were high. The extended family is the common household structure, with husbands and wives living with the husband's parents. Three decades later China now has an ageing population with a decreasing ratio of workers to dependants. Because China has always been a predominantly agrarian society the one child policy was less rigorously imposed in rural areas. The beginnings of a rural healthcare system and the emancipation and education of women have also brought significant changes to Chinese society, but one of the most significant of the social changes after 1978 was the gradual phasing out of the social security system, which resulted in rising unemployment and hardship for many. When restrictions on movement were lifted there was a wave of migration to the cities for work. China rapidly became urbanised: by 2010, 47 per cent of the population lived in cities (CIA, 2011d).

Under the Communist system the social structure was relatively flat, without major differences between the highest and lowest income levels. After 1979, however, income disparities began to grow. A distinct urban middle class started to emerge as well as a small wealthy sector. The key differences in living standards continue to be those between urban and rural China, reinforced by the eastern seaboard/rural hinterland divide. Contrast in wealth increased dramatically in the 1990s as the middle classes started to expand. In 1990 the top 20 per cent of the population earned four times the income of the bottom 20 per cent but by 1998 the difference had grown to 9.6 times (Guan 2000, cited in Sklair, 2002). The overall numbers living in poverty dropped from 648 million in 1981 to 218 million in 2001 (Brown, 2006), despite reductions in social security and the government layoffs. By 2004 the World Bank estimated that 5 per cent of the population was living below the poverty line (World Bank, 2005); the CIA estimate for the same year was 10 per cent, or 130 million people (2005). In 2007 Brown estimated that poverty levels were 16 per cent or 213 million (2009).

Until the early 1980s all Chinese had little disposable income and their lives were strictly controlled by the government. Income levels have increased 400 per cent since 1980 (Brown, 2006) and consumption levels have risen dramatically. Although foreign goods cost as much as six times the price of local products (Zuckerman, 1992), people still wanted them because the quality was better. When consumer demand was high, disposable income levels were small and there was little choice, there was no need to advertise. Competition developed quickly as more products came onto the market.

The scene was set for the expansion of advertising and marketing in the 1990s when regulations were loosened and the middle classes were growing. As we have seen, the evolution of this expansion has not been even. In a series of five-year plans the Chinese government staged economic development progressively through a system of tiers. The first stage focused on the tier one cities of Beijing, Shanghai, Guangzhou and Shenzhen, the gateway to Hong Kong. Development has now expanded down to the tier two level (20 provincial cities) and tier three (provincial capitals). The city populations constitute an enormous market: China now has more than 160 cities with a million-plus population. A study carried out by Synovate found that consumer habits in lower tier cities and rural areas were starting to converge ('Consumer habits converging in China', Synovate, 2010). The tier one cities have grown into megacities where, by the late 1990s, both a small wealthy group and a sizable middle class had emerged. In the last 15 years there has been a massive expansion of consumption in China and clearly defined niche markets have developed. These include a significant market for luxury goods, where purchases exceeded $6 billion in 2004. Other growth areas are food, recreation, health products, apparel, personal products, housing and household goods, healthcare, pharmaceuticals and financial services (Farrell *et al.*, 2006). Foreign marketers are increasingly focusing on the tier two and three cities as the markets in tier one cities become saturated. Chinese companies have a distinct advantage in provincial cities because they have more local knowledge and understanding. Foreign marketers are becoming aware that the growth areas in China are the vast central and western regions, and the rapidly expanding small cities and towns ('Consumer confidence levels mixed in China', Reuters, 2010). Procter & Gamble has been the most prominent foreign marketer moving into lower tier cities and, more recently, the rural sector.

Growth is spreading into the heartland of China. In the first half of 2010 the government introduced policies to stimulate economic activities and increase incomes in rural areas. In some places the minimum wage for migrant workers has also risen. In recent years consumers have been concerned about increasing food prices, as food still makes up a third of the consumer price index (ibid.). Since the 11th Five-Year Plan in 2004 the government has made a commitment to reducing inequalities (Farrell *et al.*, 2006) and restated this as top priority in 2010. An estimated ten million jobs were lost in China when export markets declined in 2008–09 (BBC World News, 2010).

China has a relatively young and urban population with completely different life experiences from earlier generations. In 2010 19.8 per cent of the population was under 15 and estimated 8.1 per cent over 65 (CIA, 2010d). The One Child Policy has created the 'little emperor' phenomenon. In that extended family 'every child has six pockets': access to the disposable income of two parents and four grandparents. The first children of the one child generation were hitting their teens in the early 1990s and it is estimated that television advertisers spent $313 million in 1995 targeting this market (Johnstone, 1996). This group will drive China's economic growth in the next five to ten years (BBC World News, 2010). Also of significance to marketers is the ageing population, the people who have been good savers and have disposable income to spend. Belk and Zhou (1987) noted the growth in the leisure-oriented retired sector as early as the 1980s. The whole leisure sector increased after the introduction of the five-day working week in 1995. Two decades later Tom Doctoroff (2010), the CEO of JWT China, sees enormous future potential in this 'grey' consumer market.

Urbanisation also affects the way people live and their consumption patterns. Urban dwellers consume more than, and differently from, rural people, who still spend the bulk of their income on food and clothing (Farrell *et al.*, 2006). By 2010, when the Chinese economy contracted, millions of urban jobs disappeared. The vast rural population is now the target of both Chinese and foreign producers. This sector suffered less in the economic downturn and incomes have begun to increase. Often overlooked in all the media attention China attracts, however, is the fact that only 15 per cent of the population has experienced significant increases in living standards. There is still an enormous potential market in China (Doctoroff, 2008b).

Advertising history

In the 1990s Jeffrey wrote of advertising as 'the hypodermic needle of Indian capitalism' (1997) but this description seems more apt for China, where advertising expanded alongside the spectacular post-1978 economic growth. Advertising expenditure grew 50 per cent a year in the 1980s (Swanson, 1990) and that growth continued into the next decade, averaging 46 per cent between 1986 and 1996 (Vertinsky *et al.*, 2002). It took a few years until foreign advertising agencies were established: in 1986 they were responsible for only about 6 per cent of total advertising, valued at approximately $15 million (Baudot, cited in Cheng, 1994). Between 1990 and 1999, however, expenditure grew 754 per cent. By 1999 advertising spending had reached 7.5 per cent ($14.1 billion) of global share (World Advertising Trends 2001, *International Journal of Advertising*, 2002). The expansion has continued since 2000, expenditure growing 393 per cent between 2000 and 2005 (Grech, 2006). In 2008 advertising expenditure had reached $36 billion, and continued to grow, reaching $39.7 billion in 2009 to $44.8 billion in 2010 and is projected to reach $49.6 billion in 2011 (GroupM, 2010).

The advertising sector in China has evolved in the context of massive socioeconomic changes. The high level of government intervention in the advertising sector has also made an impact. During the 1980s the government's focus was on the development of heavy industry rather than on consumer goods production. It had little interest in the advertising sector. In the 1990s, though, the government began to support the growth of advertising as a means of stimulating economic growth. The foreign agency model, with the agency having control over strategies and media placement, was also permitted, and foreign expansion into China increased during the 1990s. China was a difficult market to penetrate and it took a while for foreign companies to get established. Entering the Chinese market was also expensive. Coca-Cola first came to China in 1979 but did not make a profit until 1990. The company also invested heavily: $1.1 billion in the first 20 years (Weisert, 2001).

Although there was a very vibrant social-realist political poster tradition, there had also been limited print advertising in China before 1979, including in the government newspaper, the *People's Daily*. When commercial advertising was first introduced Chinese companies or SOEs did not appreciate its potential or understand how to market to consumers. It was managed from within the SOEs, whose managers felt that the task of advertising was to inform consumers. The SOE agencies had little autonomy; their role was to execute the ideas of the managers of the parent company, who also decided on media placement and purchased space (Stewart and Campbell, 1986). The quality of local advertisements was poor. Czepiec's study (1993) of the *People's Daily* between 1980 and 1989 found the advertisements rigid, basic and loaded with text; any product images were very simple. Few images showed the product in use or with people in them. A 1989 study found that local people enjoyed foreign advertising because it was entertaining and they appreciated the quality of the production. Chinese advertisements were seen to be less honest, attractive and entertaining (Pollay *et al.*, 1990).

But this situation was transformed by the entry of foreign companies and the advertising agencies that accompanied them. At first these agencies were compelled to set up through joint ventures with SOEs and local agencies. The Chinese market was very complex and there was a difficult regulatory environment and different value systems. Even today, the national distribution of goods continues to be difficult. Despite these problems, the commercial advertising sector began to grow during the 1980s soon after restrictions had been lifted on the entry of foreign goods and on foreign advertising. The first foreign companies to enter the Chinese market were the Japanese companies Sony, National, Mitsubishi and Sanyo (Wang, 2000). After 1986 more American and European products were advertised as more multinational corporations entered China (Xu 1990; Stewart and Campbell, 1986). There was an immediate demand for relatively expensive consumer durables such as refrigerators, televisions and watches. The first foreign advertisements in China in 1979, in both print and television, were for Rado, a luxury Swiss watchmaker (Schlevogt, 2000). Japanese companies were the largest advertisers during the 1980s and to stimulate consumer demand they often advertised products before they were available. The most advertised products were colour televisions and refrigerators (*China Daily*, 1987, cited in Ho and Chan, 1989). Another very successful approach used by the Japanese was to offer free programmes to television stations in return for advertising. This tactic secured their prominence in the media at a time when television stations were short of material (Schlevogt, 2000). The Chinese Government's focus on economic development was reflected in the products advertised. On television, consumer durable advertising represented 73 per cent of goods advertised and industrial goods accounted for 27 per cent (Stewart and Campbell, 1986). There was little advertising for repeat purchase consumables. By 1986 the leading foreign advertisers were a mix of Japanese and western companies: Toshiba, Hitachi, Mitsubishi, Konica, Philips, Canon, Ricoh, Nestlé, Maxwell House and Kodak, in descending order of importance (China Features cited in Xu, 1990).

From modest levels in the early 1980s advertising expenditure in China grew at 40–50 per cent a year between 1979 and 1987 (Cheng 1994). Estimates for 1983 were $133 million (Prabhaker and Sauer, 1994), increasing to $523 million in 1990 (de Mooij, 1994). There were some notable success stories. After J. Walter Thompson launched an advertising campaign for Lux soap in Guangzhou in 1986, sales doubled in six months (Wang, 2000). In 1984 a toothpaste company spent $100,000 on advertising and made $2.2 million profit (Reeves, 1985, cited in Pollay *et al.*, 1990).

After a fairly modest start the number of foreign agencies in China expanded during the 1980s, operating through joint ventures with local agencies or as satellites of Hong Kong agencies. The first agency to arrive in China was Dentsu of Japan, soon followed by McCann Erikson from the United States. Foreign agencies were responsible for a small portion of China's total advertising, in 1986 (Baudot, 1989, cited in Cheng, 1994) but quickly expanded their share after 1990. There were two layers in the foreign advertising agency sector in China: at the global level the agencies were part of a two-tier system of agency networks; at the local level they were involved in joint ventures with local agencies.

In the early 1990s the government changed its attitude towards advertising, which was now viewed both as a means of selling products to consumers, and as a way of stimulating both consumption and industrial production. In 1993 the government initiated a programme to expand advertising in China (Prendergast and Shi, 2001). The western agency model was now encouraged and agencies were allowed to buy media placement and create the advertisements. A further expansion of advertising in China accompanied these changes. In western industrialised societies the most advertised products tend to be FMCGs and these companies expanded into China in the 1990s, sparking explosive growth in advertising expenditure. China was the fastest growing advertising market in Asia: expenditure reached $2.91 billion by 1996. The profile of advertisers changed too. In early 1990s foreign companies dominated

Table 5.1 China leading advertisers early 1990s

Philip Morris
Matsushita (Panasonic)
Procter & Gamble
Colgate Palmolive
555 State Express (cigarettes)
Rejoice Shampoo (P&G)

Source: *Advertising Age* (1994) cited in Ha, L. 'Concerns about advertising practices in a developing country: an examination of China's new advertising regulations' (1996). *International Journal of Advertising*, Vol. 15.

advertising expenditure but by the end of the decade Chinese advertisers were the largest spenders.

The FMCG sector grew in importance. Some foreign companies faced the problem of product cloning. At one point Procter & Gamble estimated that 15–20 per cent of its products on shelves were clones (Saywell, 2000, cited in Sinclair, 2009). For multinational companies the costs of expanding into the Chinese market have been high. Based on experience in China since 1984, a spokesperson for the American company Kraft (Maxwell House coffee, Oreo cookies and Tang) said that, to grow in China, companies needed to spend more than 10 per cent of their total revenue ('China holds promise for Kraft', *Financial Times*, 2009).

Many new products, both local and foreign, have been launched onto the Chinese market in the last two decades. There is still a strong loyalty to local products. The largest foreign FMCG companies, especially Procter & Gamble, have massively increased their advertising expenditure since the early 1990s. In that decade large Chinese companies started to develop brand profiles, including computer manufacturer Lenovo (Legend), Haier whiteware, Wahaha soft-drinks and Olive shampoo. More private Chinese companies started to advertise their products. By the late 1990s some of these Chinese brands were challenging western brands for market share (Ewing *et al.*, 2001). The top brands in China in 1999 included China Telecom, Mudan Credit Card, Industrial and Commercial Bank, Sohu.com and Legend computers. Leading foreign brands such as Coca-Cola, KFC and McDonald's came lower down the list (Kilburn, 2001). By the end of the decade China was one of the few countries that managed to reverse the pattern of foreign dominance and in 2000 for the first time the ten most advertised brands were local and accounted for 7 per cent of total advertising expenditure (Madden, April 2001). The dominance of local companies in terms of advertising expenditure declined in the 2000s and by the end of the next decade there were equal numbers of foreign and local companies in the list of top advertisers.

In the early 1990s, when the Chinese Government loosened the regulations on advertising, the number of firms offering advertising services increased dramatically from 13,000 in 1991 to 86,000 in 1997 (Prendergast and Shi, 2001). The number of local advertising agencies was very high. In the mid-1990s there were 25,443 official advertising agencies employing more than half a million people (Jones, 1997). The number of foreign agencies in China was relatively small, increasing to around 550 from 1990 to 1994 (Prendergast and Shi, 2001). The billings of these agencies also grew dramatically. The revenues of the top ten agencies tripled between 1993 and 1995.

In 1992 Dentsu, Young and Rubicam, the top agency in the world that year, was the only foreign agency in the top ten agencies in China rated by business volume (de Mooij, 1994). By 1997 seven of the top ten agencies were entirely or partly run by multinational advertising companies and only three were locally owned. The concentration of the sector was reflected in the billings of the top 19 multinational agencies, which amounted to 15 per cent of all 1997 advertising

Table 5.2A China leading advertising agencies 1993

1993	Gross income (US$, millions)
1 Saatchi & Saatchi Advertising, Beijing/Guanzhou	3,600
2 Ogilvy & Mather, Beijing	3,060
3 JWT Thompson China, Beijing	2,994
4 McCann-Erickson Guangming, Beijing	2,570
5 Dentsu, Y & R China, Beijing	2,389
6 Grey China, Beijing	1,359
7 DMB&B, Guanzhou	1,303
8 Leo Burnett Ltd., Guanzhou	1,249
9 BBDO/CHUAC, Beijing	836
10 Lintas:China, Beijing	829
	Total 20,189

Table 5.2B China leading advertising agencies 1995

1995	Gross income (US$, millions)
1 Saatchi & Saatchi Advertising, Beijing/Guanzhou	12,464
2 JWT Thompson China, Beijing	8,544
3 Ogilvy & Mather, Beijing	7,877
4 Leo Burnett Co., Guanzhou	7,702
5 McCann-Erickson Guangming, Beijing	7,598
6 DMB&B, Guanzhou	6,346
7 Grey China, Beijing	4,833
8 Bates China, Beijing	3,953
9 Beijing Dentsu Advertising, Beijing	3,355
10 Euro RSCG Ball Partnership, Beijing	3,206
	Total 65,878

Source: Tharpe, M. 'Advertising Agencies in India compiled by Marye Tharpe' (no date). Online. Available www.ou.edu/class/jmc3333/india.htm (accessed 13 May 2011)

expenditure (Cheng, 2000). This pattern was similar to that in other emerging economies. Foreign agencies started to work for more Chinese clients during the 1990s, both promoting Chinese brands nationally and representing them in their international expansion (Prendergast and Shi, 2001). By 1997 the number of joint venture agencies had risen to 433 (Wang, 2000). During the 1990s more Chinese companies also began using foreign agencies (Prendergast and Shi, 2001).

Because the quality of Chinese products was not as high as that of foreign goods, in 1995 the government embarked on a programme to improve quality. Improvements were fairly rapid. Another strategy to raise the profile of Chinese brands was the introduction of the 'famous Chinese trademark' awards given to 42 brands in 1997 (Cui, 1997). Consumer preferences also started to change. A

Gallup study in 1994, which claimed to be the first national consumer survey in China, found only one Chinese brand, Tsingtao beer, among the ten most popular brands (Wang, 2000). Later in the decade there was a backlash against foreign brands (Chadwick, 1997; Saywell, 1998).

During the 1990s Chinese companies increased their advertising expenditure, especially in the annual auction for advertising on China Central Television (CCTV) (Wang, 2008). In 2000, 19 Chinese companies spent more on advertising than Coca-Cola, the largest foreign advertiser which spent $26.1 million (Weisert, 2001). In the next decade more foreign advertisers were among the top advertising spenders. Since 2000 China has been one of the most rapidly expanding advertising markets in the world. Advertising expenditure increased steadily throughout the last decades and only slowed slightly in 2009, reaching $44.8 billion in 2010 and is predicted to reach $49.6 billion in 2011 (GroupM, 2010).

Since 2000 the product profile has continued to change. In a 2001 survey the most advertised products were: medicines; tonics and vitamins; real estate; shampoos; alcohol; telecommunications facilities and services; skincare products; mobile phones and accessories; and professional services (A.C. Nielsen, 2002). The largest local advertisers were Chinese health-related products and pharmaceuticals, including non-prescription drugs, tonics, vitamins and stomach medicines. In 2003 six of the ten largest advertisers in China were Chinese companies in the health and pharmaceutical sectors, and the seventh company was China Mobile. Unilever, Colgate-Palmolive and Procter & Gamble were the only foreign advertisers, though Procter & Gamble was by far the largest advertiser, spending $517 million. The second largest advertiser, Gai Zhong Gai, spent $57.4 million. In 2004 Procter & Gamble more than doubled its spending to $1.2 billion and Gai Zhong Gai increased its expenditure to $219 million (Grech, 2006). In 2005 Procter & Gamble brands accounted for five of the ten most advertised brands (CTR Research, 2006). In 2008 Procter & Gamble's expenditure was almost double the second highest advertiser.

The agency sector grew too. From 2000 to 2001 there was an 11 per cent increase in advertising billings of transnational agencies as a result of taking on local clients (Madden, June 2001). Foreign agencies continued to remain dominant in China after 2000 and joint venture agencies were still the top revenue earners in 2006 (Dentsu/China Advertising Association 2006, cited in CTR Research, 2006). Until 2005, when this restriction was lifted under the WTO agreements, foreign ownership in agencies was capped at 70 per cent, but the complexity of marketing in China has meant that foreign agencies have tended to remain in joint ventures with local agencies. Recently agencies have followed corporations out into second and third tier cities where consumer profiles and buying preferences are quite different (Sinclair, 2009).

The product profile has begun to broaden and diversify since regulations imposed on the banking and financial sectors were loosened after 2001, enabling the marketing of such financial services as insurance and credit cards to the new class of affluent consumers (Farrell *et al.*, 2006). Other product categories to emerge in the last decade have been the digital and telecom sectors and early in the decade China Mobile was among the top ten advertisers. By the end of the 1990s a luxury goods market was beginning to emerge among the new middle classes and the 'super rich', mainly in Beijing (Schlevogt, 2000). A decade later the luxury consumer goods markets in China, along with Russia, are two of the largest in the world (O'Leary, 2008).

The growth in the auto sector provides further evidence of growing consumer affluence. Private car ownership in China has grown 20 per cent per year since 2000 ('Fire recall dents Toyota's Chinese plans', *The Times*, 2009). In 2009 China overtook the United States in auto sales, selling 13.5 million vehicles, including buses, while the US sold 10.4 million cars ('China overtakes US as world's biggest car market', *The Guardian* 2010). As foreign automakers have experienced downturns in demand in western markets since 2008, they have increasingly turned to China as their hope for the future ('China receiving unique approach from brands', *Newsweek*, 2010). Chinese manufacturers are also responding to the growth in the market and provide stiff competition for foreign companies. A recent study by Synovate found that car manufacturers were deriving the greatest benefits from television and radio advertising ('TV, radio key for automakers in China', Synovate, 2010). These companies are also embracing new technology. The Geely (company) has also built upon the informal practice of online shopping clubs set up to purchase expensive items (Calladine, 2009) to establish a system whereby a certain number of people signing up as a group get a reduced price ('China's Geely eyes online car sales', *People's Daily*, 2010).

The year of the Olympics, 2008, was nirvana for the Chinese advertising industry (Wang, 2008) and in the annual CCTV auction in 2007 advertising spending was 20 per cent higher than it had been the year before (O'Leary, 2008). The largest bidder was a Chinese firm. Procter & Gamble has not disclosed how much its failed bid was worth. Some multinationals, including Nike, Adidas, KFC, Coca-Cola and McDonald's, increased their advertising spending for the Olympics and were among the top spenders in the previous year. In contrast, the second largest sportswear company, Li Ning, increased its advertising by only 18 per cent. A later survey found that although brand recognition was a lot higher for certain products that sponsored or advertised heavily during the games, this did not translate into market share or profits. This was notably the case for Mongolian company Yili, an official sponsor of dairy products for the Olympics (Nielsen, 2008). The worldwide official sponsor for the countdown to the Olympics was Lenovo, which reportedly spent $80–100 million for the honour (Rein, 2008).

Rural markets

Although the economy has reached a stage where growth might be expected to level off, the advertising sector is likely to continue growing in the next decades because of China's many untapped consumer markets. It is mainly the first and second tier cities that have the 'gold collar workers' who are the luxury goods consumers, but this is not the largest market. The next major frontier for mass marketers are the regional centres and rural markets, where vast numbers of Chinese consumers have yet to move beyond meeting their basic needs and start expanding their consumption of non-essential items.

Media

The Chinese government's tight control over the media has had a major influence over the last two decades. The evolution of the media has been similar to that in many emerging markets, though one deviation from the pattern in China was the importance of outdoor advertising in the early 1990s, amounting to 39.1 per cent in 1990–91 (Weber, 2000). During the 1990s the two major trends were the expansion of television advertising and the increasing competition from local advertisers. The market was beginning to diversify as socio-economic differentiation grew. As competition from both local and foreign competitors has become more intense, marketers have also been faced with a much wider range of media choices. This trend has intensified in the last decade with the growth of mobile, digital and internet advertising, though television remains dominant.

Print

China is a large country where the provinces are relatively autonomous. The only national newspaper is the political *People's Daily*, which has always carried some advertising (Swanson, 1996). Magazines were the most important source of information during the 1980s, when most people did not have television. There were more than 4,000 titles, and magazines carried more advertising than newspapers (Rice and Lu, 1988). The importance of print media declined throughout the 1990s, as it did in most emerging economies. Newspaper advertising accounted for more than 30 per cent of advertising before 1990 but had dropped to 19.6 per cent by 1998 (Cheng, 2000). Print still accounted for 33 per cent of advertising in 2005, declining to 23 per cent in 2010, while television was 41 per cent in 2005 and decreased slightly to 40.4 per cent in 2010 (WAN-IFRA, 2010). As literacy levels are high – 91.6 per cent in 2007 (CIA, 2011d) – print continues to be important at the provincial level.

The recent expansion of the middle classes has stimulated the spread of the global women's magazines and the advertising of luxury goods. Many of these publications are part of the major media conglomerates: Hearst Corporation publishes *Cosmopolitan* and *Harper's Bazaar*; Condé Nast publishes *Vogue*, *Glamour*, *Brides* and *Self*; and Hachette Filipacchi publishes 238 titles worldwide, including *Elle*. There was a 26.1 per cent growth in the sector between 2005 and 2006 (China Media Yearbook 2006, cited in Frith, 2008).

The whole form and tone of these magazines are quite different from those of traditional Chinese women's magazines. Like most magazines, they are financially dependent on advertising. This means that they are tailored to please advertisers, and foreign advertisers want to target the younger, wealthier market. Content reinforces advertising and is often full of advertorials and product placements. China has more than 50 female-oriented magazines, both local and foreign (Sinomonitor Spring 2008 China Marketing and Media Survey data, cited in Frith, 2008), but they have been affected by foreign competition. Because most foreign advertisers are concentrating on foreign magazines, even if their rates are higher or their circulations lower, advertising revenues for local magazines have declined. Local magazines have responded by changing their format to follow the style of foreign magazines in order to attract multinational companies. This change has been especially evident on the covers, which used to show women as emancipated workers of the socialist state but now feature stereotyped images of beautiful women. There is little censorship in women's magazines, probably because of their focus on sex, fashion and relationships (Frith, 2008). The changing representation of women is occurring in other media too, though not the emphasis on sex. Modesty is still strongly enforced on Chinese television (Nelson and Paek, 2008).

Television

Television has been the dominant media for foreign advertisers since they arrived in China. Television advertising expanded during the 1980s though expenditure was still low – only 13.6 per cent of total advertising in 1986 (Xu, 1990). In the 1990s television became the dominant medium for both national and local advertising. The channels of the government-controlled national network, CCTV, have the widest national coverage, but there are also vibrant regional and local channels. Television ownership levels increased in the 1990s and the media profile also began to broaden with the arrival of satellite television. Rupert Murdoch's Star Television started broadcasting in 1993. By 1997 China had become one of the most cluttered television markets in the world. Chinese viewers were exposed to more than 800 commercials a week in Guangzhou, 700 in Shanghai and 650 in Beijing, compared with 300 in England and 180 in Germany (J. Walter Thompson, 1997, cited in Weber, 2000). A greater number of media options began to fracture the once homogeneous mass market, though the audiences were still the largest in the world. In 2000 the potential television audience was estimated to be 600 million (Everelles *et al.*, 2002), or even 900 million (Wang, 2000). By 2001 television accounted for 72.3 per cent of advertising spending (The Economist Intelligence Unit, 2002).

Television stations continue to be owned and controlled by central or regional government except for the satellite channels, which have always been subject to strict regulation. Direct-to-Home satellite TV was launched in October 2006 to a possible 300 million households (Grech, 2006). Currently more than 2000 television channels are offered by 600 government broadcasters (CIA, 2011d). According to Nielsen Media Research, most advertising expenditure is at provincial and city levels (cited in *Wall Street Journal*, 2008) and in areas like Shanghai and Guangzhou many provincial stations are more popular than their national counterparts (Sinclair, 2009). There are now over a billion television viewers throughout China.

Held every October since 1994, the big media event of the year in China is the CCTV annual advertising auction where the Chinese government auctions off all the television advertising for the major channels for the coming year. Prices for advertisements skyrocketed in the late 1990s when there were a few Chinese gamblers among the bidders. For some of these companies being the highest bidder was a recipe for business failure the following year (Wang, 2008). Foreign advertisers did not participate in the auctions until after 2000. A foreign company, Procter & Gamble, was 'king bidder' for the first time in 2004, when it bid more than $46.5 million for the 2005 season (Wang Jixin, 2004, cited in Wang, 2008). Prices are always extremely high for peak viewing times such as 'the golden minute' following the news and preceding the weather at 7.30pm (Wang, 2008). Special events such as the Spring Festival Gala and the Lantern Festival Gala are among the most expensive slots.

Internet

The internet first arrived in China in 1994 and the number of users grew from 18 million in 2000 to 104 million by 2006 (World Bank, 2009d). By 2009 China had the largest number of people in the world – 389 million – with access to the internet (CIA, 2011d). By 2015 internet users are predicted to increase by 47 per cent ('"Next billion" web users based in new markets', BCG, 2010). The internet market in China is already very crowded (BBC World News, Asia Business Report, 19 August 2010). Marketers are extremely interested in this market, and a lot of research is being done into online behaviour patterns. A McKinsey survey estimates the Chinese web population to be 420 million and with increased urbanisation and rural uptake that number could rise to 750 million by 2015. Only a third of those who participated in the survey had purchased products online. The groups quickest to show interest in purchasing, or actually purchasing, tended to be younger, better educated and wealthier. One of the main uses of the internet was to check out products before purchasing ('Nuanced online strategy key in China', *China Daily*, 2010). According to the research firm Propser the most popular use of the internet is surfing the net ('Chinese consumers attached to the web', Propser China, 2010). Social networking sites are less popular than playing games. Internet users tend to spend three hours a day online. The rate of e-commerce purchasing is 28 per cent in China, the highest of the BRICs ('"Next billion" web users based in new markets', BCG, 2010).

The importance of the internet advertising in China has grown rapidly, from 4.8 per cent of all media in 2005 to 18 per cent in 2010 (WAN-IFA, 2010).

According to McKinsey, 2 per cent of retail sales in China are now through the internet. An analyst from Deutsche Bank has predicted that figure will reach 7.2 per cent by 2013 ('E-commerce sales to surge in China', *Wall Street Journal*, 2010). Chinese internet users tend only to use one search engine and the most popular is baidu.com, followed by sina.com and sohu.com (*The Economist*, January 2010). The Chinese Government has always imposed strict controls by filtering content, and Google's recent experience with censorship is a clear example of the difficulties of operating in the Chinese market. When Google entered China in 2006 to set up google.cn it capitulated to government censorship and was widely criticised. In 2010, however, the Chinese Government's limitations on freedom of speech and problems with hackers forced Google to reconsider and partially withdraw from China (ibid.). Eventually it chose to close its site and diverted users to a Hong Kong-based alternative ('Google upbeat on China', *Financial Times*, 2010).

Mobile phone marketing

Mobile phones were introduced into China in 1987 and ten years later China had the most users in the world; by 2009 they numbered 747 million (CIA, 2011d). A year later, according to government statistics, there were 833 million mobile phone users ('Mobile internet usage rises in China', CTR, 2010). The smartphone is the latest addition to the media profile and its cheapness and transportability mean that millions will be able to leapfrog landline and computer technologies and access the internet with wireless handheld devices. Smartphone uptake has been rapid. The 24.1 million sold between January and June 2010 exceeded sales for all of 2009. Research by Analysys International found 214 million people logged onto the web with wireless handsets in the first half of 2010 compared with 205 million at the end of 2009. The major source of profit was from high data charges rather than advertising. Instant messaging was also popular; the main service companies were Tencent (Mobile QQ), China Mobile (Fetion) and Microsoft (MSN). Gaming is predicted to be the main driver of mobile internet revenues, with Kongsoft and Kaspersky being the key players. Security is still a major issue in China. A CTR survey of 1000 mobile internet users in ten cities found that the major reason for use was the demand for 'anytime, anywhere' content ('Mobile internet use increasing in China', Baidu, 2010).

All these media options mean that, to be effective, marketers must be increasingly sophisticated in their choices. The effectiveness of online marketing is still to be proven (World Advertising Research Council, 2009) – and a recent study by the Boston Consulting Group found that many multinational companies were far from systematic in analysing the results and effectiveness of their marketing ('Brand owners base spending on "shortcuts"', BCG, 2010). McKinsey has found that despite the entry of new media options television is still the most trusted medium in China and has the greatest reach at 85 per cent compared with 24 per cent for the web ('Nuanced online strategy key in China', *China Daily*, 2010).

Values and culture

Foreign marketers often underestimate the complexity of the Chinese market. The high failure rate for foreign product launches in China has been caused by companies not trying to find out what the Chinese consumer wanted. They assumed the Chinese would want foreign products, without researching what they actually wanted to buy ('Brand owners base spending on "shortcuts"', BCG, 2010).

Price, price, price

The average Chinese consumer is conservative and very conscious of price and value. Even if Chinese people prefer foreign brands they will usually buy a cheaper local version because of affordability. McKinsey surveys since 2004 reveal that though Chinese people are influenced by the opinions of friends and relatives, they are also swayed by in-store promotions and price always plays an important role in purchase decisions (St-Maurice *et al.*, 2008).

Confucian values persisted throughout the Communist era and remain central to Chinese life. The Chinese place emphasis on personal connections – *guanxi* – and status, rather than on the competitive meritocracy that dominates western cultures. Especially in business relations, *guanxi* is paramount. Status has a major impact on purchasing decisions and product ownership, especially among Chinese men. For businessmen the type of car they drive reflects how important they are (Macfie, 2008; 'Chinese, Indian shoppers to keep spending', Nielsen, 2009). A recent McKinsey survey discovered that 'white-collar men wanting to improve their standing' were trading up in their purchasing and balancing expensive and less expensive items. More than 70 per cent of those surveyed were cutting back on personal care, snacks and packaged food, in favour of dining out and alcohol. More than 80 per cent of the demand for higher priced clothing, footwear and accessories came from lower- and middle-income shoppers ('China's shoppers among "most complex"', McKinsey, 2010). Gift giving is another extremely important expression of relationships and also influences purchasing patterns.

Also important are family connections and clearly defined gender roles, which are embedded in Chinese advertising regulations. Other cultural traditions include arranged marriages and the centrality of the extended family, which are being undermined by contemporary social changes and by the media and advertising. Campaigns that include 'romance', love and individual choice and nuclear families contribute to this social and cultural change.

The advertisements of foreign cosmetics and personal products companies – Unilever, Procter & Gamble, Colgate Palmolive – play a key role in defining and reinforcing contemporary ideals of beauty. In Chinese advertisements and television programming pale skin and fine features characterise the images of women. Wang (2000) claims that 'white and Western' images are promoted in the media by using Eurasian models. These changes are also part of a general rejection of traditional Communist cultural propaganda. In the Communist era images of tanned peasants were glorified. Pale skin has become associated with 'the new China' and with beauty. With an estimated 90 per cent of sales, the international cosmetics companies dominate the market for skin whitening cream. Global brands also rely on the cachet of being foreign (Jakes and Xu, 2005). The cosmetics industry is one of the fastest growing in China, with enormous potential for further growth. In 2005, when it was estimated that only about 7 per cent of the population bought cosmetics, sales were still around $21 billion, having increased from $24 million in 1984 (ibid.). Stereotypes of beauty are also being extended to body shape. In 2002 *Time* reported that cosmetic surgery was also becoming more popular and some of the most common treatments were for wider eyes, longer noses and fuller breasts to make women look 'more Caucasian' (Cullen, 2002).

One of the most notable features of contemporary advertising is its focus on youth and this is an area of great potential cultural change in China. Empowerment through consumption, along with education, independence and migration, is weakening the tradition of the extended family and arranged marriages. A cross-cultural study of global youth in the late 1990s, based on The New World Teen Survey conducted by D'Arcy, Masius, Benton & Bowles, revealed that the universal dream of world youth is much the same: 'to lead a good life with a rewarding job, have satisfying family relationships, good relationships, enjoy rich experiences, manifest freedom and individual expression and possess lots of consumer goods' (Moses, 2000). But apart from that young people in China were relatively unconcerned about fashion brand awareness (ibid.). Another study comparing middle class urban Chinese and Indian young people found the Chinese group less traditionally focused. They were much more relaxed about consumerism, making individual choices that included selecting their own marriage partners (Sharma *et al.*, 2008). Wang (2008) has also found that Chinese youth are less passionate about music than their western counterparts. These characteristics tend to support de Mooij's argument (2003) that there is not a global universal youth culture.

According to Paolo Gasparini, president of L'Oréal, 'Chinese people now like to try new things and advanced products, and are more brand-conscious and receptive to new ideas' ('Cosmetics giants look to China', *China Daily*, 2009). But as we have seen, the Chinese buy chiefly on price, then status, and prioritise based on whether the product is consumed in public or privately. As overall quality improves, products are differentiated by the values associated with them. McKinsey surveys show that lack of brand loyalty is a distinctive characteristic of Chinese consumers (Farrell *et al.*, 2006). They also like to shop around and try different options. As happened in the late 1990s when local brands briefly dominated advertising expenditure, local brands may in future dominate the local market (Doctoroff, 2008).

The Chinese market is becoming more competitive and Doctoroff has revised his former opinion about local companies. In 2005 he considered many emerging companies in China unsophisticated about advertising and media buying. He spoke of Chinese advertising using 'the sledgehammer approach' and being like 'the 1950s but in color' (Ni, 2005). In 2008 Doctoroff described Chinese brands as 'tactically ruthless, a school of piranhas smelling blood and instinctively detecting weakness in the primordial soup that is China's brand universe' and warning foreign companies they were in danger of losing out to local brands.

Strategies

Advertising in China is one of the most tightly regulated environments in the world. Foreign advertisers have had to adjust to China's cultural and regulatory complexity, while local advertisers have become increasingly sophisticated and market savvy. The regulatory environment plays an influential role in the types of strategies used by companies and agencies in China. Foreign advertisers get frustrated with the opaqueness and almost arbitrariness of the Chinese regulations. The enforcement of regulations is stringent, especially when depicting such 'western' values as individualism and defiance of authority. Some practices such as comparison advertising, or claiming to be 'the best', which are commonplace in the west, are illegal in China (Ha, 1996). It is not acceptable to show tattoos, pierced ears or women kicking and punching the air in aerobics classes. A classic Pepsi commercial that had Michael J. Fox climbing out of a window and dodging traffic to get a woman a can of Pepsi was modified in the local version where the Chinese pop star had to stop for the traffic light. Not permitted either was a Pizza Hut advertisement that showed a boy standing on a desk to tell his friends how good the pizza was (Doctoroff, cited in Ni, 2005). Cultural differences and lack of understanding of core Chinese cultural values meant that imported campaigns often did not resonate with the local audience. Chinese people did not understand the Nike slogan, 'Just do it' (Sinclair, 2009).

Advertising laws introduced in 1993 made operations for foreign companies more difficult, and agencies and the media were made responsible for any infractions. Foreigners were also discriminated against, having to pay as much as three times more than local advertisers (Roberts, 1995). There were also specific laws defining what visual material was allowed. Forbidden were sexual images, including a woman's body from the shoulders to 15 centimetres above the knee, and images that could cause fear, horror and pain or result in dangerous or bad behaviour. Also restricted was the use, for local products, of Caucasian models to encourage aspirations of 'a western lifestyle'. Advertising for foreign products could not use Chinese models unless the product was clearly identified as foreign. Censorship is still in force and all advertisements have to be approved before launching.

The start of 2004 saw the introduction of further television advertising regulations, one of which forbade the advertising at mealtimes of medical products for treating beriberi and haemorrhoids, and female hygiene products. The number of advertisements shown per hour was limited and the frequency of advertising during serials was reduced to only once per episode (*People's Daily Online*, 2003a, September 25). In 2005 advertising time was limited to 20 per cent of daytime broadcast hours and 15 per cent of hourly programming from 7–9pm (Xie, 2005, cited in Wang, 2008). Advertisements for alcohol were reduced from 17 to 12 per day. These reductions led to an increase in rates (Wang, 2008). Recently there have been indications that the Chinese advertising environment is becoming even more difficult and discriminatory ('Many foreign firms grow frustrated in China', European Chamber of Commerce in China, 2010).

Significant language and cultural differences are reflected in Chinese and foreign approaches to advertising strategies, though both foreign and local companies are aware of the importance of product branding (Landreth, 2006). During the 1990s Chinese companies started to realise the importance of branding products and the decade was characterised by the emergence of the major Chinese brands. The big Chinese brands were developed at this time: Legend, Haier and Wahaha. The most popular brand of the 1990s was the Chinese cigarette brand Hongtashan (Madden, April 2001). The companies' approach to branding tends to follow trends in the overall product categories. Those in the consumer durable categories, such as Haier and Legend, have tended to favour a branded house approach (Wang, 2009). In the FMCG sector companies like Procter & Gamble tend to follow the house of brands approach. Procter & Gamble's key brands included Dove soap. By 2005 it dominated the haircare market with three key brands: Rejoice, Pantene and Head & Shoulders (Wang, 2008). Coca-Cola also favours a suite of brands in China.

During the 1990s a consumer reaction to foreign brands set in, reinforced by a government campaign urging people to buy local goods. Around the same time there was an improvement in the quality of local products so 'foreign' was no longer equated with 'quality'. As we have seen, Chinese companies were the largest advertisers in the late 1990s, and the largest bidders in the annual CCTV auctions. A brand recognition survey conducted by Gallup found that seven of the most popular brands in China were Chinese in the late 1990s. The foreign brands Head & Shoulders and Santana (Volkswagen China) were both thought to be Chinese (Madden, April 2001).

Standardised advertising

Branding, especially for cosmetics and personal products, naturally lends itself to global and standardised campaigns (Belch and Belch, 2007). In the 1990s 31 per cent of multinational companies were using standardised campaigns in China compared with 66 per cent using differentiated campaigns (Tai, 1997). Another study in 1996, which claimed to be the first comprehensive review of strategies used by foreign advertisers in China, found that most companies were using a combination of standardised and localised strategies. The factors that influenced these choices were: the number of company subsidiaries, the perceived importance of using local language, and product attributes and whether they used Chinese cultural values (Yin, 1999). Many of the major brands were employing a modified branding strategy, such as using local heroes to promote the same products in all countries (celebrity endorsement). In the late 1990s film star Cindy Crawford was the endorser for Omega watches while Procter & Gamble used Chinese tennis star Michael Chang to promote shampoo (Cui, 1997). Procter & Gamble tend to use the testimonial strategy in all markets (de Mooij, 2005). Some brands like Dove (Unilever) have a clear brand mandate laid down at their home office in London (author interview, Ogilvy & Mather, Mumbai, 2010). The cosmetics and personal products sectors have become some of the largest sectors for advertising expenditure in China, largely driven by Procter & Gamble, Unilever and L'Oréal. Cosmetics are seen as one of the growth categories of the near future ('China receiving unique approach from brands', *Newsweek*, 2010), but China has been a key destination for such multinationals over the last two decades. Brands will need to address the problem of China's low per capita income, which stood at $3,567 in 2010, against $37,510 in Japan and $40,500 in the US ('China set for prolonged spending boom', Bloomberg, 2010). Consumers currently prefer skincare products which are three times more popular than make-up (*Time Magazine* Style and Design Supplement, Spring 2007). Because English is rarely spoken in China, it is necessary to translate the text of international advertisements. A 2004 study of female Chinese consumers' attitudes towards cosmetics advertising found that standardised advertising, both on television and in magazines, was well received. Expert opinions and endorsements were important but consumers also relied heavily on the opinions of boyfriends, girlfriends and sisters (Barnes *et al.*, 2004).

Doctoroff (2008) considers that Chinese brands have become a real threat to multinational company brands in the last ten years because the latter target only the top level of consumers and leave the broad base exposed. The 'cool' foreign brands are still popular but they are too expensive; the local brands such as Bird mobile phones, Lenovo, Haier, Wahaha (soft drinks) and Tsingtao (beer) are growing in importance because, according to the Chinese Statistical Bureau, only 15 per cent of urban Chinese have experienced significant increases in income and standards of living, which leaves 85 per cent with limited disposable income. Local brands have the dominant market share in many brand categories based on price and now control more than 50 per cent of the shampoo market and 30 per cent of the mobile phone market (mostly in tier two and three cities). Even in the auto market a new brand, Cherry, is making inroads in the mid-tier market (ibid.). 'Upper mass' brands like Olay are still 250 per cent more expensive, and female hygiene brands like Whisper are 75 per cent more costly than local brands.

The recent acquisition of foreign firms by Chinese companies provides evidence that the environment is changing, and that local brands have become a threat in some areas. TCL has acquired Thompson Television and Lenovo purchased IBM's PC division (Pieterse, 2011). The multinationals dominate categories like mobile phones and some of the personal products, but local players dominate the appliance, furniture and apparel industries. For example, clothing manufacturer Li Ning is becoming strong competition for Nike ('Many multinationals grow hesitant about China', *Daily Telegraph*, 2010). Chinese brands also frequently have the resources of massive state-funded budgets (often irrationally allocated) and knowledge of distribution channels. However multinational advertisers still advertise better than brands that are still 'hobbled by key weaknesses including inconsistent messages, failure to distinguish between consumer-relevant copy and corporate propaganda and confusion between brand awareness and brand equity' (Doctoroff, 2008).

Localisation

There are many ways in which advertising campaigns are customised. The simplest use local language, actors and situations, while the most complex develop culturally specific campaigns or even products. Early advertisements tended to use celebrity endorsement by famous Chinese athletes as a key strategy (Li and Shooshtari, 2007). Nike modified their advertising campaigns to be more relevant to Chinese young people, changing their focus from the 'empowerment' campaigns developed for the American market to an 'achievement-orientation' approach more suitable for the Chinese consumer. When it was understood that, in China, Nike trainers were often worth a month's salary and were considered too expensive to wear in the playground and get dirty, the company introduced a less expensive shoe (Madden, 1999). Because there is enormous pressure on Chinese young people to be successful they localised the brand by showing a player scoring on a playground. While visiting in 2003, I noticed that Nike still did not have a strong enough profile to use the 'Swoosh' symbol without the brand name. During the Olympics official sponsor Adidas used the slogan 'the impossible is nothing', the idea being that the Chinese athletes could draw strength from their 1.3 billion supporters (Nielsen, 2008).

Despite its desire for market relevance, Nike got one strategy badly wrong when it launched its 'Chamber of Fear' campaign in 2004. The advertisement featured LeBron James, a forward for the Cleveland Cavaliers basketball team, who was depicted overcoming a series of animated characters that included a white-haired kung fu master, two women in traditional clothing and a pair of dragons. The dragon is revered as a national icon in China and its use in a campaign was seen as deeply offensive. The government hastily stopped the advertisements, citing the 'offending of national feelings' and claiming they broke the rule that all advertisements had to 'uphold national dignity and interest and respect the motherland's culture'. Nike was forced to make a public apology ('Nike apologises for footwear ad in China', *China Daily*, 2004). Toyota created a similar uproar when, in a magazine advertisement, it featured a Toyota vehicle pulling an unidentified truck that was the same shape as a Chinese military truck.

The image brought back vivid memories of the brutal Japanese occupation in the 1940s. Both campaigns sparked significant debate on the major Chinese internet sites (Li and Shooshtari, 2007).

Branded entertainment has been a more successful strategy in China. Companies are starting to sponsor television shows like *SuperGirl*, an *American Idol* clone, with the same format of SMS voting (Wang, 2008). In this case, the sponsorship, by Mengniu Dairy, generated $185 million in sales of its new yoghurt drink (Madden, 2005).

Multi-strategy approach

Foreign advertisers still consider television the most effective medium for advertising in China, but some of the largest players like Coca-Cola and Procter & Gamble have successfully used a multi-strategy approach. Coca-Cola has a mixture of strategies in China, blending-in in some contexts and standing out in others. It uses localisation as part of its global branding strategy. In 1997, for example, the company shot its New Year commercial in a remote village, using local actors engaged in traditional festivities. As Wang pointed out, the whole execution was simply a local application of a western formula with strong visual clues and warm fuzzy emotional messages (Gao, 2003, cited in Wang, 2008). McDonald's customises its marketing to China but also adapts it in some cities, such as Shanghai (Sinclair, 2009). As in India, it has also tried to integrate itself into local communities by sponsoring sports teams and providing facilities.

The largest foreign advertiser, Procter & Gamble, has been very strategic and successful in its entry to the Chinese market ('P&G adapts approach in emerging markets, *New York Times*, 16 December 2009). The company embarked on a multifaceted programme of cultivating strong relationships with government officials at national, provincial and local levels, developed a strong local organisation, introduced the latest technology and researched the effectiveness of their imported advertising before developing customised content (Dyer *et al.*, 2004). Procter & Gamble, which was the top advertiser in China between 1995 and 1999 (Gao, 2003) and has held that position since 2003, still sees plenty of potential for growth in China. The Chinese consumer currently spends on average $3 per year on Procter & Gamble products ($3.9 billion) compared with an average of $100 per person in the US, and $1 per person in India ('P&G adapts approach in emerging markets', *New York Times*, 2009). Procter & Gamble's dominant strategy across product groups is the 'problem–solution', while its competitor L'Oréal, the second largest advertiser in China, tends to use the celebrity endorser (de Mooij, 2005). Strategy profiles vary with product category. Personal products have not embraced digital media as successfully as other categories ('Cosmetics, beauty brands fail on digital', Consultancy L2, 2010) probably because of the way women buy products and their enjoyment of the process and aesthetics of purchasing.

In response to the growing popularity of local brands in the late 1990s some foreign companies like Coca-Cola took over local brands, or developed new brands with Chinese names: for example Xingmu (Smart) and Tianyud (Heaven and Earth), a practice Wang (2008) calls 'brand camouflaging'. Coca-Cola has also become a player in the bottled water category with Ice Dew and Sensation. Whirlpool sells washing machines in China under the local brand name Kelon and Maytag International uses its partner's brand name Rongshida (Schlevogt, 2000). The complexity of contemporary brands, many of which are hybrids, is reflected in customer perceptions. Some companies are seen as Chinese when they are not. Wahaha, for instance, is 51 per cent owned by French food products group Danone, but continues to market itself as a 'local' brand (Wang, 2008).

Because many foreign products are too expensive for local people, another option is what Doctoroff (2005) calls 'downward brand extension' – developing a cheaper line of products. Procter & Gamble has tried this approach, keeping the same brand name but coming up with cheaper formulae (ibid.). Other companies like L'Oréal have developed cheaper products with different names as well as moving into the previously untapped male segment with products like L'Oréal Men Expert, which was expanding rapidly in 2010 ('L'Oréal anticipates global "sea change"', L'Oréal, 2010).

Internet, mobile phones and word of mouth

Internet advertising is the largest growth area in international advertising but it is still a relatively small percentage of overall advertising, and it probably will never overtake television, despite all the hype. Some companies have successfully made the transition to internet advertising, and a recent McKinsey survey of web users found that marketers with a diverse online strategy in China quickly gained a competitive edge. Their advice was to 'craft a compelling online experience', on their own and other websites, and bring together video sharing, social networking, online forums and industry reviews ('Nuanced online strategy key in China', *China Daily*, 2010).

The internet also provides opportunities for consumer research and relies on the fact that mobile and email messages are not private. Samsung, Nokia and Sony are among the technology brands delivering the most online word-of-mouth marketing (WOMM) in China. Internet campaigns are often event driven. The 2008 Olympic Games was the first international event that really used internet and mobile phones. In 2010, for the FIFA World Cup in South Africa, China's three main mobile operators, China Mobile, China Unicom and China Telecom, all offered facilities to watch the games on the move. Samsung allied with popular portals sina.com, sohu.com and tom.com to run social ads and hold competitions, which boosted its status ('Samsung, Sony top buzz charts in China', Edelman, 2010). The Chinese social networking sites Kaixin001 and Renren hosted contests and other events. Marketers are finding Sina Weibo, the Chinese version of Twitter, a useful location for marketing. In an assessment of 736 websites by Edelman (a PR network) and Brandtology (a business intelligence firm) at the time of the FIFA World Cup, more than half of the 89 key companies in the technology sector were using it. BlackBerry signed up 7,000 'fans' on Sina Weibo between June and September 2010 (ibid.).

Product placement

Product placement is another growing area in China. The president of Ogilvy-One China, Chris Reitermann, claims that because there are fewer entertainment options in China people do not mind if a brand appears during a programme. Product placement has migrated to the internet and some multinational companies are developing online interactive films and 'mini-films' that combine short stories with high levels of product placement. Unilever used Catherine Zeta Jones to star in a seven-minute mini-film promoting Lux shampoo, and developed another series for China based on US television programme, *Ugly Betty*, renamed *Ugly Wudi*, which featured Dove and Lipton's tea ('Product placement growing in China', *Wall Street Journal*, 2009).

Local campaigns

As well as local companies gaining a grip on the Chinese market, local – *bentu* – agencies are connecting with consumers because they have more of a feel for local nuances and cultural subtleties than foreign advertisers. As Wang suggests (2008), they have a much greater insight into selling to the 700 million rural Chinese and their relatives who have recently come to the cities. Foreign advertisers may laugh at the corny and somewhat trashy local advertising campaigns but in Wang's words, '*bentu* advertising agencies [have] evolved their own advertising strategies based on local aesthetics', which are 'earthy, noisy and [have the] straightforward aesthetic of mass appeal'. She describes an advertisement for Naobaijin health tonic using 'an unabashed display of spectacle that translates into the sensational, hustle-bustle crowd effect' (ibid.). Where foreigners are sympathetic to the visual, Chinese people are pleased by audio aesthetics, double entendre and word plays. Also extremely successful were the commercials made by Ye Maozhong for Mengnui Dairy, which blended the local with emotional resonance and western references (ibid.).

Local marketing in China is often undertaken with a kind of war strategy mentality. One tactic, documented by Wang, is the 'spider warfare' strategy, which takes a leaf from Mao and spreads out to the villages around cities. Wahaha used this strategy very successfully to push Future Cola deep into the countryside after its launch in 1998. By 2001–02 it had 10 per cent market share. Wang (2008) notes, however, that Wahaha's branding strategy was unfocused and some brilliant marketing endeavours were accompanied by mixed and unclear messages. As competition increases, advertisers in Chinese need to be aware of the many subtleties of the market and perhaps follow Euromonitor's recommendation that companies may need to develop different models in markets like India and China ('Companies must adapt in emerging markets', 2010).

Snapshot study of outdoor advertising 2003 and 2010

In 2003 I documented outdoor advertising in central and eastern China. I was particularly struck by the scale of economic development in China and the size and extent of the outdoor advertising. Enormous billboards covered the sides of building construction sites, especially in the interior provinces at an earlier stage of development compared with Shanghai and Beijing. In the cities of the interior, such as Xian, billboards sometimes extended for almost half a kilometre, too long to get in a camera frame.

The product profile of advertising varied significantly in each of the cities I visited, as did the types of signage. In Beijing, one of the first cities to experience change, advertising reflected the maturity of the market (Xu, 1990). Many foreign companies were just raising their profile with the company name on buildings rather than advertising actual products. In Shanghai there was a much greater diversity of products advertised, and a lot of advertising for new housing developments and shopping centres. The cities of the interior had enormous billboards promoting industrial development, and many celebrating tourism and growth. There was a certain amount of social service and government advertising. High-tech products such as mobile phones and computers were common, as were services such as banking. The advertising reflected optimism and a country proud of its own development, success and growth.

The size and extent of the outdoor advertising was more extensive than in most other countries I have visited. There seemed to be saturation advertising on street signs for products such as Sprite, Pepsi and China Mobile. Billboard space appeared to be sold by distance (in units of roughly half a kilometre). One company would have all the street signs on lamp-posts down a certain section of a street. China Mobile was the most prominent Chinese company. There were also significant amounts of outdoor advertising for alcohol, but not for cigarettes. There was little evidence of foreign lifestyles or the use of foreign models, though the women featured tended to be very pale with western features. The youth market was targeted heavily by the soft drinks marketers and by McDonald's, using their standard strategy of 'attitude' advertising based on hedonism and consumption. As you would expect in less developed cities, there was more social service advertising in the interior provinces, including images of armed people in uniform. There were also more billboards advertising industrial products, real estate and industrial development zones.

In terms of branding the most visible company was China Mobile, which used a variety of strategies from product alone, to product in use, to people without product (lifestyle association). Foreign companies were not prominent. Coca-Cola and McDonald's followed their usual policy of picking high-profile locations with maximum visibility, for example at the foot of the Great Wall and in the square in front of the Shanghai railway station. The only foreign company shop in the Forbidden City was Starbucks, but it had only a minimal sign.

Figure 5.1 Often celebrity endorsements in China were not closely linked to brand association. Basketball star Yao Ming (Kaifeng, 2003).

Figure 5.2 Large-scale outdoor advertising on building sites. New production methods have enabled printing on massive vinyl sheets (Nanjing, 2003).

Figure 5.3 White-facing China: Global company, local campaign. This advertisement for L'Oréal White Perfect skin-whitening cream, reinforces traditional values with new products (Shanghai, 2003).

Figure 5.4 Cosmopolitan advertisement. Foreign magazines have dramatically changed the female magazine sector in China, duplicating formats used to target women internationally. Their popularity has stimulated local publications to follow western formations and content (Beijing, 2010).

Figure 5.5 Strong Chinese brands have emerged in recent years. Top Chinese advertiser Li Ning is challenging the global players Nike and Adidas (Beijing, 2010).

6 An environmental audit of the BRIC economies

'The two defining challenges of the 21st century are the battle against poverty and the management of climate change. If we fail on one, we will fail on the other.'
(Nicholas Stern, 2010 cited in S. Feldman. 'Lord Stern charts a "green" industrial revolution').

Introduction

This chapter focuses on the environmental effects of advertising and consumer culture in the BRIC economies, and how they will be changed by sustainability concerns. These economies are becoming increasingly important in the global economy. Their growth significantly increases the world's consumption of resources. Through an environmental audit of the BRIC economies I explore their environmental history, their current environmental profile (ecological footprint and bio-capacity) and the potential implications of their continuing development. The key factor in that projected growth will be the expansion of the middle classes, mainly in India and China.

The resources of the planet are being consumed faster than they are being renewed. Every aspect of contemporary life in high-income nations, from industrial production and the construction of infrastructure right through to everyday products, uses both materials and energy. Heavy industry and consumer goods industries are mutually dependent. Advertising links the latter with the market by stimulating product purchases. In wealthy countries consumers often have far more than they need to meet their basic needs. At the end of their short life cycles, accelerated by inbuilt obsolescence, many products are discarded, generating pollution. As resources become scarce, consumer capitalism and advertising cannot continue in their present form. Advertising will play a central communication role in facilitating the transition to a low carbon, resource-efficient green economy.

The environmental impact of contemporary lifestyles

High levels of consumption not only deplete resources but also generate high levels of carbon emissions, accelerating climate change. The Global Footprint Network estimated that in 2010 humanity was consuming the equivalent of 1.5 planets to supply the resources in current use and to absorb the waste produced (Global Footprint Network (GFN), *Living Planet Report*, 2010). Earth Overshoot Day 2010, when the earth had consumed its annual resource budget for the year, was 21 August (ibid.; Simms, 2010). Any further consumption that year took the planet into resource deficit. The effects of current and future levels of consumption will be extreme. Increases in consumption seem inevitable as the rapid growth of India and China continues. As income levels rise it is essential that these countries do not replicate the production and consumption patterns of the industrialised nations, which must also alter the quantity and nature of their consumption.

Unless carbon emissions are lowered and increases in global temperature are kept to two degrees this century, our planet is on the verge of an irreversible climate change crisis (International Panel on Climate Change (IPCC), 2007). Necessary changes in the way societies produce and consume goods will require massive communications programmes. Advertising can harness its skills to effect positive change. Change is most urgently required in the industrialised countries with the highest per capita ecological footprint and largest bio-capacity deficits. In 2007 the high-income nations had a total population of 1.1 billion people, while their average per capita carbon footprint was 6.1 hectares (Global Footprint Network, 2010). The most rapidly developing countries, especially India and China, need to manage their development sustainably or they will be crippled by food and resource shortages, as well as generating increasing levels of carbon emissions. There are not enough resources for the high-income nations to continue at their current consumption levels, let alone to meet rising demand from India and China.

Economic background

Growth figures are the main measures economists use to evaluate national economic well-being, but they hide many costs, most significantly the environmental and human costs of production and consumption. Prices that ignore subsidies, trade restrictions, low wages and the environmental costs of production and disposal do not reflect true costs. Sustainable resourcing and production must be incorporated into prices. Subsidies on resources like oil and agriculture transfer costs to the taxpayer rather than the producer. In India government subsidies on electricity encourage excessive pumping of ground water for irrigation, while subsidies on fuel keep prices down. In China key SOEs received subsidised energy. Fair wages also need to be included in prices. Currently, cheap goods for consumers in high-income nations are being produced by low-income workers in low- and middle-income nations such as India and China. The working conditions and wages would be unacceptable to workers in high-income countries, where, in many cases, governments also subsidise the agricultural and energy sectors. World trade is far from being equitable for all players. If full costs and higher wages were included in prices they would increase and demand would decrease, along with consumption and possibly profits – which is why so many businesses resist such changes.

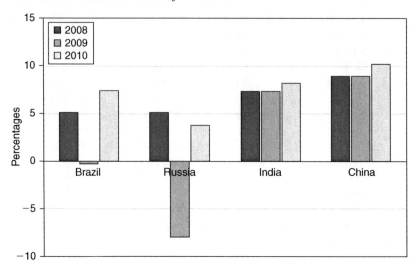

Figure 6.1 Growth profiles of the BRICs 2008–2010 (source: CIA. (8 March 2011a,b,c,d); CIA (8 March 2011a) World Factbook Country profile: Brazil. Online. Available https://www.cia.gov/library/publications/the-world-factbook/geos/br.html (accessed 21 March 2011); (8 March 2011b) World Factbook Country profile: Russia. Online. Available https://www.cia.gov/library/publications/the-world-factbook/geos/br.html (accessed 21 March 2011); (8 March 2011c) World Factbook Country profile: India. Online. Available https://www.cia.gov/library/publications/the-world-factbook/geos/br.html (accessed 21 March 2011); (8 March 2011d) World Factbook Country profile: China. Online. Available https://www.cia.gov/library/publications/the-world-factbook/geos/br.html (accessed 21 March 2011)).

The recent economic downturn has increased the importance of emerging economies as potential markets for western companies, especially in the BRIC economies. Consumption levels in the industrialised countries are likely to be flat for some years to come. The Centre for Economics and Business Research has predicted that corporations will change their focus as countries like India and China lead the recovery from the slowdown ('Recession boosts status of emerging markets', Bloomberg, 2010). Growth figures continued to be high for both India and China during the recent economic crisis and have recovered quickly. India's economy grew at 8.3 per cent in 2010 and China's at 10.3 per cent. These growth figures are likely to continue to be high as internal markets expand and income levels rise. Living standards have risen much more rapidly in China than India in the last decade. India is about ten years behind China but expanding rapidly.

The middle classes

The growth of the middle classes is closely tied to the expansion of consumption. Although the industrialised economies make up only a small proportion of the world's population, they have large middle class populations with high levels of consumption and high per capita ecological footprints (averaging 6.1 hectares).

The BRIC economies make up 40 per cent of the world's population, but only Russia is classified as a high-income nation. The recent rapid industrialisation of Brazil, India and China is changing lifestyles in those countries. With a per capita footprint of 2.2 hectares China is classified as a middle-income nation, along with Brazil, which has a per capita footprint of 2.9 hectares, while India is definitely a low-income nation with a per capita footprint of 0.9 hectares. Most people in these countries do not have a high standard of living, though the middle classes are expanding. There are simply not enough resources on the planet for the population of China to achieve a western middle class consumer lifestyle (Yang, 2010), let alone India as well.

As Martin Ravallion (2009) of the World Bank has pointed out, there is no agreed definition of middle class and different criteria are used for different purposes, but Wilson and Dragusanu's definition (2008) is a useful measure for assessing the environmental impact of consumption. They identify the 'world middle class' as earning $6,000–$30,000 per annum (adjusted for PPP across nations). They estimate the middle class in India to be 5 per cent of the

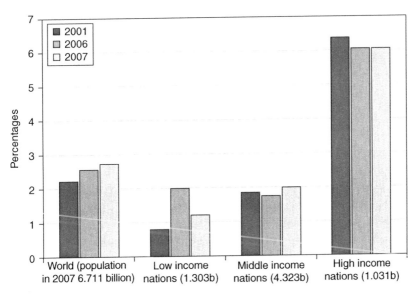

Figure 6.2 Global per capita footprint 2001/2006/2007 (sources: Global Footprint Network (2004, 2008, 2011); Global Footprint Network. (2004) *Living Planet Report 2004*. Online. Available www.footprintnetwork.org (accessed 3 March 2011); (25 November 2009) Ecological footprint and biocapacity (2009). Online. Available www.footprintnetwork.org (accessed 2010); (13 October 2010). Ecological footprint and biocapacity (2011). Online. Available footprintnetwork.org (accessed 16 January 2011); (2010). *Living Planet Report*. Online. Available www.footprintnetwork.org (accessed 3 March 2011)).

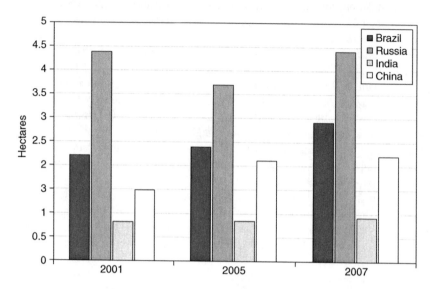

Figure 6.3 BRICS per capita footprint 2001/2005/2007 (sources: Global Footprint Network (2004, 2008, 2011); Global Footprint Network. (2004) *Living Planet Report 2004*. Online. Available www.footprintnetwork.org (accessed 3 March 2011); (25 November 2008) Ecological footprint and biocapacity (2005). Online. Available www.footprintnetwork.org (accessed 2010); (2010). *Living Planet Report*. Online. Available www.footprintnetwork.org (accessed 3 March 2011)).

population (55 million) and in China 55 per cent (715 million). Average incomes in India and China fall below the middle class threshold, between $2,000 and $4,000 per annum. Even if, as predicted, the GNP of the BRIC economies brings them into the G7 – the seven powerful industrialised nations comprising France, Germany, Italy, Japan, Britain, the United States and Canada – by 2030, per capita incomes will not be equivalent to those of the other G7 countries. I consider Wilson and Dragusanu's estimate for China to be too high; Doctoroff's (2008) figure of 15 per cent (195 million) based on Chinese Government estimates seems more realistic in terms of data about levels of consumption in China, and the Chinese government's commitment to raise the wages of 200 million migrant workers (BBC News, 14 February 2011). In India and China the living standards of some 2.15 billion people have yet to improve. In 2007 O'Neill of Goldman Sachs (2008) predicted a 400 per cent growth in the middle classes of the BRICs by 2017. Such an increase will have a significant impact on the environment. China is already the world's largest carbon emitter and India the third largest (Sharma, 2010).

Two key indicators of higher living standards are changing patterns of food consumption – moving up the food chain and increasing meat, dairy and milk consumption – together with levels of car ownership. Other sectors predicted to grow in the BRIC economies in the near future are energy consumption and automobile purchasing, both of which have major environmental impacts. People do not buy cars until their annual income levels are around $9,000 (Wilson and Dragusanu, 2008). If oil continues to be the primary energy source, escalating consumption will have a devastating impact on carbon emission levels. Car ownership levels in the BRICs are currently much lower than in the west, but they have already increased significantly since 2002. In India ownership levels went from 17.3 million vehicles in 2002 (United Nations Statistics Division, 2008c) to 20.3 million in 2010 (O'Neill and Stupnytska, 2009). In China the increase in vehicle ownership has risen from 20.1 million vehicles in 2002 (UN Environmental Statistics, 2008d) to a predicted 55 million in 2010 (O'Neill and Stupnytska, 2009).

Brazil

Brazil's economic growth in the last decade has been driven not by rising living standards and increasing internal demand – it has a relatively small population – but by its vital role as a supplier of raw materials, notably timber, oil and minerals, to the rest of the world. Brazil also has large areas of agricultural and pastoral production and is one of the world's largest exporters of agricultural products. Many of its resources are exploited unsustainably and some are under threat of depletion. In the Amazon Basin Brazil has the largest area of forest cover in the world, so its management has major global implications both for climate change and for continued supplies of resources. Brazil's industrial production and consumption also has an impact: it is still one of the world's top ten carbon emitters. In 2007 its per capita footprint was 2.9 hectares (Figure 3), which makes it a middle-income nation. Brazil's ecological reserve of 6.1 hectares per capita (the ecological resources it has to draw on) is by far the largest of all the BRICs (GFN, 2010), but the ongoing depletion of the country's resources to meet overseas demand has major global environmental implications.

For the first 200 years after Brazil became a Portuguese colony its main function was supplying wood and sugar to Europe. Most of the coastal forests were destroyed and plantation agriculture was also environmentally damaging. The system of monoculture production depleted the soil of nutrients and polluted waterways with by-products. The plantation model was later used for cocoa and coffee production. In the seventeenth century the main export was gold and in the nineteenth century coffee replaced sugar as the major agricultural export (*New Internationalist*, 2007). In the twentieth century the Brazilian economy remained fairly static, especially from the 1930s to the 1960s, but then development accelerated, affecting the environment through industrialisation, agribusiness, deforestation of the Amazon Basin and expansion of agricultural production in the Cerrado, Brazil's vast tropical savannah.

The total area of the Amazon Basin is 4,143,980 square kilometres and already 20 per cent has been destroyed. The ongoing pace of destruction recorded in satellite data is rapid. Between 2000 and 2005 Brazil lost more than

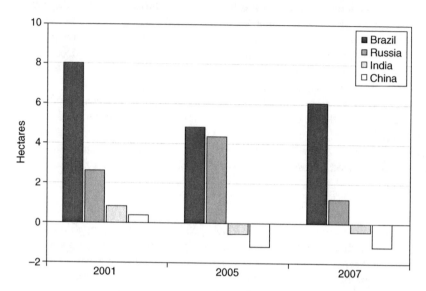

Figure 6.4 BRICs National Ecological Reserve (hectares) 2001/2005/2007 (sources: Global Footprint Network (2004, 2008, 2011); Global Footprint Network. (2004) *Living Planet Report 2004*. Online. Available www.footprintnetwork. org (accessed 3 March 2011); (25 November 2008) Ecological footprint and biocapacity (2005). Online. Available www.footprintnetwork.org (accessed 2010); (2010). *Living Planet Report*. Online. Available www.footprintnetwork.org (accessed 3 March 2011)).

129,999 square kilometres of rainforest. The Amazon also provides much of its own precipitation so the destruction of the forest also results in drought, as happened in the summer of 2010 (Wallace, 2007). The building of roads has played a major part in the exploitation of the rainforest. Apart from the state highways, the east-west Trans-Amazonian Highway and the 'soy highway' (the BR-163), there are more than 170,000 km of unauthorised roads, most of them constructed by illegal logging enterprises. Eighty per cent of illegal activity occurs near these roads (ibid.). Valuable timber is often felled and the land cleared by burning to exploit the timber and mineral resources or to turn it into grassland for raising cattle (*New Internationalist*, 2007). Fires often get out of control and burn large areas. By 2006, 721 species were threatened as a result of the cutting down the Brazilian rainforest (UNSD, 2008a). Deforestation is destroying the habitats of plants along with the livelihood and cultures of local indigenous peoples (*New Internationalist*, 2007).

Attempts to curb this unregulated exploitation have been weakly enforced and are largely ineffective. The problem of exploitation covers the full spectrum from businesses, political allegiances and regional power holders to illegal timber cullers and poachers, as well as landless farmers simply trying to survive (ibid.). International decisions are being ignored by the government. In 2004

Petrobras, the state oil company, signed an agreement with Ecuador to drill in Yasuni National Park, a UNESCO-declared biosphere reserve. Oil development is also causing toxic contamination and forest destruction (Worldwatch Institute, 2004). Both water sources and wetlands are being destroyed through mining. Cattle ranches have been established in the interior on unforested grasslands that cover vast areas, and the forests of the Cerrado are being cut more rapidly than in the Amazon (*The Economist*, 2009c). This onslaught is a response to increasing world demand for soy, beef and timber. Meat has become a major export in recent decades. In 2005 the European Union (EU) sourced 49 per cent of its soybeans, 34 per cent of its beef and 28 per cent of its hardwoods from Brazil. China imports 20 per cent of Brazil's soybeans; the United States imports 50 per cent of its hardwoods and Russia 19 per cent of its beef (Wallace, 2007). It has been illegal to export protected wood from Brazil since the 1970s but trees are still cut if buyers can be found.

Brazil's energy production also has significant environmental implications. After the 1970s oil crisis the Brazilian government made a commitment to being self-sufficient in energy. Large subsidies were provided for developing ethanol from sugarcane, and Brazil is now the second largest ethanol producer in the world. By-products from ethanol production are another source of pollution (Brown, 2009). The expansion of agriculture into grassland and marginal land has also created a range of environmental problems that include soil depletion, erosion (caused by wind) and desertification. Intense use of irrigation has reduced groundwater levels and lowered the water table. Fertilisers have penetrated the water table as a result of heavy use and polluted the water. The latest Brazilian oil discoveries lie almost 300 km from its coastline some five to six kilometres below the ocean. Petrobras is already developing wells in high-risk areas (*The Economist*, 2009c).

During the twentieth century Brazil's historical profile was similar to that of other South American countries: political instability and military dictatorships, high levels of corruption and low levels of tax collection. In the twenty-first century Brazil is becoming an emerging global power and developing into a major industrial economy. Between 1999 and 2009, thanks to the surge in commodity prices, Brazil's share of world GDP increased from 1.9 to 2.3 per cent (Anderlini *et al.*, 2009). As the Amazon's role as the world's major carbon sink becomes increasingly vital, Brazil is likely to play an increasingly prominent role on the world political stage in the next 40 years.

Brazil has a sound legal environmental framework but not the resources to implement and enforce it (United States Library of Congress, 2011a). The outlook for the growth of a widespread sustainability movement in Brazil does not look hopeful. The emerging middle classes, and those becoming consumers for the first time, are not interested in sustainable consumption and the environment. Such interest tends to be a feature of mature economies. The Gfk Roper consumer survey found that Brazilians, and Latin Americans in general, recycled less and cared less about the environment than people in other countries (Salles, 2006). The case of Brazil highlights the contradictions inherent in reducing poverty, in this case with governmental welfare programmes: increased prosperity means increased environmental impact. As caretaker of the Amazon, Brazil has the most environmentally important role of all the BRICs. The destruction of the rainforest releases large amounts of carbon into the atmosphere, which accelerates the greenhouse effect and climate change. Protecting this rainforest deserves and requires concerted international action similar to international relief efforts organised by the United Nations in disaster areas and war zones, or to the post-war Marshall Plan. Lester Brown (2009) has recommended such a wartime mobilisation model in his book, *Plan B: Rescuing a Planet under Stress and a Civilization in Trouble*. A multi-strategy approach is needed to protect the forest and peoples of the Amazon. These strategies would include international aid, financial support and people on the ground to monitor and police illegal activities and support the new initiatives. Local people need alternative employment in protecting the forest and they, and the government, must be properly compensated for loss of revenue. In 2010 the governments of Sweden and Norway provided a role model by paying the Indonesian government to stop logging the rainforests for two years (*The Economist*, September 2010; Barnett, 2010). Potential income could also come from carbon tax credits, though little progress was made on this topic at the Copenhagen Climate Change Conference in 2009. The Amazon Basin could well be the carbon emission lifeline of the planet but current rates of destruction could reduce it to a third of its current size. Brazil's main export markets – China, the United States, Argentina, the Netherlands and Germany (CIA, 2011a) – are the key drivers of the exploitation of Brazil's resources and should front efforts to protect the Amazon rainforest.

Russia

Russia, as the world's largest country and home to a wealth of natural resources, has a crucial role in the environmental sustainability of the planet. Russia has been an industrial economy for more than half a century. Its per capita footprint of 4.4 hectares – higher than that of the other BRICs (Figure 6.4) – puts it at the low end of high-income nations (Figure 6.2). Population pressure will not be a future problem because Russia's population is small relative to its land area, and is declining rather than increasing: it is predicted to reach 103 million by 2050 (US Census, 2010b). Even if most of the Russian population had a western middle class lifestyle, the increased consumption that brought with it would not have a major effect on the sustainability of the planet (O'Neill, 2001). Russia's biggest environmental challenges are dealing with the high levels of environmental degradation that are the legacy of the Soviet era.

It was industrialisation that enabled Soviet Russia to become a world power in the second half of the twentieth century. This was a command economy in which goals were set by politicians. There were no incentives to modernise or to consider efficiency or the environmental impact of industry. Production methods were wasteful, factories became outdated and the country's industrial plant was allowed to deteriorate. The results of these practices have been high levels of industrial pollution, the dumping of industrial waste, contamination, acid rain and also an accumulation of hazardous waste from nuclear and chemical munitions (United States Library of Congress (USLC), 2011b). The 1986 Chernobyl nuclear disaster was the first Russian environmental disaster that hit the international headlines. In the 1990s the government categorised 40 per cent of Russia, an area three-quarters the size of the United States, as under high or moderately high ecological risk (ibid.). The decline in industrial activity in the last two decades has reduced the levels of industrial pollution, but this may change as the government tries to diversify its economy.

Before 1989 environmental degradation was a public issue in Russia, but in the next two decades people became more preoccupied with economic survival. Since 1991 the government has continued to show little interest in environmental issues. Government spending on the environment declined to $480 million in 1997, less than 0.5 per cent of federal budget spending (National Intelligence Council (NIC), 1999). In 2007 the OECD reported environmental spending in the Russian Federation as only 1.2 to 1.6 per cent of GDP (OECD Policy Brief, 2007). Russia's environmental problems are compounded by corruption and indifference. Environmental protection bureaucracies have extensive ties to the industries they are regulating. The Forestry Service, for example, earns half its income from lumber sales. Nuclear energy has been used in Russia since 1954 and the Russian government has illegally dumped nuclear waste into the oceans (NIC, 1999). Other environmental problems included radioactive leakages and poor monitoring of chemical weapons. When the economic environment was insecure firms exploited resources for cash value rather than planning for the future. Black market economic activities, which included the exploitation of such natural resources as timber, meat and fish, amounted to an estimated 60 to 90 per cent of GDP in the 1990s (ibid., 1999). There are 161 threatened species in Russia, which is the lowest of all the BRICs (UNSD, 2008b), possibly because development has focused on urban industrialisation.

Urbanisation has also created environmental problems. As Russian cities expanded people adopted western consumption patterns and levels of solid waste increased significantly. Because there is little expertise in managing disposal, many waste disposal systems came under pressure in the 1990s (NIC, 1999). Air pollution, caused by rising levels of motor vehicle ownership, is another problem. Because Russian vehicles still use leaded fuel, and many are old and poorly maintained, they produce high levels of carbon and other emissions (UNSD, 2008b). Ownership levels are also increasing, from 27 million motor vehicles in 2003 (18 per cent of the population), to a predicted 36.9 million in 2010 (O'Neill and Stupnytska, 2009). Vehicle ownership levels are much higher than in India and China: in 2006, 27 per cent of Russians households owned a car (*European Marketing Pocket Book 2006*, cited in Grech, 2006c).

Russia's strength in the coming century will be as a source of primary resources. Much of its recent wealth has been derived from mineral and oil reserves, though the latter have already passed their peak. The Russian economy continues to be dominated by resource extraction, especially minerals – lead, bauxite, manganese, tin, copper, zinc, oil, coal and iron – in the Urals, Caucasia and Siberia (*New Internationalist*, 2007). International companies have taken part in developing these resources and become involved in regional politics: the oil giants ExxonMobil, Unocal and Chevron were all involved in the Russia–Chechen conflict. Since the collapse of the Soviet Union these companies have also encroached into the Caspian Sea area. The fight for control of Russian oil led the United States to support the construction of a 1,750 km pipeline to transport a million barrels of oil a day from Baku to Turkey to avoid going through politically unstable Iran (*New Internationalist*, 2007). Russia also has a vested interest in the oil and minerals lying under the northern icecap. Because of the decline in external demand for its resources Russia was one of the hardest hit economies in the 2008–09 economic crisis. The government has responded by attempting to move the economy away from resource extraction.

In the last half-century Russia's main focus has been on industrialisation and then resource extraction rather than agriculture, which accounted for only 4.8 per cent of GDP in 2008 (World Bank, 2008b). Some agricultural initiatives during the Soviet era created major environmental damage. In an effort to increase wheat production, between 1954 into the 1960s the government initiated the Virgin Lands Project, in which a large area of marginal land in Kazakhstan was ploughed to grow wheat. By the 1980s this area had been transformed into an unproductive dustbowl; 40 per cent of Kazakhstan's grain-producing land has been abandoned since 1980 (Brown, 2009). As in the industrial sector, there has been little regulation in agriculture. There is a huge stock of old, unused and deteriorating pesticides. Although Russia has abundant water resources, and is one of the six countries that account for more than half of the world's total renewable fresh water supply (Worldwatch Institute, 2004), poor water quality is a major problem. Only one third of the population has safe drinking water (UNSD, 2008b). Rivers have been polluted by agro-chemicals and inadequate systems for waste and sewage treatment. The Volga River, the Sea of Azov in the north, the Black Sea, the Caspian Sea and Lake Baikal all suffer from severe water contamination (US Library of Congress, 2011b). Solutions to these problems often deal only with effects but fail to tackle the basic causes. For instance, the declining level of the Red Sea is to be 'solved' by piping in water. Russia's agricultural and other resources have great potential for future development, especially with the prospect of future global food shortages and increased emphasis on food security. International commodity prices for wheat have already been affected by a heatwave and bushfires which reduced the Russian harvest in the summer of 2010.

Russia's resources have been overexploited and they are diminishing rapidly. Its per capita ecological reserve was 1.3 hectares in 2007 (Figure 6.4). Environmental damage and pollution has damaged the health and well-being of its citizens, and the environmental future continues to look bleak in the face of government indifference, a large black market economy, little regulation and enforcement and high levels of corruption. There is growing evidence of public concern about the environment: in 2010 there was a massive response when President Vladimir Putin approved the reopening of a paper mill that would discharge waste into Lake Baikal.

Although most of Russia's environmental problems are internal, Russia demonstrates the global nature of some ecological problems. After the 1998 floods, when China banned the cutting of trees in the Yangtze Basin, there was an increase in the logging of forests in Russia, most of it illegal (Brown, 2006). Another cross-border issue is the result of global warming. The melting of the large permafrost areas of Siberia generates methane gas, which also stimulates the production of greenhouse gases.

India

India has always had a large and mostly poor population. Resulting from the lifestyle of the rajahs, and 200 years of British colonial rule, the wildlife population has been severely reduced. Since Independence in 1947 deforestation for agriculture and fuel, poaching, pesticides and increasing population have created further environmental pressures (UNSD, 2008c). After Independence two of the new government's key goals were self-reliance and improved living standards, and in the 1960s it embarked on initiatives that became known as the Green Revolution, funded by loans from the United States, the World Bank and the IMF, which were all fearful of India's alignment with Russia. The programme included introducing high-yielding seeds and fertilisers to increase crop yields. These innovations intensified already inequitable traditional patterns of land ownership. Levels of dispossession, landlessness, poverty and rural inequality all increased and prompted the first wave of urban migration. The seeds and pesticides caused soil depletion, loss of biodiversity and pollution of rivers and water sources (*New Internationalist*, 2007). By 2006 the number of threatened species in India had reached 569 (UNSD, 2008c).

For many decades the Indian economy was inward looking and the economy remained inert until the 1980s, when gradual changes were introduced. Growth and development began to accelerate only after the liberalisation of the economy in the early 1990s and, as we have seen, India is a decade behind China. As is shown by the poor quality of its roads, electricity supply and social services, India lacks the financial resources of its totalitarian neighbour. India's future growth is likely to have a massive impact on the environment through industrial development, the building of infrastructure and cities and the expansion of energy supplies, often poorly regulated. The growth of cities has led to encroachment upon surrounding land, as well as increasing demand for resources and energy. Social inequality and levels of poverty are also much higher in India than in China, and are compounded by the rigidity of the caste system.

Many of India's environmental issues are the result of a growing population and the resulting pressure on resources. India is already in water deficit and in the north-west aquifers are drying out and many lakes are disappearing. There have been suicides among farmers dependent on this water (Brown, 2009).

When surface wells dry up mining technology has been used to access deep groundwater, which is causing water table levels to drop (ibid.). Water quality is also a problem and there is a shortage of clean drinking water throughout the country. Government subsidies intensify the water and energy problems. There is little incentive to conserve resources when Indian farmers received subsidised energy worth $4–5 billion a year and collectively they pump 150 billion litres of ground water (Worldwatch Institute, 2004). It is predicted that crop yields in the Ganges Valley will decline because of water shortages (Brown, 2009). The vast delta plains will also be in jeopardy if sea levels rise. Desertification and salination are also forcing people off the land. Food scarcity will be another key issue as population pressure pushes up demand. The size of harvests is affected by the weather, particularly bad monsoons and droughts, and extreme weather events are becoming more frequent. The poor are particularly vulnerable during these crises. India will be one of the countries most affected by climate change.

India remains a predominantly rural agricultural nation. Most people live in the countryside and agriculture is the main form of employment despite only accounting for 18 per cent of GDP in 2007 (World Bank, 2008c). India's agricultural sector has a major chemical pollution problem: 32 of the 180 registered insecticides currently in use in India have been banned in other countries. Between 1998 and 2001 India produced 40,000 tonnes of these compounds a year (Worldwatch Institute, 2004). India is also the world's third largest producer of cotton, the world's best-selling fibre. Cotton production is one of the most polluting forms of agriculture. It uses pesticides in large quantities, which causes sickness and even death among farm workers, harms birds, fish and wildlife and pollutes local water supplies; herbicides are also used to defoliate the plants before harvesting. Later in the production cycle chemical dyes are used, and these often contain copper, zinc and other heavy metals that are toxic and pollute water through factory runoff. Fabric finishes like stain and wrinkle repellents can contain petrochemicals such as formaldehyde (Worldwatch Institute, 2004).

The introduction of genetically modified seeds is causing major environmental and social problems. Many cotton farmers have been told that Monsanto seeds will increase harvests and are resistant to certain pests, but they need to be bought annually, they deplete the soil and eventually they require more fertilisers and pesticides. An estimated 200,000 of these cotton farmers have committed suicide because of debt. Genetically modified seeds also exacerbate the loss of biodiversity (*Dying in Abundance*, Russian Television, March 2011). India depends on cattle for milk, power and fuel and the dairy sector is one area that is environmentally sustainable. Cattle are fed agricultural residues and hay (Brown, 2009) and practices are excellent. India has the largest dairy herd in the world and in 1997 overtook the United States as the world's largest producer of milk.

The liberalisation policies of the early 1990s gave Indian industry a major boost. More multinational companies set up production, and local industry also grew. Industry has slowly increased as a proportion of GDP from 26.3 per cent in 1987 to 26.8 per cent in 1997 and 29 per cent in 2007 (World Bank, 2008c). The future growth of India's economy will come from the industrial and service sectors. Meeting the needs of the internal market enabled the Indian economy to continue growing throughout the economic crisis. India is, however, increasingly dependent on imported fuel and food. Rising prices and inflation are becoming major problems, especially for the poor. Industrial development must be managed so that India does not replicate the environmental disaster that is occurring at local level in China. The major environmental issue facing India is its population; its birth rate is higher than China's, and by 2025 it will overtake its neighbour as the world's most populous nation (USCD, 2011c). India's population increases by about 16 million per year (Worldwatch Institute, 2004) and is projected to increase to 1.6 billion by 2050 (ibid., 2011c). Although poverty levels have been declining for some decades they are still high and India has the world's largest population living in poverty and the highest numbers of both illiterate and under-fed people. The CIA (2011c) estimated poverty levels to be 275 million in 2007. Using Brown's estimate of the world poor as 1.1 billion people (2009), India has 25 per cent of the world's poor, or 20 per cent if one uses Stiglitz's estimate that the world's poor number 1.4 billion (2009). The poor need access to safe water, food, medicine, education and healthcare. Brown (2009) has estimated that the costs of meeting the social needs of the poorest 1.1 billion of the world's population is $77 billion, so by extrapolation meeting the social needs of India's poor would cost about $19 billion, roughly six times the cost of the 2010 Commonwealth Games held in India. Poverty, illiteracy and gender inequalities could hinder India's future growth and must be addressed to avoid the entrenchment of 'two Indias'.

India is not a major consumer of world resources but if the government facilitates the reduction of poverty, and the middle classes continue to expand, resource consumption will increase dramatically. The Indian middle classes grew from 1 per cent of the population in 2000 to 5 per cent – 55 million – in 2008 (Wilson and Dragusanu, 2008). If, as predicted, they reach 50 per cent of the population by 2030, that would amount to 730 million people (ibid.; USCD, 2010c).

As living standards and disposable incomes rise, so do the quantity and types of products consumed. The increased food consumption of the Indian middle classes could have a major impact on global food prices, and higher incomes could also mean greater vehicle ownership leading to more demand for energy and more air pollution. There were 17.3 million motor vehicles in India in 2002 (UNSD, 2008c), a number predicted to rise to 20.3 million in 2010 (O'Neill and Stupnytska, 2009). The world's cheapest car, the Tata Nano costing $1,500, came onto the market in 2009. Increasing consumption levels resulted in India's per capita ecological footprint increasing from 0.8 hectares in 2001 to 0.9 in 2007, while the per capita ecological reserve declined from a surplus of 0.8 hectares to a deficit of 0.4 hectares (Figures 6.3, 6.4) India is already the world's third highest producer of carbon emissions at a time when half the population has no access to electricity (Sharma, 2010). The Indian government has recognised that though its carbon emissions are only 5 per cent of the world total, future growth and higher living standards for the poor cannot be accompanied by rising emission levels (ibid.).

China

China is a nation of many contradictions. In 2007 it overtook the United States as the largest producer of greenhouse gases (Vidal and Adam, 2007) and in August 2010 it overtook Japan as the second largest economy in the world after the United States. Yet China is still a developing country and its per capita income is not in the top 100 countries (BBC World News, 13 September 2010). China's environmental issues – there are high levels of both urban and rural pollution – are the result of rapid and unregulated development. Pollution and environmentally unsustainable economic practices have been having an impact since the 1990s. Environmental pollution has damaged health and the toll of water and air pollution in 1997 was as estimated as being $54 billion, 8 per cent of GDP (World Bank, cited in Economy, 2004).

China's history has always been shaped by the sheer size of its population and its future will be dominated by the consumption of both its own resources and those of the world. Until the late twentieth century most of the population lived in poverty and the reversal of this situation over the last 30 years has been one of history's greatest social achievements. China has raised the living standards of nearly 1.3 billion people, approximately 20 per cent of the world's population. Although those standards are still much lower than in high-income nations, the numbers of people living in poverty in China dropped from 685 million in 1990 to 213 million in 2007 (Brown, 2009), but the accompanying high economic growth rates have inflicted major damage to the environment. Water and food scarcities, environmental pollution and degradation – in a country already prone to major flooding and famines – are the key issues China will face in the next decades.

Many of China's environmental problems are caused by government development policies. The country has always had a large population but in the Maoist era pressure to feed the population encouraged policies that brought inappropriate land into agricultural production. The consequence has been increased desertification and soil erosion in an interior which was once the food bowl of imperial China. After 1979 this damage was intensified by removing constraints on the ownership of grazing animals. Soaring stock numbers damaged the groundcover in extensive areas of marginal land (Brown, 2006), which in turn has increased the incidence of major dust storms in northern China.

The economic growth of the Chinese economy averaged 9 per cent between 1975 and 2000 (ibid.). In a short period China has managed to achieve results that took the industrialised nations in the west more than a century to achieve. In the 1980s central government delegated the responsibility for development to the TVEs, the township and village enterprises, in the provinces and regions. Local bureaucrats made the growth of industry their goal, regardless of the environmental cost. A proliferation of unregulated small-scale polluting industries has caused immeasurable environmental pollution and degradation (Economy, 2004). Many industrialised nations and companies have contributed to the pollution by transferring to China their most polluting industries, including steel, aluminium, paper, cement and petrochemicals (ibid.; Magnier, 2007). China has become the 'factory of the world', producing half of the world's cement and flat glass and a third of its aluminium. China has emerged as a producer of cheap, low-end consumer goods exported primarily to the United States. Its surplus with the United States rose tenfold from $10 billion in 1990 to $103 billion in 2002 (Worldwatch Institute, 2004) and has continued to grow. The trade imbalance reached its highest level in 2008 ($426 billion), then dropped in 2009 as a result of the global economic crisis, but soon began to expand again, reaching $305.4 billion in 2010 (State Administration of Foreign Exchange of the People's Republic of China, 2011). Growth figures for 2010 were expected to reflect lower demand from the EU and the United States ('Official: China's trade surplus to drop in 2010', *People's Daily*, 2010).

In the last three decades China has undertaken massive building programmes, including industry, energy plants, infrastructure development, cities and roads. Urbanisation both encroaches on the land and is also very resource intensive, especially in the high use of cement, which is one of the most environmentally damaging products. China has also been extending its energy production. The Three Gorges Dam Project is the world's largest and seriously threatens the local ecology as well as displacing thousands of people (*New Internationalist*, 2007). China has an abundance of low-grade brown coal, which is its main energy source, and coal-based industrial production is the largest source of air and land pollution. Even if these coal plants are made to be more efficient and produce fewer emissions they will still contribute to global warming. Although China has become a world leader in wind farm technology, and is also developing energy plants to harness wave power, it is continuing to build coal-fired power stations and 70 per cent of its energy needs are still being met by coal (Yang, 2009). This is likely to remain the case for the foreseeable future.

The Chinese Government has also put growth before the safety of the population. Cheap labour (which results in low prices for western consumers) can be attributed in part to China's lax labour laws and the absence of a comprehensive social welfare system. Health and safety in industry and construction are a low priority and there are high accident levels on building sites and in factories. China has the highest rate of mining deaths in the world. By transferring production to China, companies from industrialised nations have capitalised on cheap labour and avoided the stricter labour and environmental legislation in their home countries. Wal-Mart, which controls 15 per cent of the American apparel market, could squeeze manufacturers to pay workers as little as 13 US cents an hour, far below the normal rate in China of 25 US cents. Prices can also be kept low by the threat of taking business elsewhere. Sixty per cent of American toys are made in China under similar conditions (Worldwatch Institute, 2004).

China's pollution and environmental problems are partly driven by the high consumption levels of the west and its demand for cheap products. China produces a huge amount for the 'global consuming classes' and many products, such as clothes and electronics, have actually got cheaper for western consumers in the last decade. A good example is cotton T-shirts: China is the world's largest producer of cotton and it is the top producer of T-shirts. As was mentioned in the Indian section, many aspects of cotton production are environmentally damaging. Other consumer goods industries with high environmental impacts include textiles, children's toys, cars and paper.

Industrial disasters, environmental damage and the human cost of lax labour laws are having a major social impact. There have been a number of large industrial disasters in China, including the National Petroleum Corporation explosion near Chonquin in 2003 and the poisoning of the waters of the Songhua River after an explosion at a chemical plant in 2005 (*New Internationalist*, 2007). There has been a human cost, too, during natural disasters such as the 2009 Sichuan earthquake. Many children died unnecessarily because of the use of inferior materials and the use of inadequate reinforcement in the construction of school buildings because of the corruption of local officials.

China is also home to 20 of the world's 30 most polluted cities. Other environmental problems are also extracting a human cost. People are dying of pollution-related illnesses and children are being born with birth defects as a result of pollution. Acid rain falls on 30 per cent of the country, and on the adjacent countries of Korea, Japan and Vietnam. Many of the waterways and coastal areas are polluted and most cities do not have safe drinking water (Magnier, 2007). Polluted water contributes to stomach, bladder and bowel cancer (Macfie, 2010). Cancer is the now the leading cause of death in China, and the populations of some 'cancer villages' have been decimated by disease (Brown, 2009).

China's economy has been largely dependent on external consumer demand, but there is also a large potential internal market, which the government is keen to develop. An estimated 20 million migrant worker jobs were lost during the economic crisis in 2009 (BBC World News, April 2010). Using Doctoroff's estimate of the size of the middle classes, 1.105 billion Chinese are yet to join 'the consuming classes' (2008). China has also started modifying and relaxing its one child policy to compensate for the ageing population and decline in the workforce, so this figure could increase (Dickie, 2008). Consumption of raw materials and food in China already affect the rest of the world and will have a major impact on future global commodity prices. China has replaced the United States as the world's highest consumer of basic commodities. As living standards rise, people consume more energy and more products. Patterns of food consumption also change – what Brown (2009) calls 'moving up the food chain'. One of the key indicators is the increased consumption of meat and dairy products: already China is the world's largest consumer of chicken (ibid.). A recent McKinsey survey found that Chinese purchasers are starting to display similar preferences to those in the west and that their shopping patterns are changing from shopping daily to shopping less frequently but buying more goods. Buyers were starting to report that they treated shopping as a leisure activity. Product choice was also being influenced by factors such as perfume and packaging ('China's shoppers among "most complex"', McKinsey, 2010).

Chinese people lead the world in ownership of mobile phones, televisions and refrigerators. It may soon catch up in car ownership, another indicator of middle class aspiration. China has the fastest growing automobile market in the world; although current ownership levels are still very low they are growing rapidly. In the early 2000s domestically designed and manufactured cars had the biggest negative environmental impact because they were poorly maintained, less fuel-efficient and produced more pollution than foreign cars. There were 20.14 million cars in China in 2002 (UNSD, 2008d), predicted to rise to 55 million in 2010 (O'Neill and Stupnytska, 2009). China overtook the US as the world's largest car market in 2009, with sales of 13.6 million vehicles, including buses, and 10.3 million cars (*The Economist*, 14 January 2010a). All the big auto manufacturers are looking to China for future growth in sales and many have established production facilities ('China will be VW's biggest market, says CEO', *China Daily*, 2009). The expansion of credit lending in emerging economies, especially China, is facilitating this growth in automobile sales (Worldwatch Institute, 2004). China is a major oil consumer, doubling its consumption to 6.5 million barrels between 1994 and 2004, although this is still low when compared with America's 20.4 million barrels (Brown, 2006). The fact that car sales are the force behind the Chinese economy, and that expansion is likely to continue, is a cause for environmental concern even though China's fuel efficiency standards are now higher than the United States. The government is now subsidising the uptake of electric cars (Macfie, 2010).

Environmental issues have become a priority for the Chinese government. It faces internal pressure because pollution, degradation and desertification are causing social unrest and creating environmental refugees. Inflation, price increases and low wages are also leading to labour unrest. Energy is a key priority and the government has committed to finding replacements for coal. It has started planning for a different economic and environmental future. China is now a leader in developing alternative sources of energy. There are still inconsistencies in the system, though, and certain sectors of the economy dominated by SOEs are privileged with cheap loans from state-owned banks and cheap energy from the state utility companies (*The Economist*, October 2010).

There is also external pressure on China to address environmental issues. The national per capita footprint in China increased from 1.5 hectares in 2001 to 2.2 hectares in 2007, while the per capita ecological reserve declined from 0.4 hectares to a deficit of 1.2 hectares (Figures 6.3, 6.4) The size of this footprint, however, is still less than a fifth of that left by the average American. As China has four times the population of the United States the impact of rising standards of living is potentially disastrous (Watts, 2007). When the Chinese government released its first national plan on climate change in June 2007 it pledged to follow a new path to industrialisation that would not cause high levels of emissions and consumption, even though it still maintained that industrialised countries were responsible for most of the planet's global warming. The key future strategies were to increase renewable energy, forestation and efficiency. China signed the Kyoto Agreement in 2002, committing to curbing greenhouse emissions, but was not required to meet targets as it was still a developing country. China has also shown an interest in global carbon trading to bring down carbon dioxide outputs (Magnier, 2007).

China can no longer meet its agricultural needs and is already a net food importer. There are moves to adopt 'cradle to cradle' technologies for industries and energy as part of a strategy to address its needs (Worldwatch Institute, 2004). Climate change is accelerating the melting of the Himalayan snows which will have major impacts on the country's future water supplies. China is one of the world's main grain producers and production is already affected both by falling water tables in the North China Plain and lower river levels (Brown, 2006). The government's immediate response to addressing water shortages in Beijing has simply been to pipe in water from far away. Other major problems include deforestation (which causes flooding and soil loss), industrial and chemical pollution, air pollution and toxic waste disposal. The cost of pollution is estimated at 10 per cent of China's economy. Much of that cost is in the consumer goods industries, where pollution causes ill-health and subsequent loss of productivity (Magnier, 2007). China has even become a destination for the waste disposal of other countries (Economy, 2004). China also has the largest number of threatened species (804) of all the BRICs (UNSD, 2008d).

According to Ma Tianjie, who runs the Greenpeace campaign against toxic waste in China, there is nothing wrong with China's environmental laws; the problem is enforcement, compliance and the absence of data. China has welcomed the international community as part of its long-term strategy to improve environmental conditions. Intergovernmental organisations, including the UN, the World Bank, the Asia Development Bank and NGOs such as Greenpeace, have stepped in with assistance. Recently, however, the government reduced the amount of external funding that NGOs are allowed to receive, which hampered their activities (Macfie, 2010). The significant impediments to implementing environmental regulations identified in 2004 remain the same: lack of infrastructure for effective technology implementation, inconsistent enforcement of environmental laws, lack of transparency, poor management and weak incentives for environmental protection. Focus on economic development has directed attention away from environmental issues (Economy, 2004). In a recent interview, Ma Tianjie claimed that environmental protection in China is moving towards greater efficiency, transparency, the rule of law and introduction of managerial expertise (Interview with Economy, cited Macfie, 10 July 2010).

How do the environmental records of the BRICs stack up?

> 'When environmental issues start affecting growth, development and even lives the environment gets more attention.'
>
> (United Nations Statistics Division, 2008)

The BRIC economies encompass more than a quarter of the world's land mass, 40 per cent of its population and a combined GDP (adjusted to reflect PPP) of $15.4 trillion. Their percentage of world output increased rapidly from 7.5 per cent in 1998 to more than 15 per cent a decade later (Anderlini *et al.*, 2009). But the global role of each of these countries is quite different. Brazil and Russia are resource rich and have smaller populations relative to their resources, whereas India and China have enormous populations and high demand for resources. Brazil and Russia have ecological capacity that enables them to export primary products, though those resources are shrinking rapidly. The main exports for India and China are industrial and manufactured goods. China is a major importer and consumer of global raw materials. The Indian and Chinese governments are committed to raising standards of living, reducing inequality and developing internal markets to protect their economies from the impact of fluctuating export demand, though India is less vulnerable than China. They have low per capita footprints, though these are growing because of rising standards of living.

Dealing with climate change is inseparable from dealing with global poverty, which should be a top international priority (Stern, 2010). Reducing poverty levels and providing for the basic needs of the poor will have less environmental impact compared with the expansion in the size and consumption patterns of the middle classes but current and future patterns of consumption need to change for both groups. Crucial to controlling population growth is providing poor women with education, healthcare and support so that child mortality and family sizes are reduced.

How do we change the model of production and consumption?

Changing the model of production and consumption requires a multi-level strategy, including international, governmental and civic organisations, corporations and individual action. Governments and corporations play an essential role in driving change, along with the cumulative individual actions of people.

The European countries have a stronger commitment to public service and social welfare than the United States, with its dominating individualistic and privatising ethos. The United States is also lagging behind the EU and China in its environmental commitments and has yet to sign the Kyoto Protocol. Because the American electoral process has been hijacked by the corporations and the conservatives, a political resolution seems to be almost impossible to achieve in time to be effective (Oreskes and Conway, 2010). China, at the other end of the political spectrum, is an authoritarian society and can implement change more easily than a democracy, though ensuring the implementation of such policies is much more difficult. In its 2010 Five-Year Plan China set a benchmark of government leadership in sustainability. The US could ultimately face a trade boycott by other nations if it does not address climate change as a key issue (Stern, 2010).

Apart from Russia the per capita footprints of the BRIC economies are low compared with the high-income nations, but the cumulative effects are significant. The BRICs are among the top global carbon emitters (Figure 6.5). Leaders in China and India have recognised that continuing development is unsustainable if it is accompanied by rising carbon emissions. When India overtook Russia to be the third largest carbon emitter in 2010 the Indian environmental minister stated clearly that India was committed to a high-growth, low-carbon development model (Sharma, 2010). The Chinese Government has signed the Kyoto Protocol and has also committed to having 20 per cent of its electricity from renewable energy sources by 2020, up from 7 per cent in 2005. It is also targeting a 40–45 per cent reduction in greenhouse gas emissions as a proportion of GDP by 2020 (Macfie, 2010). The Chinese Government could become a role model for governmental leadership in sustainable development in the next decades. If both the EU and China embrace sustainability they could lead the way in addressing the keys issues of the century: sustainability and poverty. As these countries make the changes and move toward more sustainable economies the United States will get left behind (Hansen, 2011).

At the Mesa 18 Alternative Global Forum in Cancun in 2010 business leaders, including Virgin's Sir Richard Branson and CNN's Ted Turner, made the case for independent individual and corporate action. Businesses that base their planning on the assumption that current patterns of production and consumption are unsustainable will be the leaders in the new sustainable economy. Some of the first companies to embrace climate change and sustainability in their future planning are the insurance companies, but other organisations such as Deutsche Bank are astute enough to realise that those that do not embrace change will be the losers (Walsh, 2010).

If resource depletion and the environmental impact of production are included in business planning and analysis – for example, cost benefit analysis or SWOT

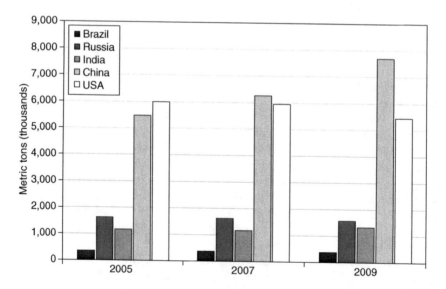

Figure 6.5 BRICs and USA carbon emissions 2005/2007/2009 (source: US Energy Information Administration (EIA). (2010). Online. Available www.eia.doe.gov/countries/ (accessed 5 May 2011)).

analysis (strengths, weaknesses, opportunities and threats) – it soon becomes obvious that current patterns of resource consumption and carbon emission production will have major impacts on future business viability. Planning for the impact of climate change and diminishing world resources should be a part of risk analysis. The true costs of resources and production need to be built into business models. Sustainability is becoming more mainstream in the corporate sector. In an interview with *Time* in 2010 Kevin Parker of Deutsche Asset Management said, 'We have to ask whether it's going to be possible to feed nine billion people. It's clear the planet can't sustain the rate of growth the way we live.' But there are significant opportunities for forward-thinking companies that get ahead of the major trends. In 2006 Deutsche Bank launched the first climate change investment funds – still only a small proportion of its overall investment funds – which have so far invested in energy efficiency, environmental management, agriculture and emerging clean technology. Deutsche Bank has also has erected the Carbon Counter Clock which measures metric tons of carbon dioxide in the atmosphere outside New York's Penn Station (Walsh, 2010). It does need to be remembered, however, that Deutsche Bank, like my other key source of material, Goldman Sachs, was a major contributor to the 2008–09 banking crisis, a fact that might be considered to counterbalance any environmental contributions it is making.

There is also a growing public awareness of the need for ethical investment, especially when public money and pension funds are involved. People are also showing a preference towards working for companies with good corporate social responsibility (CSR) profiles (McKinsey, February 2009). These factors can have a positive influence on shareholder value (Bonini *et al.*, February 2009). Business leaders are recognising that customers value their acting as 'good corporate citizens'. Most of the FMCG companies, and firms like Nokia, have high CSR profiles. The activities of oil companies are more suspect: they advertise their commitments to CSR and alternative technologies, yet more than 95 per cent of their profits come from oil. Such companies have been implicated in lending the most financial support to climate change deniers (Oreskes and Conway, 2010).

Advertising and the sustainable society

Expansion of the middle classes goes hand in hand with the growth of advertising expenditure. Before 2005 the BRICs accounted for 8 per cent of global advertising but 30 per cent of world growth in advertising ('Asia key global ad growth driver; internet spends skyrocket', ZenithOptimedia, 2005). The global growth of advertising has been hit by the global economic crisis but the largest BRIC economies were among the least affected. Russia was the hardest hit but by 2010 advertising was growing in all of the BRICs.

The advertising industry needs to change and there are already champions for new directions. OgilvyEarth was established on the assumption that we are at the dawn of the age of sustainability. In its philosophy and policies, laid out in

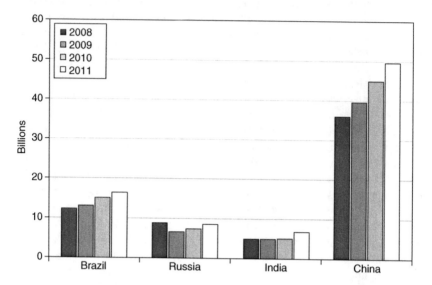

Figure 6.6 BRICs advertising expenditure 2008–2011 (source: GroupM (Autumn 2010). *This Year, Next Year: Worldwide Marketing and Media Forecasts*).

the 2009 paper, 'From Greenwash to Great' (2009), the fundamental premise is that the transition to a sustainable economy is inevitable. The company remains motivated by a profit-driven business model but is also committed to being part of the new market environment, which embodies many business and marketing opportunities. There is a need for new sustainability-driven products, and those products will need to be marketed. Change requires clear and transparent communication. Both production and marketing need to be 'compelling and stand up to the highest scrutiny'. Sustainability-oriented marketing can transform the way we look at the world and be a catalyst for positive change, offering consumers concrete ways to take action. There is plenty of evidence that ordinary people want to be involved in such change. A *Time Magazine* study found that 38 per cent of US consumers over the age of 18 regularly make an effort to purchase products from socially responsible companies (Stengel, 2009).

Advertising plays a key role in promoting products that have a negative impact on the environment, like Sports Utility Vehicles (SUVs) and vehicles in general. A radical response to climate change proposed by climate activist George Monbiot would be to treat the industries that cause most carbon emissions the same way that tobacco has been treated in recent decades. In the article 'Is it time to consider a ban on the adverts which help to cook the planet?' (*The Guardian*, 2008) Monbiot looked at banning adverts for holidays requiring airline travel, as well as vehicle advertising.

At the level of individual action attitudes vary in different countries, including in the BRICs. Strong environmental movements and an awareness of sustainability and the environment tend to be a characteristic of mature rather than emerging economies. One GfK Roper study identified six key consumer segments of what it called the value compass. The segment most likely to be interested in environmental issues were the 'altruists'. In none of the BRIC countries did this group make up a significant proportion of consumers (Amir and Chow, 2006). Another GfK Roper consumer survey found that Brazilians, and Latin Americans in general, recycle less and care less about the environment than in other countries (Salles, 2006). In Russia in the 1990s people were too concerned about personal economic survival to worry about the environment (NIC, 1999), but there is evidence of mounting environmental concern and protest (BBC World News, 22 March 2011). Though there is a history of environmental action from groups adversely affected by specific events, in India economic concerns tend to displace environmental concerns. India did, however, experience one of the world's worst industrial accidents, at Bhopal in 1986, so there is an awareness of the dangers of unregulated industrial development. Though the executives I interviewed at Ogilvy & Mather Mumbai claimed there was little interest in environmental issues in India, spokesperson Gaurav Grover, from the research firm Datamonitor, claimed that environmental concern amongst consumers in India was increasing. Datamonitor discovered a high level of interest amongst shoppers: 60 per cent considered it important to buy brands with eco-friendly credentials ('India offers huge potential for green brands', *Business Standard*, 2010). There was also a relatively low incidence of 'altruists' in China (Amir and Chow, 2006). However, in 2009 the highest level of social unrest was registered in China to date. The country is grappling with more acute social problems, rising food prices and the widening urban–rural gap and deep resentment towards unfairness and power abuse by government officials (Chen, 2009). The 2008 Dutch film *Rainmakers* documented examples of grass-roots regional social activism against environmental pollution. Many, however, also feel powerless in the face of corruption and the power of government interests (Zhang, 2011).

A 2005 report on a cross-cultural TGI survey tells a different and more hopeful story. The sample base was urban and middle class, and tended to be from two or three core cities in each country. Environmental issues, especially pollution and traffic congestion in the cities, were causing concern for 76 per cent of the Brazilian sample, 68 per cent in Russia and 56 per cent in India; the Chinese figures were not available. There was also evidence that consumer awareness has the potential to translate into buying power. The numbers prepared to pay more for environmentally friendly products were 71 per cent in Brazil, 57 per cent in Russia, 49 per cent in India and 54 per cent in China (Wicken *et al*, 2006).

A new economic model will require major advertising and communication campaigns to convince people to change their consumption patterns and change to new products, processes and behaviours. There is also an enormous need to develop the new industries and products required by new technologies for energy production, and to design products for sustainable living. The biggest problem will be to change models of consumption so that people pay more and consume less, and to prioritise social justice for the world's poor, whether they live in wealthy or developing countries. 'Socialism collapsed because it did not allow the market to tell the economic truth. Capitalism may collapse because it does not allow the market to tell the ecological truth,' according to former vice-president of Exxon Norway, Oystein Dahle (cited in Brown, 2006). The market needs to tell the ecological truth: in its analysis, prices and the processes it uses. Industrialised economies must lead the way.

7 Conclusion

Advertising has used emotional appeals to sell products since the nineteenth century, but this approach was taken to another level with the popularity of psychology in the United States in the 1920s. Psychology harnessed to advertising played on both social insecurities and realistic concerns about health and well-being. Strategies evolved in the following decades until branding, which associated products with emotions and key cultural values, changed the essence of advertising in the 1980s. During these years, too, and especially in the 1990s, large advertising agencies expanded internationally. As a result of the much freer access provided by the BRICs – Brazil, Russia, India and China – during the 1990s, consumer goods industries descended on these countries, followed by the big advertising agency complexes. Advertising expenditure expanded dramatically. The global economic crisis had a major impact on advertising in 2008–09, but although expenditure decreased in the BRIC economies in 2008–09, especially in Russia, these figures were growing again by 2010 (Figure 6.6). This growth is changing the profile of international advertising.

The four BRIC economies had very different profiles in the 20th century. Both Russia and China had Communist backgrounds. The Russian economy was bankrupt by the early 1990s and, with the assistance of the IMF, capitalism was introduced using a 'shock therapy' approach of rapid liberalisation. This led to major economic and social dislocation. China, on the other hand, gradually introduced 'market socialism' during the 1980s under the tight control of the Communist Party, which was determined not to permit protest and democracy. Foreign goods were not widely available until the 1990s, when advertising restrictions were loosened as the government began to view advertising as a stimulus to consumption and thus economic growth.

India had been a British colony before it became independent in 1947, though colonial influences were stronger in the cities and in certain regions. Most of the population continued to live in the countryside. As a colony India had always been on the fringes of capitalist culture and had a tradition of advertising that dated back to the nineteenth century. One of the main legacies of the British was the strength of the print media. Print advertising was dominant in India until television began to challenge that pre-eminence in the 1990s. Even today print media advertising expenditure is a slightly higher than television.

Brazil was the most mature of the BRIC economies in the 1990s. Like India, it had always been part of the capitalist system, and had also been protected by tariffs and regulations until the end of the military dictatorships. Most of the population was of European descent and Brazil had always had strong links to European cultural traditions. The feudal economic system had left a legacy of extreme social inequality which persists; the middle classes were very small even in the 1990s. Despite the high levels of poverty, however, the population was in touch with global cultural trends and television ownership was high. The maturity of the Brazilian market was reflected in the high quality of Brazilian advertising since the 1960s.

As restriction and tariffs loosened in all the BRICs during the 1990s, foreign goods became more widely available as the numbers of foreign companies and advertising agencies increased. Liberalisation of the media at the same time resulted in a proliferation of media options. When foreign companies and their agencies entered these countries, television tended to be their chosen medium because it reached the largest number of people. The expansion of satellite television, which tended to be funded by advertising, provided a further marketing vehicle, especially as its audiences were more affluent. With many more channels now available the market became increasingly fractured. After 2004 the internet and social networking sites became attractive options for advertising. The uptake of mobile phones has been astonishingly rapid in the last decade and the smartphone, especially as it becomes cheaper, will give millions of people in lower income countries access to the internet. The smartphone also enables more targeted marketing and research data collection. New media seem to hold the promise for the future and there is a buzz about their potential ('On the other hand: online advertising', WARC, 2009). It will be interesting to see if new media will displace television as the mass market vehicle of choice for major advertisers. New media use has tended to be a middle class phenomenon, but as mobile connectivity becomes widespread among poorer groups in emerging economies the marketing options will increase.

When markets are relatively small and poverty levels are high, the biggest foreign advertisers tend to be the FMCG companies because they sell cheap repeat-purchase consumables to the mass market. Though their products are usually more expensive than local products, they are still more accessible to the poor, who will often sacrifice necessities to buy what they regard as global, prestigious, foreign brands. In countries like India, China and Russia local product quality was often poor, especially for consumer durables, so when foreign products came on the market demand was high, limited only by disposable income levels.

The profile of top advertisers has varied across the BRIC economies, though Procter & Gamble and other FMCG companies tend to dominate advertising expenditure. Procter & Gamble, L'Oréal, Reckitt Benckiser, Nestlé, Coca-Cola and McDonald's are major advertisers that have increased their presence in emerging markets in the last two decades. Though these are not the largest global companies, they have the highest profit margins and spend the highest proportion of their revenues on advertising.

Procter & Gamble has been the top global advertiser for most of the last two decades after significantly increasing its advertising expenditure in the 1990s. The company's entry into the BRIC economies has been uneven. By the late 1990s Procter & Gamble was the top advertiser in both Russia and China. For a brief period around the end of the decade local Chinese firms outspent the foreign companies, mainly because of the high level of spending at the CCTV annual auctions, but after Procter & Gamble joined the auctions in 2004 (Madden, 2006) it dominated the Chinese advertising profile for the rest of the decade. By 2005 five of the ten most advertised brands were from Procter & Gamble (CTR Market Research, 2011). The company arrived relatively late in Brazil in the 1980s. Competitor Unilever, which had arrived in the 1930s, continues to dominate the personal product market in Brazil. Unilever has also dominated Indian advertising for most of the twentieth century. Brazil is the only BRIC country where the top advertiser for the last decade has been a local company, Casas Bahia (a company similar to Wal-Mart) which reinforces its position by providing the poor with cheap loans to buy its products.

The dominant advertising product categories also differ across the BRICs. In Russia the most advertised products in the early 1990s were the escapist categories: cigarettes, chocolate and spirits (Goldman, 1993). Procter & Gamble sells over 70 different brands in Russia and soon came to dominate many product categories. In contrast consumer durables were the most advertised foreign products in China during the 1980s and the market reflected the early entry of the Japanese firms. It was not until the 1990s that FMCGs became dominant in China. In the early 2000s pharmaceutical and health foods were the largest advertisers. The top advertiser in 2003 was a calcium supplement, Gai Zhong Gai. By 2008 three of the top ten advertisers in China were local (GroupM, 2010), compared with two in Russia (GroupM cited at www.adbrands.net/ru/, 2011), three in India (Group M cited at adbrands.net/in/, 2011) and two in Brazil (GroupM, 2010).

Though some agencies had been in markets like India and Brazil for most of the twentieth century, notably JWT and Ogilvy & Mather, there was a massive international expansion of advertising agencies in the 1990s. This expansion followed a decade of mergers and acquisitions that had created a small number of large agency complexes. Advertising agencies followed their multinational clients to emerging markets and by the 1990s dominated the sector in most countries. In Russia, China and India they were required to enter into joint ventures with local agencies, but in Brazil local agencies willingly entered joint venture partnerships with foreign agencies. In China, when restrictions on such joint ventures were lifted in 2005, most agencies continued with the arrangement because it brought the benefits of local cultural knowledge (Sinclair, 2009).

Foreign agencies brought finance and expertise, but lacked local knowledge. In the former Communist countries western style advertising was an alien concept. Local advertisers focused on communication of information rather than stimulating consumer demand and understanding the wants and needs of buyers. Advertising campaigns developed in head offices in New York or London were sometimes incomprehensible to local people. As a result, foreign agencies began to localise their advertising campaigns during the 1990s. At the same time local advertising agencies became more experienced, and local personnel were often trained in foreign agencies and joint ventures.

As foreign agencies discovered, local values and beliefs are important in determining the success of advertising campaigns. The BRIC economies cover a spectrum of political, economic and religious value systems. A cross-cultural study by Amir and Chow (2006) identified six key consumer types: striver, fun-seeker, creative, devout, intimate and altruist. The defining values of the BRICs were as follows: Brazilians were devout (31.4 per cent), Russians were strivers/intimates, while 43 per cent of Chinese and 49.5 per cent of Indians were strivers, reflecting the rapid development of their countries. China and Russia are predominantly secular nations though traditional religious beliefs persist, including the resurgence of the Russian Orthodox Church and the continuity of Confucian values. Catholicism is still strong in Brazil, while nearly 80.5 per cent of Indians are Hindu, 13.4 per cent Muslim, 2.3 per cent Christian, and 1.9 per cent Sikh (World Factbook: India).

India and China have traditions of arranged marriages, though this persists more strongly in India. The traditional extended family is also the normal structure in India and China, compared with the nuclear family in Russia and Brazil. Family values remain important in traditional value systems, where parents will sacrifice much for their children. Education is especially important in China, India and Brazil, where it is perceived as essential for economic and social advancement, and education in these countries is an important advertising category. The social profiles of the BRICs differ too. Brazil and India have profiles dominated by the younger age groups while China and Russia have ageing population profiles. Russia is the only country where the population is declining. The youth and younger affluent professional markets are of most interest to contemporary foreign marketers.

In the areas of gender stereotypes and beauty ideals there are more cross-cultural similarities and there are more global campaigns for associated products. In most cultures women are identified with the family and as primary care-givers, as well as being the main targets for personal products and cosmetics. Modesty is part of the cultural tradition in India and China, where displays of nakedness are regulated more strictly than in Russia and Brazil. Although Brazil is known for its worship of the body beautiful and sexuality, studies of television advertising have revealed that the amount of nudity does not differ greatly from that of other countries. Brazil also has strict rules about using sex as a selling strategy. A recent advertisement for Devassa Bem Loura beer, starring Paris Hilton, was banned for being sexually provocative (Wentz, 2010). Advertising regulations are particularly tight in China, which is the only BRIC country to have a censorship policy. All the BRICs have regulations on the advertising of alcohol and tobacco and the amount of advertising permitted.

Another significant trend in most 'emerging economies', including the BRICs, has been the growth of consumerism since the 1990s. As people have become more affluent they have increased their spending on non-essential consumer goods, both FMCG and consumer durables. Consumerism, though persisting alongside traditional values, reinforces the devaluing and displacement of those values, especially among the young. Cultural change is reinforced through reinforcement or omission of certain values. Global advertisers have used a wide range of advertising strategies in the BRIC economies to stimulate product sales, from the global saturation approach used by such companies as Marlboro and Mars to very specific customisation. The trend has been for companies to tailor their campaigns to local values.

Cosmetics companies are among the largest global advertisers. 'Looking good' has become increasingly important in many cultures (Salles, 2006) and this is certainly true in the BRIC countries. Cosmetics companies tend to use image advertising and global campaigns commonly use a large close-up of a heavily airbrushed woman's face. Eva Longoria of *Desperate Housewives*, who is of Mexican origin and regarded as generically 'multicultural', is currently used in many countries to market L'Oréal products. In Asia the major global cosmetics companies promote skin-whitening creams with campaigns that blatantly promote white and western stereotypes. The models in such campaigns tend to be Eurasian, with very pale skin and westernised features, though eye colour and shape are more Asian.

There are marked contrasts between the advertising strategies used in different product categories. Major advertisers often have their own signature styles. Procter & Gamble tends to use problem–solution format while its main competitor L'Oréal uses the celebrity endorsement approach (de Mooij, 2005). Companies like Procter & Gamble, which sells as many as 70 products in Russia alone, takes a house of brands approach, which disguises companies that dominate the sector in certain product categories, and even have competing brands within the same category.

The house of brands approach tends to be used by companies in the electronics, technology, vehicle and oil sectors, where there has been major investment in research and development, and the quality of the product is significant. The consumer durable categories are generally characterised by rapid product obsolescence, new models and constant renewal of the product range. The launch of the Apple iPad in 2010 is a recent example of excessive marketing hype, though technology companies are finding it increasingly difficult to create this 'wow' factor (Salles, 2006).

In 2003 A.C. Nielsen claimed that there were 63 megabrand franchises and this seems to be borne out by cross-cultural studies which have found that only a small number, 20 at most, will be known in any specific country. The 20 largest global brands tend to be in the FMCG sectors. The very biggest companies also use a range of media and strategies so their advertising efforts have the widest reach. A cross-cultural study over 25 countries between 2004 and 2006 compared recognition levels for 35 brands. The average number of brands that people are familiar with is 20; the number of brands that people really like increased from six in 2004 to seven in 2006; the average number of brands people often recommended was between 2.3 and 4.3. There was a renewed interest in global brands and brand appreciation was increasing in countries like China and Russia while declining in industrialised countries (Salles, 2006). The next challenge for the BRICs, and particularly India and China as the main exporters of consumer goods, is to lift their status in terms of national branding so that 'Made in China' and 'Made in India' come to symbolise quality rather then 'cheap and cheerful'. China started to do this in 2010 with its campaign on BBC World News: 'Made in China, designed by the world'. Foreign companies like Apple are doing something similar in China. Staff at the Apple Store in Shanghai wear red T-shirts, instead of the customary black, bearing the message 'Designed in California, Made for China' ('China receiving unique approach from brands', *Newsweek*, 2010).

Consumers in emerging markets became market-savvy quite quickly and by the late 1990s in Russia and China there was a consumer backlash against foreign goods. Governments were also promoting local goods. Even in India there was a vogue for 'Indianisation' in the late 1990s. Rather belatedly foreign advertisers started to customise their campaigns for local markets, as well as increasing their advertising expenditure. Their market share grew in the next decade.

The addition of new media to the spectrum of advertising options has added further complexity for marketers. Although ownership levels of new media are relatively low among the BRIC economies, the middle classes and the younger age groups are the main adopters, and these are increasingly important market segments. Mobile phones and the smartphone are the latest additions to the marketing mix. The internet is a rapidly growing advertising sector and some companies have started redeploying their television budgets to new media.

The pervasiveness and expansion of advertising promotes consumption. Rising consumption levels have major implications for global sustainability. The real impact of increased population lies with the industrialised countries, where having a child is the most environmentally damaging individual activity because of the high per capita footprint of each person. The per capita footprints of high-income nations, which make up less than 20 per cent of the world's population, are much higher than is sustainable (6.1 hectares per person), compared with middle-income nations at 2.0 hectares, and low-income nations, where a large proportion of the population still live in poverty, an average per capita footprint of 1.2 hectares. When people who are very poor have children the increase in per capita footprint is not large. However the cumulative effect of even small increases of consumption by large numbers of people is huge. The increases in consumption of potential consumers in India and China have major global environmental implications. International consumption is grossly unequal. Resolving these inequalities sustainably means both raising the standards of living of the poor and reducing the consumption levels of affluent nations. International consumption is grossly unequal, but reducing the impact of high levels of consumption is more of a challenge for the high-income nations than the low-income countries. When people who are very poor have children the increase in per capita footprint is not large.

The key challenges of the twenty-first century are to manage environmental sustainability and climate change and address world poverty. The dominant economic model is capitalism in all its variants, but the problem with capitalism is that its main economic focus is on growth and profit. The corporate sector is a key driver of economic growth and international expansion. Companies are constantly seeking to expand product sales. Advertising agencies assist corporations in selling those products to consumers. Because the use of resources is outstripping supply, industrialisation and consumption are creating a global environmental crisis that is accelerating climate change. To avoid environmental disaster every level of society must change. Astute businesses are embracing the new model of society and planning for a sustainable future, and some advertising agencies have joined the trend. Governments in both India and China are committed to ongoing development, raising the standard of living of the poor and low-carbon economic growth. The earth simply does not have enough resources for the global consumption of industrialised nations to continue at current levels, let alone expanding dramatically to enable 85 per cent of the Chinese and 95 per cent of Indian populations to join the 'consuming classes'.

Bibliography

Accenture. 'Smartphones change consumer habits' (9 December 2010). Original material sourced by WARC. Online. Available at: www.warc.com/News/PrintNewsItem. asp?NID=27615 (15 December 2010).

Ad News/ Ad Village. 'Brazilian consumers see value in advertising' (15 April 2010). Original material sourced by WARC. Online. Available at: www.warc.com/News/ PrintNewsItem.asp?NID=26577 (accessed 7 August 2010).

Adams, R. *If You Build It Will They Come? Three Steps to Test and Validate Any Market Opportunity*, Hoboken New Jersey: John Wiley & Sons. 2010.

Adese, Carlos. 'Tuning in: Lower income consumers are fuelling business in Latin America which is good news for advertisers' (October 2006). *Latin Trade.*

Advertising Age. 'Advertising Age's Top 50 Marketing Groups Worldwide in 2009 by revenues' (2011). Online. Available at: www.adbrands.net/agencies_index.htm (accessed 14 February 2011).

Advertising Age. 'Coca-Cola India Pulls Ad After Another Child Dies' (4 July 1997). Online. Available at: www.adage.com/news:cms?newid=12466 (accessed 5 August 2002).

Advertising Age. 'India permits foreign ads' (4 October 1993). Vol. 64 (42): p. 61.

Advertising Educational Foundation. 'The GBU (Good, Bad and Ugly) Awards' (2011). Online. Available at: www.aef.com/exhibits/awards/gbu/index.html (accessed 25 April 2011).

Aiken, L. 'Wiping out "Greenwash"' (2007). *The Guardian.* Online. Available at: www. guardian.co.uk/media/2007/nov/19/mondaymediasection.climatechanger/print (accessed 26 January 2009).

Aleksandrov, F. *Khroniki rossiskoi reklmay*: Moscow: no publisher cited: pp. 115–117. 2003.

Amir, S. and S. Chow. 'The universality of values: implications for global advertising strategy' (2006), *Journal of Advertising Research.* Vol. 46 (3).

Anderlini, Giles, C.J. Gorst, I. Leahy and J. Wheatley. 'Quartet defined by differences' (16 June 2009). *Financial Times.*

Anderson, C. *The Long Tail: Why the Future of Business Is Selling Less of More.* New York: Hyperion. 2006.

Araújo, E. *Principais Rotos do Trafico de Escravos np Atlantico 1574–1870.* Np Atlantico: pp52–53.

Art Direction. 'Inside Russian Advertising: A Few Steppes to Go'. (December 1992).

Ascheberg, C. 'Russia's new lifestyle elites: from show-off to sophistication' (March 2008). European Society for Opinion and Market Research (ESOMAR). Online. Available at: www.warc.com (accessed August 2009).

Assadourian, E. 'Rise and fall of consumer cultures', in Assadourian, E. (ed.) *State of the World 2010: Transforming Cultures: from Consumerism to Sustainability*, The Worldwatch Institute Report, New York: W.W. Norton and Company. 2010.

Baidu. 'Mobile internet use increasing in China' (6 October 2010). Original material sourced by WARC. Online. Available at: www.warc.com/News/PrintNewsItem. asp?NID=27330 (accessed 7 October 2010).)

Bajpai, S. and Unnikrishnan, N. *The Impact of Television Advertising on Children*, New Delhi: Sage. 1996.

Barnes, B., P. Kitchen, G. Spickett-Jones and Q. Yu. 'Investigating the impact of international cosmetics advertising in China' (2004), *International Journal of Advertising*, Vol. 23: pp. 361–87.

Barnett, S. 'Saw points' (12 June 2010). *New Zealand Listener*: p. 55.

BBC News. 'Americas, Country Profiles. Timeline: Brazil' (2008). Online. Available at: http://newsvote.bbc.uk (accessed 10 October 2008).

BBC News. 'Brazil Country Profile' (broadcast date 5 October 2010). Online. Available at: http://news.bbc.co.uk/2/hi/europe/country_profiles/1227110.stm#leaders (accessed 31 October 2010).

BBC News. 'Chinese Government planning to raise the wages of 200 million migrant workers' (14 February 2011).

BBC World News. 'The Bottom Line' (broadcast date 6 March 2010). Series 4, Episode 6. Panel discussion: Martin Sorrell, CEO WPP; Rita Cifton, CEO Interbrand and Wol Kolade of Let's Start.

BBC World News. 'World Business Report' (broadcast date 5 March 2010).

BBC World News. 'World Business Report' (broadcast date 23 April 2010).

BBC World News. 'World Business Report' (broadcast date 23 May 2010).

BBC World News. 'Working Lives: Human Trafficking' (broadcast date 31 May 2010).

BBC World News. 'World Business Report' (broadcast date 7 July 2010).

BBC World News. 'World Business Report' (broadcast date 17 July 2010).

BBC World News. 'Asia Business Report' (broadcast 19 August 2010).

BBC World News. 'India Business Report' (broadcast date 27 September 2010).

BBC World News. 'Hard Talk' (broadcast date 13 September 2010). Former Vice-Chairman of the 10th NPC Standing Committee Cheng Siwei interviewed by Stephen Sackur.

Beinhocker, Eric D., Diana Farrell and Adil S. Zainulbhai. 'Tracking the growth of India's middle class' (August 2007). *McKinsey Quarterly*. Online. Available at: www. mckinseyquarterly.com/Tracking_the_growth_of_Indias_middle_class_2032 (accessed 28 September 2010).

Belch, G.E. and M.A. Belch. *Introduction to Advertising and Marketing*, Burr Ridge, Illinois: Irwin. 1990.

Belch, G.E. and M.A. Belch. *Introduction to Advertising and Marketing* (6th edition), Burr Ridge, Illinois: Irwin. 2004.

Belch, G.E. and M.A. Belch. *Introduction to Advertising and Marketing* (7th edition), Burr Ridge, Illinois: Irwin. 2007.

Belk, R. W. and N. Zhou. 'Learning to want things' (1987). *Advances in Consumer Research*, Vol. 14 (1): pp. 478–82.

Biagi, S. *Media Impact*, Belmont: Wadsworth. 1996.

Bloomberg and *Institutional Investor*. 'China set for prolonged spending boom' (18 August 2010) Original material sourced by WARC. Online. Available at: www.warc. com/News/TopNews.asp?NID=27123 (accessed 10 September 2010).

Bloomberg. 'Recession boosts status of emerging markets' (15 September 2010). Original material sourced by WARC. Online. Available at: www.warc.com/News/PrintNewsItem.asp?NID=27243 (accessed 16 September 2010).

Bloomberg/ HUL. 'Hindustan Unilever boost adspend levels' (27 January, 2010). Original material sourced by WARC. Online. Available at: www.warc.com/News/PrintNewsItem.asp?NID=26241 (accessed 28 January 2010).

Bonini, S., N. Brun and M. Rosenthal. 'Valuing corporate social responsibility' (February 2009). *McKinsey Global Survey Results.* Online. Available at: www.mckinseyquarterly.com/PDFDownload.aspx?ar=2309 (accessed 3 March 2011).

Boston Consulting Group (BCG). 'Brand owners base spending on "shortcuts"' (13 September 2010). Original material sourced by WARC. Online. Available at: www.warc.com/News/PrintNewsItem.asp?NID=27231(accessed 14 September 2010).

Boston Consulting Group (BCG). 'Next billion web users based in new markets' (3 September 2010). Original material sourced by WARC. Online. Available at: www.warc.com/News/PrintNewsItem.asp?NID=27194, (accessed 10 September 2010).

Bowes, E. 'India to Ban Tobacco Advertising' (2003) *Advertising Age*, Vol. 74: p. 20.

Boyce, S. 'BrandZ 2007: Top 100 most powerful brands: Second Annual Millward Brown Optimor/Financial Times Brand Ranking' (2007). WARC Report. Online. Available at: warc.com (accessed December 2009).

Brand Republic. 'Indian tourism up for grabs' (28 August 2009). Original material sourced by WARC. Online. Available at: www.warc.com/News/PrintNewsItem.asp?NID=25597 (accessed 17 August 2010).

Brashear, T., V. Kashyap, M. Musante and N. Donthu. 'A profile of the internet shopper: evidence from six countries' (Summer 2009). *Journal of Marketing Theory and Practice*, Vol. 17 (3): pp. 267–81.

Brown, Lester R. *Plan B 2.0: Rescuing a Planet under Stress and a Civilization in Trouble*, New York: W.W. Norton & Company. 2006.

Brown, Lester R. *Plan B: 4.0: Mobilizing to Save Civilization*, New York: W.W. Norton & Company. 2009.

Buckman, G. *Globalization: tame it or scrap it?* London: Zed. 2004.

Burgoyne, P. 'Russia's Creative Block' (August 1995) *Creative Review*, Vol. 15: pp. 42–3.

Business Standard. 'India offers hugh potential for green brands' (1 September 2010). Original material sourced by WARC. Online. Available at: www.warc.com/News/PrintNewsItem.asp?NID=27181 (accessed 10 September 2010).

Byrne, C. 'Kate Stanners proves how wrong WPP's Neil French was when he said women were crap' (24 October 2005). *The Telegraph*. Online. Available at: http://news.independent.co.uk/media/article321853.ece (accessed 25 October 2005).

Calladine, D. 'The trends in digital media in early-adopting regions' (October 2009). *Admap Magazine*. Online. Available at: www.warc.com/admap (accessed 16 March 2011).

Cao, Y., Y. Qian, and B. Weingast. 'From federalism, Chinese style, to privatization, Chinese style' (1999). *Economics of Transition*, Vol. 7: pp. 103–31.

Carramenha, P., L. Dougnac, and N. Marangoni. 'Evaluating the value of global brands in Latin America' (April 1999) in Santiago ESOMAR conference paper 'Marketing in Latin America Conference.' Online. Available at: www.warc.com (accessed December 2009).

Caryl, C. 'We will bury you … with a Snickers Bar' (26 January 1998). *US News & World Report.*

Central Intelligence Agency (CIA). World Factbook 2001: Russia. Online. Available at: www.umsl.edu/services/govdocs/wofact2001/index.html (accessed 8 September 2011).

Central Intelligence Agency (CIA). 'World Factbook Country profile: Brazil' (8 March 2011a) Online. Available at: www.cia.gov/library/publications/the-world-factbook/geos/rs.html (accessed 21 March 2011).

Central Intelligence Agency (CIA). 'World Factbook Country profile: Russia' (8 March 2011b) Online. Available at: www.cia.gov/library/publications/the-world-factbook/geos/in.html (accessed 21 March 2011).

Central Intelligence Agency (CIA). 'World Factbook Country profile: India' (8 March 2011c) Online. Available at: www.cia.gov/library/publications/the-world-factbook/geos/ch.html (accessed 21 March 2011).

Central Intelligence Agency (CIA). 'World Factbook Country profile: China' (8 March 2011d). Online. Available at: www.cia.gov/library/publications/the-world-factbook/geos/br.html (accessed 21 March 2011).

Chadwick, J. 'Navigating through China's new advertising law: the role of market research' (1997). *International Journal of Advertising*, Vol. 16: pp. 284–94.

Chandra, A., D.A. Griffith, and J.K. Ryans 'Advertising standardisation in India' (2002). *International Journal of Advertising*, Vol. 21 (1): pp. 36; 47–66.

Chakraborty, A. 'Zenith Media's Ad Forecast foresees growth for television and radio in India' (19 July 2002). Online. Available at: www.agencyfaqs.com/www1/news/stories/2002/07/19/4636.htm (accessed 16 October 2002).

Chaturvedi, Preeti. 'One billion into one won't always go: how regional and national brands vie for India's FMCG shoppers' (May 2008). Online. Available at: www.warc.com (accessed January 2010).

Chen, S. 'Social unrest rising in China' (21 December 2009). BBC News. Online. Available at: http://newsvote.bbc.co.uk/mpapps/pagetools/print/news.bbcco.uk/2/hi/asia-pacific/8425119.stm?ad=1 (accessed 16 March 2011).

Cheng, H. 'China: advertising yesterday and today', in J.P. Jones (ed.) *International Advertising, Realities and Myths* (pp255–84), London: Sage. 2000.

Cheng, H. 'Reflections of cultural values: a content analysis of Chinese magazine advertisements from 1982 and 1992' (1994). *International Journal of Advertising*, Vol. 13: pp. 167–83.

China Daily. 'Advertisers turn to social media in China' (16 December 2009). Original material sourced by WARC. Online. Available at: www.warc.com/News//PrintNews-Item.asp?NID=26081 (accessed 28 January 2010).

China Daily. 'China will be VW's biggest market says CEO' (16 April 2009). Original material sourced by WARC. Online. Available at: www.warc.com/News/PrintNews-Item.asp? NID=25003 (accessed 18 April 2009).

China Daily. 'Chinese women go "crazy" for cosmetics' (7 June 2005). Online. Available at: www.chinadaily.com.cn/english/doc/2005–06/07/content_449333.htm (accessed 18 December 2010).

China Daily. 'Cosmetic giants look to China'. (8 July 2010) Original material sourced by WARC. Online. Available at: www.warc.com/News/PrintNewsItem.asp?NID=25373 (accessed 11 August 2010).

China Daily. 'Nike apologises for footwear ad in China' (12 September, 2004). Online. Available at: http://chinadaily.com.cn/English/doc/2004–12/09/content_3998845.htm (accessed 8 February 2010).

China Daily. 'Nuanced online strategy key in China' (1 October 2010). Original material sourced by WARC. Online. Available at: www.warc.com/News/PrintNewsItem. asp?NID=27313 (accessed 3 November 2010).

CIOL News. 'Nokia targets India for growth' (21 August 2009). Original material sourced by WARC. Online. Available at: www.warc.com/News/PrintNewsItem. asp?NID=25566 (accessed 17 August 2010).

Consultancy L2. 'Cosmetics, beauty brands fail on digital' (2 December 2010). Original material sourced by WARC. Online. Available at: www.warc.com/News/PrintNews-Items.asp?NID=27585 (accessed 6 December 2010).

CTR Market Research. 'Mobile internet usage rises in China' (17 November 2010). Original material sourced by WARC. Online. Available at: www.warc.com/News/Print-NewsItem.asp?NID=27516 (accessed 22 November 2010).

CTR Research. 'China's biggest brands by advertising expenditure in 2005' (2006). *China: Advertisers/Agencies*. Online. Available at: www.adbrands.net/cn/ (accessed 4 June 2006).

Cui, G. 'The name game' (1997). *China Business Review*, Vol. 24 (6): pp. 40–43.

Cullen, L. 'Changing faces' (5 August 2002). *Time Magazine*. Online. Available at: www.time.com/time/world/article/0,8599,2047454,00.html#ixzz1LtYYMSz6(accessed 10 May 2011).

Cullity, J. 'Sex appeal and cultural liberty: a feminist inquiry into MTV India', (2004) *Frontiers*. Online. Available at: BNET.com (accessed 20 December 2007).

Cutler, B., M.K. Erranilli and R. Javalgi. 'The visual components of print advertising: a five-country cross-cultural analysis' (1992). *European Journal of Marketing*, Vol. 26 (4): pp. 7–20.

Czepiec, H. 'Promoting industrial goods in China: identifying the key appeals' (1993). *International Journal of Advertising*, Vol. 13 (3): pp. 257–64.

Daily Telegraph. 'Many multinationals grow hesitant about China' (31 August 2010). Original material sourced by WARC. Online. Available at: www.warc.com/News/ PrintNewsItem.asp?NID=27173 (accessed 1 September 2010).

Data Axis Intelligence: News. 'Russian TV market falls 13% in 2009' (20 July 2010). Online. Available at: www.dataxisnews.com/?p=19655 (accessed 2 January 2010).

de Mooij, M. 'Convergence and divergence in consumer behaviour: implications for global advertising' (2003). *International Journal of Advertising*, Vol. 22 (2).

de Mooij, M. *Advertising and the Globalising of the Economy*, London: Prentice Hall. 1994.

de Mooij, M. *Global Marketing and Advertising*, Thousand Oaks, California: Sage. 2005.

Dentsu/ China Advertising Association. 'China's leading agencies in 2006 by revenue' (2006). Cited in CTR Research. *China: Advertisers/ Agencies*. Online. Available at: www.adbrands.net/cn/ (accessed 4 June 2006).

Dickie, M. 'China mulls "one-child" policy shift' (28 February 2008). *Financial Times*. Online. Available at: www.ft.com/cms/s/0/4dbeca68-e62e-11dc-8398-0000779fd2ac. html#ixzz1BAfSTDNB (accessed 16 January 2011).

Dinakar, S. 'Choice and no choice; Hindustan Lever is being attacked from below and is opting to sacrifice margins to reach choosy Indian consumers of all stripes' (8 November 2005). *Forbes Magazine*.

Doctoroff, T. 'Advertising agencies in China: glorious opportunities, easily squandered' (27 August 2008). *The Huffington Post*. Online. Available at: www.huffingtonpost.com/tom-doctoroff/advertising-agencies-in-c_b_121951.html (accessed 9 January 2011).

Doctoroff, T. 'China's gray consumers are a golden opportunity' (19 January 2010). Online. Available at: www.adage.comarticle_id-141577 (accessed 22 January 2010).

Doctoroff, T. 'Chinese consumers, brands and the MNC learning curve' (Summer 2008a). *Market Leader*, Vol. 41.

Doctoroff, T. *Billions: Selling to the New Chinese Consumer*, New York: Palgrave Macmillan. 2005.

Dyer, D., F. Dalzell and R. Olegario, *Rising Tide: Lessons from 165 years of Brand Building at Procter & Gamble*, Cincinnati: Procter & Gamble. 2004.

Economic Times. 'Coke targets Indian energy drinks market' (16 December 2009). Original material sourced by WARC. Online. Available at: www.warc.com/News/PrintNewsItem.asp?NID=26083 (accessed 17 December 2009).

Economic Times. 'Drinks brands look to India' (23 September 2010). Original material sourced by WARC. Online. Available at: www.warc.com/News/PrintNewsItem.asp?NID=25711 (accessed 24 September 2010).

Economic Times. 'Indian ad industry to defy downturn' (1 May 2009). Original material sourced by WARC. Online. Available at: www.warc.com/News/PrintNewsItem.asp?NID=25076 (accessed 1 May 2009).

Economic Times. 'Nokia, Colgate, most trusted brands in India' (2 September 2010). Original material sourced by WARC. Online. Available at: www.warc.com/News/PrintNewsItem.asp?NID=27184 (accessed 4 September 2010).

Economic Times. 'Use of celebrities has mixed results in India' (4 February 2010). Original material sourced by WARC. Online. Available at: www.warc.com/News/PrintNewsItem.asp?NID=26276 (accessed 18 March 2010).

Economist Intelligence Unit Limited. 'Growing Up' (August 1997). India Business Intelligence.

Economist Intelligence Unit Limited. 'Industry Monitor' (24 August 2002).

Economist Special Report. '2 Americas' (12 November 2009a).

Economist Special Report. 'A better today: Brazil's growing middle class wants the good life, right now' (12 November 2009b).

Economist Special Report. 'Condemned to prosperity: Brazil has learned to love its commodity sector' (12 November 2009c).

Economist Special Report. 'Getting it together at last: "Brazil used to be all promise. Now it is beginning to deliver", says John Prideaux' (12 November 2009d).

Economist. 'A radioactive subject: Clamping down on the trade in illicit nuclear materials sometimes offends Russia' (1 February 2007). Online. Available at: www.economist.com/node/8633393 (accessed 16 January 2011).

Economist. 'Sticky issue' (24 August 2002). p. 51

Economist. (14 January 2010) Business this week. Online. Available The_Economist-business-admin@news.economist (accessed 18 January, 2010).

Economist. (21 October 2010) 'China's economy: A new epic. China's new five-year plan is at odds with itself'. Online. Available at: www.economist.com/node17314578 (accessed 22 October 2010).

Economist. (23 September 2010) 'A special report on forests'. Online. Available at: www.economist.com/node/17062663/ (accessed 3 March 2011).

Economy, E. *The River Runs Black: the Environmental Challenge to China's Future*, Ithaca: Cornell University Press. 2004.

Edelman. 'Samsung, Sony top buzz charts in China' (17 August 2010). Original material sourced by WARC. Online. Available at: www.warc.com/News/PrintNewsItem.asp?NID=27117 (accessed 10 September 2010).

Emerging Markets Economy. 'India's advertising industry grows by 23% in 2000–01'

(28 January 2002). Online. Available through Business Source Premier (accessed 8 July 2003).

Etcoff, N., S. Orbach, J. Scott and H. Agostino. 'Beyond stereotypes: rebuilding the foundation of beauty beliefs' (September 2004) Online. Available at: www.campaignforrealbeauty.com/Dove/beyond/StereotypesWhitePaper.pdf (accessed 2010).

Euromonitor. 'Companies must adapt in emerging markets' (8 September 2010. Original material sourced by WARC. Online. Available at: www.warc.com/News/PrintNewsItem.asp?NID=27213 (accessed 9 September 2010).

Euromonitor Global Market Information Database. 'Consumer lifestyles in India' (November 2001). Online. Available at: www.euromonitor.com/gmidv1/ShowTopic.asp (accessed 10 September 2002).

Euromonitor Global Market Information Database. 'Retail trade international India. Household cleaning products in India' (July 2001). Online. Available at: www.euromonitor.com/rti/default.asp (accessed 10 April 2002).

Euromonitor International. 'Country Report: Alcoholic drinks in Russia' (December 2010). Online. Available at: www.euromonitor.com/alcoholic-drinks-in-russia/report (accessed 8 September 2011).

European Chamber of Commerce in China. 'Many foreign firms grow frustrated in China'. (7 September 2010) Original material sourced by WARC. Online. Available at: www.warc.com/News/PrintNewsItem.asp?NID=27202 (accessed 10 September 2010).

Everelles, S., F. Morgan, I. Buke, and R. Nguyen. 'Advertising strategy in China: an analysis of cultural and regulatory factors' (2002). *Journal of International Consumer Marketing*, Vol. 15 (1): pp. 91–123.

Ewing, M., J. Napoli and L. Pitt. 'Managing Southeast Asian brands in the Global Economy' (2001). *Business Horizons*, Vol. 44 (3): pp. 52–59.

Eyeblaster. 'Web ads have biggest impact in South America' (14 May 2010). Original material sourced by WARC. Online. Available at: www.warc.com/News/PrintNewsItem.asp?NID=26703 (accessed 7 August 2010).

Fannin, R. 'Q&A, ask the expert' (8 February 1999). *Advertising Age International*, Vol. 6.

Farrell D., U.A. Gersch and E. Stephenson. 'The value of China's emerging middle class' (June 2006). *McKinsey Quarterly*. Online. Available at: www.mckinseyquarterly.com/The_value_of_Chinas_emerging_middle_class_1798 (accessed 8 September 2011).

Fast Company/ IAB. 'Agencies still adapting to digital era' (18 November 2010). Original material sourced by WARC. Online. Available at: www.warc.com/News/NID=27521 (accessed 22 November 2010).

Feldman S. 'Lord Stern charts a "green" industrial revolution' (2010). Online. Available at: http://insideclimatenews.org/news/20101206/lord-stern-charts-green-industrial-revolution (accessed 5 May 2011).

Fergusson, Niall. *The Ascent of Money*, Camberwell, Victoria: Allen Lane. 2008.

Financial Times. 'Branded radio takes off in Brazil' (7 September 2009). Original material sourced by WARC. Online. Available at: www.warc.com/News/PrintNewsItem.asp?NID=25637 (accessed 13 August 2010).

Financial Times. 'China holds promise for Kraft' (8 June 2009). Original material sourced by WARC. Online. Available at: www.warc.com/News/PrintNewsItem.asp?NID=25240 (accessed 9 June, 2010).

Financial Times. 'Google upbeat on China' (2010).

Financial Times. 'India set for consumer spending boom' (22 July 2010). Original material sourced by WARC. Online. Available at: www.warc.com/News/PrintNewsItem.asp?NID=27005 (accessed February 2011).

FIPP/ZenithOptimedia. World Magazine Trends 2004/2005 (no date). Online. Available at: www.warc.com/LandingPages/Data/MagazineTrends/PDF/Russia (accessed 10 December 2010).

Ford India. 'Ford sets its sights on India' (31 August, 2010). Original material sourced by WARC. Online. Available at: www.warc.com/News/PrintNewsItem.asp?NID=27176 (accessed 1 September 2010).

Fowler, G. 'Ad agencies booking a passage to India' (22 March 2006). *Wall Street Journal*. Online. Available at: http://online.wsj.com, cited at: http://yaleglobal.yale. edu/print/305 (accessed 22 September 2010).

Frith, K. 'Globalising women: How global women's magazines in China and Singapore transmit consumer culture' (2008). *Media International Australia*, Vol. 133: pp. 130–45.

Frumin, B. 'Once-taboo cosmetic surgery on rise in India' (2008). *San Francisco Chronicle*. Online. Available at: www.sfgate.com/cgi-bin/article.cgi?file=c/a/2008/06/13/MN8MV9CE7.DTL (accessed 8 September 2011).

Gao, Z. 'The future of foreign advertising in China: the lessons of history' (2003). *Advertising and Society Review*. Online. Available at: http://muse.jhu.edu/journal/advertising_and_society_review/v2004/4.1gao.html.

Gartner Research. 'Social media stays local in Asia Pacific' (22 October 2010). Original material sourced by WARC. Online. Available at: www.warc.com/News/PrintNewsItem.asp?NID=27405 (accessed 3 November 2010).

Gladstone N. and R. Passikoff. 'The great partnership: the right brand and the right medium' (June 2008). *ESOMAR Conference Paper*. Online. Available at: www.warc.com (accessed December 2009).

Global Footprint Network. *Ecological footprint and biocapacity 2005* (2008). Online. Available at: www.footprintnetwork.org (accessed 29 September 2009).

Global Footprint Network. *Ecological footprint and biocapacity 2006* (25 November 2009) Online. Available at: www.footprintnetwork.org (accessed 2010).

Global Footprint Network. *Ecological footprint and biocapacity 2007*. (13 October 2010). Online. Available at: footprintnetwork.org (accessed 16 January 2011).

Global Footprint Network. *Living Planet Report* (2010). Online. Available at: www.footprintnetwork.org (accessed 3 March 2011).

Global Footprint Network. *Living Planet Report 2004* (2004). Online. Available at: www.footprintnetwork.org (accessed 3 March 2011).

Goldman, D. 'The Final Frontier' (29 March 1993). *Adweek*, pp. 26–35.

Goodson, Scott. 'Southern Exposure' (2007) *Adweek*, Vol. 48 (43): p. 17.

Grech, P. (ed.) *Country focus: China* (September 2006a). Online. Available at: www.warc.com (accessed January 2010).

Grech, P. (ed.) *Country Focus: India* (2006b). Online. Available at: www.warc.com (accessed January 2010).

Grech, P. (ed.) *Country Focus: Russia* (2006c). Online. Available at: www.warc.com (accessed January 2010).

GroupM. India's leading advertisers in 2009 by advertising expenditure. (2011) Online. Available at: adbrands.net/in/index.html (accessed 10 June 2011).

GroupM. *This Year, Next Year: Worldwide Media & Marketing Forecasts*, London: GroupM. 2010.

GroupM. Russia's leading advertisers in 2009 by advertising expenditure. (2011) Online. Available at: adbrands.net/ru/index.html (accessed 10 June 2011).

Guardian. 'China overtakes US as world's biggest car market' (8 January 2010). Online.

Available at: www.guardian.co.uk/business/2010/jan/08/china-us-car-sales-overtakes (accessed 3 December 2010).

Gupta, R. 'Rural consumers get close to established world brands' (June 2002). *Advertising Age Global*, Vol. 2 (10): p. 5.

Ha, L. 'Concerns about advertising practices in a developing country: an examination of China's new advertising regulations' (1996). *International Journal of Advertising*, Vol. 15: pp. 91–102.

Hamilton, C. and R. Denniss. *Affluenza – When Too Much is Never Enough*, Crows Nest, Australia: Allen and Unwin. 2005.

Hansen. J. Public lecture: Coal in a carbon-constrained world (17 May 2011). Symposium on the future of Coal, hosted by Victoria University of Wellington, New Zealand.

Hanson, P. *Advertising and Socialism*, London: Macmillan. 1974.

Hertz, N. *Silent Takeover: Global Capitalism and the Death of Democracy*, London: William Heinemann. 2001

Hindustan Times. 'Indian Government turns to Facebook, Twitter' (30 September 2009). Original material sourced by WARC. Online. Available at: www.warc.com/News/PrintNewsItem.asp?NID=25745 (accessed 11 August 2010).

Hindustan Times. 'Young consumers lure big brands in India' (16 November 2010). Original material sourced by WARC. Online. Available at: www.warc.com/new/PrintNewsItem.asp?NID=27506 (accessed 22 November 2010).

Hindustan Unilever Limited (HUL/HLL). Company website (2010). Online. Available at: www.hul.co.in/aboutus/ourhistory/ (accessed 10 October 2010).

Ho, S. and C. Chan. 'Advertising in China-problems and prospects' (1989). *International Journal of Advertising*, Vol. 8: pp. 79–87.

Hooper, B. 'Globalisation and resistance in post-Mao China: the case of foreign consumer products' (December 2000). *Asian Studies*, Vol. 24 (4).

Hunt, T. 'Eric Hobsbawm: a conversation … about Marx, student riots, the new Left and the Millibands' (16 January 2011). *Guardian*. Online. Available at: www.guardian.co.uk/books/2011/jan/16/eric-hobsbawm-tristram-hunt-marx (accessed 21 January 2011).

India TradePoint. Doing Business in India (1995). New Delhi, India. Online. Available at: http://sphere.rdc.puc-rio.br/parceerias/untpdc/incubator/ind/tpdel/doingbus.html (accessed 16 October 2002).

Indiantelevision.com. 'India will be the fourth largest product placement market: study' (2007). Online. Available at http://us.indiantelevision.com/mam/headlines/y2k7/mar/marmam66.php (accessed 12 August 2008).

International Development Bank (IDB) Country summary. Online. Available at: www.census.gov/ipc/www/idb/informationGateway.php (accessed 6 October 2008).

International Journal of Advertising. 'Adspend in the Americas – a tale of 2 regions' (1998). Vol. 17 (3).

International Labour Office Social Security Department. 'Bolsa Familia in Brazil: context, context and impacts' (2009). Online. Available at: www.ilo.org/global/about-the-ilo/press-and-media-centre/insight/WCMS_103947/lang–en/index.htm (accessed January 2011).

International Panel on Climate Change (IPCC). *Climate Change Report* (2007). Online. Available at: www.picc.ch (accessed 21 January 2009).

Jakes, S. and J. Xu. 'From Mao to Maybelline' (Autumn 2005). *Time Style and Design*: p. 16.

James, L. *World Federation of Advertisers Annual Report 2009: WFA global advertising and economic data 2007–2008 and outlook for 2009* (March 2009). Online. Available at: www.warc.com (accessed December 2009).

Jeffrey, R. 'Advertising and English language newspapers: how capitalism supports (certain) cultures and (some) states 1947–96' (1997). *Pacific Affairs*, Vol. 70 (1): pp. 57–85.

Johnstone, H. '"Little emperors" call the shots' (September1996). *Asian Business*, pp. 67–70.

Jones, M. 'China's media boom rewards those willing to endure growing pains' (October 1997). *Advertising Age International*, Vol. 16.

Jones, S. 'World advertising trends 2009'. (2009a) Online. Available at: warc.com (accessed December 2009).

Jones, S. (ed.). 'The Russian advertising market in 2009' (2009b). Online. Available at: www.warc.com (accessed December 2009).

Kelly, C. 'Creating a consumer: advertising and communication' in Kelly, C. and D. Shepherd, D. (editors). *Russian Cultural Studies: an Introduction*, Oxford: Oxford University Press. pp223–46. 1998.

Keys, T. and T.W. Malnight. 'Corporate clout: the influence of the world's largest economic entities' (14 January, 2011) Online. Available at: www.globaltrends.com/features/shapers-and-influencers/66-corporate-clout-the-influence-of-the-worlds-largest-100-economic-entities (accessed 15 March 2011).

Khairullah, H. Z. and Z.Y. Khairullah. 'Dominant cultural values: content analysis of the U.S. and Indian print advertisements' (2002). *Journal of Global Marketing*, Vol. 16 (1–2), pp47–70.

Kilburn, D. 'Chasing Chinese consumers' (27 July 2001). *Campaign*: p. 27.

Kilburn, D. 'Marketing to reach rural India' (13 November 2000). *Marketing Magazine*, Vol. 105 (45): p. 6.

Kishkovsky, S. 'Hammers & symbols' (May-June 2005). *Print*, pp. 96–99.

Klein, N. *No Space, No Choice, No Logo: Taking Aim at the Brand Bullies*, 1st edition (USA), New York: Picador. 2000.

Korten, D. *When Corporations Rule The World*, West Hartford: Kumarian Press and Bernett-Koeler. 1995

Kuznetsova, E. 'Russia's booming drinks market' (March 2008). Online. Available at: www.warc.com (accessed December 2009).

L'Oréal. 'L'Oréal anticipates global "sea change"' (27 August 2010). Original material sourced by WARC. Online. Available at: www.warc.com/News/PrintNewsItem.asp?NID=27162 (accessed 30 August 2010).

Landreth, J. 'China advertising' (14 March 2006). *The Hollywood Reporter*. Online. Available at: www.hollywoodreporter.com/hr/search/article_display.jsp?vnu_content_id=1002157847 (accessed 8 February 2010).

Leme, P. 'Unlocking the 'B' in BRICS: Brazil's growth potential' (4 December 2007) in O'Neill, J. (ed.) *BRICS and Beyond*, Goldman Sachs Global Economics Group. Online. Available at: www.360.gs.com (accessed 16 July 2010).

Lenta. 'Advertising expenditure levels rise in Russia' (13 August 2010). Original material sourced by WARC. Online. Available at: www.warc.com/News/PrintNewsItem.asp?NID=27101 (accessed 13 August 2010).

Levitt. 'The globalization of markets' (1983). *Harvard Business Review* (May-June), pp. 2–11.

Li, F. and N. Shooshtari. 'Multinational corporations' controversial ad campaigns in China – lessons from Nike and Toyota' (2007). *Advertising and Society Review*. Online. Available at: http://muse.jhu.edu/journals/asr/v008/8.1li_shooshtari.html (accessed 8 February 2010).

Livemint. 'Ad-funded mobiles coming to India' (9 June 2010). Original material sourced by

WARC. Online. Available at: www.warc.com/News/PrintNewsItem.asp?NID=25244 (accessed June 2010).

MacFarquhar, R. 'Russia: a smooth political transition' (2007) in O'Neill, J. (ed.) *BRICS and Beyond*, Goldman Sachs Global Economics Group. Online book. Available at: www.360.gs.com: pp. 28–45.

Macfie, R. 'Key to the kingdom' (17 May 2008). *New Zealand Listener*, pp.18–28.

Macfie, R. 'The greening of the monster' (10 July 2010). *New Zealand Listener*, pp. 26–33.

Mad Men. Television series. United States. Created by Matthew Weiner. (19 July 2007).

Madden, N. 'Asia-Pacific ad spend shows signs of slowing' (19 April 2001). Online. Available at: www.adage.com/newcms?newsid=15240 (accessed 5 August, 2002).

Madden, N. 'China's WTO advertising revolution' (December 2001). *Advertising Age Global*, Vol. 2 (4): p. 4.

Madden, N. 'Chinese brands turn to western agencies' (June 2001). *Advertising Age Global*, Vol. 1 (10): p. 21.

Madden, N. 'P&G reigns supreme at China's wild TV upfront' (26 November 2006). *Advertising Age*. Online. Available at: http://adage.com/print?article_id=113428 (accessed 10 February 2011).

Madden, N. 'Pepsi, Coke duke it out in India and China' (October 2000). *Ad Age Global*: p. 6.

Madden, N. 'Real winner in SuperGirl is Mengnui Dairy' (10 October 2005). *Advertising Age Global China*. Online. Available at: http://adage.com/china/article.php?article_id=46903 (accessed August 2006).

Madden, N. 'Target: 380 million Chinese emperors' (12 April 1999). *Advertising Age International*: p. 26

Madid, M. 'Are Latin America's children becoming globalized?' (September 2005). *ESOMAR Conference Paper*. Online. Available at: www.warc.com (accessed December 2009).

Magnier, M. 'Prosperity buys problems' (2007). *Los Angeles Times*, reprinted in *The Dominion Post* (11 April 2007).

Majumder, S. 'India's politicians keep it in the family' (10 June 2009). Online. Available at: http://newsvote.bbc.co.uk/mpapps/pagetools/print/news.bbc.co.uk/2/hi/south_asia/8089734.stm?ad=1(accessed 28 September 2010).

Mandese, J. 'Online ad networks will rule' (February 2009). *Admap Magazine*. Online. Available at: www.warc.com/admap (accessed 2009).

Marketing Charts. 'Chinese consumers take to mobile web' (1 June 2009). Original material sourced by WARC. Online. Available at: www.warc.com/News/PrintNewsItem. asp?NID=25207 (accessed 3 June 2010).

Marur, M. 'Fair trade? Indian advertising has a not-so-hidden message: change your skin colour to get the perfect job or mate' (Winter 2007). *Eye Magazine*: Vol. 66. Online. Available at: www.eyemagazine.co.uk/issue.php?id=152 (accessed 30 September 2010).

Mattelart, A. *Advertising International: The Privatization of Public Space*, London: Routledge. 1991.

Mazzarella, W. *Shovelling Smoke? Advertising and globalization in contemporary India*, New Delhi: Oxford University Press. 2003.

McDonald, J. 'China tops Japan as world's 2nd biggest economy' (17 August 2010). Online. Available at: http://articles.sfgate.com/2010–08–17/business/22222406 (accessed 30 January 2011).

McKinsey. 'China's shoppers among 'most complex' (13 October 2010). Original material sourced by WARC. Online. Available at: www.warc.com/News/PrintNewsItem. asp?NID=27363 (accessed 14 October 2010).

McMann, B. *The Throes of Democracy: Brazil Since 1989*, Halifax: Fernwood Publishing; London: Zed Books. 2008.

Media Asia. 'Chinese adspend growth set to slow' (27 January 2010). Original material sourced by WARC. Online. Available at: www.warc.com/News/NID=26238 (accessed 28 January 2010).

Meirelles, H. 'A giant awakens in Brazil' (Jan-Feb 2009) *Foreign Affairs*, Vol. 88 (1).

Millward Brown. 'Digital consumers more loyal to brands' (8 June 2009). Original material sourced by WARC. Online. Available at: www.warc.com/News//PrintNewsItem. asp?NID=25237 (accessed 17 December 2010).

Millward Brown. 'Great Global Brands: the secret of success' (2009). Online. Available at: www.warc.com (accessed 2009).

Monbiot, G. 'Selling Ecocide' (14 August 2008, originally published 14 August 2007). *The Guardian*. Online. Available at: www.monbiot.com/2007/08/14/selling-ecocide/ (accessed 2009).

Monbiot, G. 'Toxic Assets' (22 September 2009). *The Guardian*. Online. Available at: www.monbiot.com/2009/09/22/toxic-assets (accessed September 2009).

Monye, S. O. (ed.) *The Handbook of International Marketing Communications*, Oxford: Blackwell. 2000.

Morris, J. (2005) 'The empire strikes back: projections of national identity in contemporary Russian advertising' (October 2005 October). *The Russian Review*: Vol. 64, pp. 642–60.

Moscow Times. 'Middle class is back and growing' (27 September 2000). Online. Available at: www.russiatoday.com/mostimesphp3?id=203160 (accessed 2000).

Moses, E. *The $100 billion Allowance: Accessing the Global Teen Market*, New York: John Wiley and Sons. 2000.

Mueller, B. *International Advertising: Communicating Across Cultures*, Belmont, California: Wadsworth. 1996.

Multinational Monitor. Essential Information (May/June 2005). Published by Essential Information.

Munshi, S. 'Wife/mother/daughter-in-law: multiple avatars of homemaker in 1990s Indian advertising' (1998). *Media, Culture and Society*, Vol. 20: pp 573–91.

National Intelligence Council. *The Environmental Outlook in Russia: National Intelligence Estimate* (January 1999). Online. Available at: www.dni.gov/nic/special_russianoutlook.html (accessed 8 February 2011).

National Law Center for Inter-American Free Trade. 'It's the law' (December 2003). *Latin Trade*, Vol. 11 (12).

Nelson, M. and H-J Paek. 'Predicting cross-cultural differences in sexual advertising content in a traditional women's magazine' (2005). *Sex Roles*: Vol. 53 (5–6), pp. 371–83.

Nelson, M. and H-J Paek. 'A content analysis of advertising in a global magazine across seven countries (2007). *International Marketing Review*, Vol. 24 (1): pp.64–86.

Nelson, M. and H-J Paek. 'Nudity of female and male models in primetime TV advertising across seven countries' (2008). *International Journal of Advertising*: Vol. 27 (5). Online. Available at: www.warc.com (accessed December 2009).

New Internationalist. *The World Guide*, 11th edition, Oxford: 2007.

New York Times. 'P&G adapts approach in emerging markets' (16 December 2009).

Original material sourced by WARC. Online. Available at: www.warc.com/News/ PrintNewsItem.asp?NID=26080 (accessed 28 January 2010).

Newsweek. 'China receiving unique approach from brands' (12 October 2010). Original material sourced by WARC. Online. Available at: www.warc.com/News/PrintNews-Item.asp?NID=27356 (accessed 13 October 2010).

Ni, C. 'Careful courting as west woos virgin market' (21–28 Feb 2005). *Los Angeles Times/ Washington Post* reprinted in *Otago Daily Times*: p. 15.

Nielsen Company. 'Chinese, Indian shoppers keep spending' (25 May 2009). Original material sourced by WARC. Online. Available at: www.warc.com/News/PrintNews-Item.asp?NID=25178 (accessed 26 May 2010).

Nielsen Company. 'Global adspend posts double-digit rise' (12 October 2010). Original material sourced by WARC. Online. Available at: www.warc.com/News/PrintNews-Item.asp?NID=27353 (accessed 13 October 2010).

Nielsen, A.C. '63 global mega brand franchises exist, 51 are available in New Zealand' (2003) Online. Available at: www.acnielsen.co.nz/news.asp?newsID=328 (accessed 18 November 2003).

Nielsen, A.C. 'China Leads the Asia-Pacific advertising market' (3 October 2002). *Emerging Markets Economy*. Online. Available at: Business Source Premier (accessed 15 January 2002).

Nielsen, A.C. 'Who were the real winners of the Beijing Olympics?' (September 2008). Online. Available at: http://cn.en.acnielsen.com/pubs/documents/Olympic_en.Pdf (accessed 10 January 2011).

Nixon, S. *Advertising Cultures*, London: Sage. 2003.

Noble, J., A. Draffen, R. Jones, C. McAsey and L. Pinheiro. *Brazil* (5th edition), Melbourne: Lonely Planet. 2002.

O'Barr, William. 'Advertising in Brazil' (2008) *Advertising and Society Review*, Vol. 9 (2). Online. Available at: http://muse.jhu.edu/journals/advertising_and_society_review/ v009/9.2.o-barr (accessed 17 August 2009).

O'Barr, William. 'Advertising in China' (2007). *Advertising and Society Review*. Online. Available at: http://muse.jhu.edu/journals (accessed 17 September 2009).

O'Barr, William. 'Advertising in India' (2008). *Advertising and Society Review*, Vol. 9 (3). Online. Available at: www.muse.jhu.edu/journals/advertising_and_society_review/ v009.39-barr.html (accessed 7 October, 2008).

O'Flannery, T. Interview with Finlay McDonald (16 October 2010). National Radio New Zealand.

O'Leary, Noreen. 'The rise of the BRIC' (4 February 2008). *Adweek*, Vol. 49 (4): pp. 32–65.

O'Neill, J. 'The World Needs Better Economic BRICs' (2001). Global economics paper: Goldman Sachs. Online. Available at: www.gs.com (accessed 11 October 2010).

O'Neill, J. 'Welcome to the BRICS' (2008). Online video. Available at: https://360.gs. com (accessed 2010).

O'Neill, J. (ed.) (2007) *The Brics and Beyond*, Goldman Sachs Global Economics Group. Online. Available www.360.gs.com (accessed 5 October 2010).

O'Neill, J. and A. Stupnytska. 'The long-term outlook for the BRICs and the N-11 post-crisis' (4 December 2009). Goldman Sachs Global Economics, Commodities and Strategy Research: Global Economics Paper 192 (2010). Online. Available at: https://360. gs.com (accessed 10 October 2010).

OECD Policy Brief. 'Making environment spending count'. (September 2007). Online. Available at: www.oecd.org/dataoecd/1/18/39376495.pdf (accessed 15 January 2011).

OECD. *Purchasing Power Parity* (2011). Online. Available at: www.oecd.org/std/ppp (accessed 24 May 2011).

OgilvyEarth. 'From Greenwash to Great' (2009). Online. Available at: http://ogilvyearth.com/greenwash (accessed 2 June 2010).

Oreskes, N. and E. Conway. *Merchants of Doubt: How a Handful of Scientists Obscured the Truth on Issues from Tobacco Smoke to Global Warming*, Bloomsbury: London. 2010.

Osbourn, A. 'Russia fails to ban drinking in public despite soaring alcoholism' (18 November 2004. *British Medical Journal*, Vol. 1202: p. 329).

Parsons, A. and R. Makwana. 'Sharing in the global economy: an introduction' (2007, August 13). *Global Policy Forum*. Online. Available at: www.globalpolicy.org/globaliz/econ/2007/0813stwr.htm (accessed 3 February 2009).

Pashupati, K. and S. Sengupta. 'Advertising in India: the winds of change' in Frith, K.T. (ed.) *Advertising in Asia: Communication, Culture and Consumption*, Ames: Iowa State University Press: pp155–86. 1996.

Penteado, Claudia. 'Ads central to Brazil presidential race' (30 September 2002). *Advertising Age International*, Vol. 73 (39): p. 6.

Penteado, Claudia. 'Recession fears end' (9 August 1999). *Advertising Age International*: p. 22.

People's Daily and Reuters. 'China's Geely eyes online car sales' (10 December 2010). Original material sourced by WARC. Online. Available at: www.warc.com/News/PrintNewsItem.asp?NID=27619 (accessed 20 December 2010).

People's Daily Online. 'China tightens control of TV advertising'. (2003a, September 25). Online. Available at: www.english.people.daily.com.cn (accessed 19 August 2004).

People's Daily Online. 'Official: China's trade surplus to drop in 2010' (16 November 2010) *Online*. Available at: http://english.peopledaily.com.cn/90001/90778/90862/7201441.ht2010 (accessed 16 January 2011).

PepsiCo Corporate website. (2010) Online. Available www.pepsico.com/PressRelease/PepsiCo-Completes-Acquisition-of-66-of-Wimm-Bill-Dann02032011.html (accessed 13 September 2011).

Perkins, J. *Confessions of an Economic Hit Man*, London: Edbury Press. 2006.

Petrov, A. 'Advertising in Russia: Language and Other Pitfalls' (2000). Centre for Russian and Eurasian Studies. Monterey: Monterey Institute of International Studies.

Pieterse, J-N. 'Global rebalancing: crisis and the east-south turn' (2011). *Development and Change*, Vol. 42 (1): pp. 22–48.

Poddar, T. and E. Yi. 'India's rising growth potential' in O'Neill, J. (ed.) *BRICS and Beyond*, Goldman Sachs Global Economics Group (2007). Online. Available at: www.360.gs.com (accessed 16 July 2010).

Pollay, R. and Gallagher, K. 'Advertising and cultural values: reflections in the distorted mirror' (1990) *International Journal of Advertising*, Vol. 9: pp359–72.

Pollay, R.W. 'Distorted mirror: reflections on the unintended consequences of advertising' (April 1986). *Journal of Marketing*, Vol. 50: pp. 18–36.

Pollay, R.W. 'Measuring the Cultural Values Manifest in Advertising' (1983). *Current Issues & Research in Advertising*, Vol. 6 (1): pp. 71–93.

Pollay, R.W. 'Quality of life in the padded sell: common criticisms of advertising's cultural character and international public policies' (1989). *Current Issues and Research in Advertising*, Vol. 9 (2): pp. 173–250.

Pollay, R.W., D.K. Tse and Z. Wang. 'Advertising, propaganda, and value change in economic development: The new Cultural Revolution in China and attitudes towards advertising' (1990). *Journal of Business Research*, Vol. 20: pp. 83–95.

Powel, C. 'Global agencies gain ground in 2004' (18 April 2005). *Marketing Magazine*, Vol. 110 (14): p. 6.

PQ Media. 'European product placement set for double-digit growth' (24 August 2010). Online. Available at: www.businessandleadership.com/marketing/item/25274-european-product-placement (accessed 29 October 2010).

Prabhaker, P. R., and P. Sauer. 'Global and multinational advertising' in Basil G. Englis (ed.) *Global and Multinational Advertising*, Hillsdale: Lawrence Erlbaum Associates: pp. 159–70. 1994

Precourt, G. 'The global media index: a map for social media trends' (October 2009). Online. Available at: www.warc.com (accessed December 2009).

Precourt, G. 'Research intervenes in developing markets including Russia and China' (September 2008). ESOMAR Conference Paper. Online. Available at: www.warc.com (accessed January 2010).

Prendergast, G., and Y.Z. Shi 'Client perceptions of advertising and advertising agencies: a China study' (2001). *Journal of Marketing Communications*, Vol. 7: pp. 47–63.

Prendergast, M. *For God, Country and Coca Cola*, London: Weidenfeld and Nicholson. 1993.

PRN Newswire. 'Pepsi to invest $1 billion in Russia' (7 July 2009). Original material sourced by WARC. Online. Available at: www.warc.com/News/PrintNewsItem. asp?NID=25366 (accessed 10 August 2010).

Procter & Gamble corporate website. Available at: www.procterandgamble.ru/english_ info/ (accessed 6 Sept 2010).

Proctor & Gamble. 'Social media boosts Indian sales for P&G' (3 June 2009). P&G presentation at Conversational Marketing Summit, Washington. Online. Available at: www.warc.com/News/PrintNewsItem.asp?NID=25219 (accessed 14 February 2011).

Propser China. 'Chinese consumers attached to the web' (17 September 2010). Original material sourced by WARC. Online. Available at: www.warc.com/News/PrintNews-Item.asp?NID=27255 (accessed 3 November 2010).

Purushothaman, R. and D. Wilson. 'Dreaming with the Brics: the path to 2050' (October 2003). *Global Economics Paper No. 99*. Goldman Sachs. Online. Available at: www. gs.com (accessed 6 January 2011).

Qiao, H. 'Will China grow old before getting rich?' (14 February 2006) in O'Neill, J. (ed.) *BRICS and Beyond*, Goldman Sachs Global Economics Group. 2007. Online. Available at: www.360.gs.com (accessed 16 July 2010).

Ramzy, A. 'Coke's recession boomlet' (21 September 2009). *Time Magazine*, pp. 37–39.

Raval, A. 'Bollywood: revolutionising product placement' (29 September 2010). Online. Available at: http://blogs.ft.com/beyond-brics/2010/09/29/bollywood-in-film-branding/# (accessed 27 January, 2011).

Ravallion, M. 'The Developing World's Bulging (but Vulnerable) "Middle Class"' (January 2009). *Policy Research Working Paper 4816*. The World Bank, Development Research Group. Online. Available at: http://econ.worldbank.org (accessed 24 November 2010).

Rein, S. 'Beijing Olympic Sponsorship's A Waste' (24 April 2008). *Forbes*. Online. Available at: www.forbes.com/2008/04/23/china-olympics-sponsors-oped-cx_sre_0424olympics. html (accessed 16 March 2011).

Renton, A. 'India's hidden climate change catastrophe' (2 January 2011). *The Independent*. Online. Available at: www.independent.co.uk/environment/climate-change/indias-hidden-climate-change-catastrophe-2173995.html (accessed 30 January 2011).

Repiev, A. 'A Glimpse of Advertising in Russia' (June1997). *Marketing Russia*.

Rial, C. 'Racial and ethnic stereotypes in Brazilian advertising' (2001). *Anthropologia em Primeira Mao*, Vol. 44: pp. 1–23.

Rice, M. D., and Z. Lu. 'A content analysis of Chinese magazine advertisements' (1988). *Journal of Advertising*, Vol.17 (4): pp. 43–48.

Ritzer, G. *The McDonaldization of Society*, (revised edition), Thousand Oaks, California: Pine Forge. 1996.

Roberts, D. 'Winding up for the big pitch' (23 October1995). *Business Week*: p.52

Rosenwald, P. 'Pointed advice for direct marketers in Brazil (5 October 1998). *Advertising Age International*, p. 6. Online. Available at: ephost@epnet.com (accessed 11 December 2009).

RT (Russian Television). *Dying in Abundance* (broadcast 4 March 2011).

Sabonis-Chafee, T. (1999) 'Communism as Kitsch', in Barker, A.M. (ed.), Consuming Russia, Durham, NC: Duke University Press.

Sachdeva, S. 'Trends in advertising in the Indian corporate sector' (1984). Institute for Studies in Industrial Development. New Delhi. Online. Available at: isid.org.in/pdf/sudha.pdf (accessed 2004).

Salles, J. 'How to turn Latin American trends into market opportunities' (2006). Esomar Latin American Conference, October 2006. Online. Available at: www.warc.com (accessed December 2009).

Savage, Mike. 'Region all set to boost adspend in 2006' (4 November 2005). *Media: Asia's Media and Marketing Newspaper*: p. 5.

Savchenko, L. 'Advertising Market' (1999). Industry Sector Analysis Series. Moscow: US and Foreign Commercial Service and US Department of State.

Savva, S. 'Rising beer consumption in Russia' (2001) *Addiction*, Vol. 96: p. 661.

Saywell, T. 'Curious in China' (1998). *Far Eastern Economic Review*, Vol. 161: pp. 74–76.

Schell, O. *To Get Rich is Glorious: China in the Eighties*, New York: Pantheon Books. 1984.

Schlevogt, K.A. 'The branding revolution in China' (2000). *China Business Review*, Vol. 27 (3): pp. 52–58.

Schmeichel, N., M. Barbarena and B. Corrales. 'Latin American profile, demographics and socio-economic date – an update'. ESOMAR Latin American Conference Paper. October 2006. Online. Available at: www.warc.com (accessed December 2009).

Seghal, R. 'India clamps down on vice, piracy' (25 September 2000c). *Multinational News International*, Vol. 21 (39): p. 49.

Seghal, R. 'India's renaissance' (July/August 2000b). *Multinational News International*, Vol. 6 (7): p. 10.

Seghal, R. 'Kiss and Sell: Don't Try it in India' (May 2001). *Multichannel News International*, Vol. 8 (10): p. 8.

Seghal, R. 'Sunny skies ahead for Indian channels' (April 2000a). *Multinational News International*, Vol. 6 (4): p.10.

Sethi, A. 'Shaadi.com: a match made in cyberspace' (7 June 2008). Online. Available at: www.telegraph.co.uk/education/3356403/Shaadi.com-a-match-made-in-cyberspace.html (accessed 12 January 2011).

Shah, G. 'A new chapter in Indian advertising with ad novellas' (2008). *The Wall Street Journal*. Online. Available at: www.livemint.com/2008/0616222244/A-new-chapter-opens-in-india.html (accessed 15 July 2008).

Sharma, A. 'Anti-aging cream goes young' (2 June 2008). *The Economic Times*. Online. Available at: http://economictimes.indiatimes.com/news/News_By_Industry/Cons_Products/Anti-aging_cream_goes_young/articlesshow/3091429.cms.

Sharma, G. 'India says is now third highest carbon emitter' (2010). *Reuters*. Online. Available at: www.reuters.com/article/2010/10/04/us-india-climate-idUSTRE6932PE20101004 (accessed 10 February 2011).

Sharma, S. K. Sinha, and J. Ling. 'New routes from old roots, comparing Indian and Chinese middle class' (Summer 2008). *Market Leader*, p. 41. Online. Available at: www.warc.com (accessed December 2009).

Shemesh, A. 'New beer law sends ripples through sports beer industries' (12 October 2004). *The Russia Journal*, Issue 571.

Simms, A. 'We've gone into the ecological red' (22 August 2010). *The Guardian*. Online. Available at: (www.footprintnetwork.org/en/index.php/GFN/page/earth_overshoot_day/ (accessed November 20).

Sina/ Reuters. 'Consumer confidence levels mixed in China' (16 August 2010). Original material sourced by WARC. Online. Available at: www.warc.com/News/PrintNewsItem.asp?NID=27106 (accessed 10 September 2010).

Sinclair, J. 'Globalization and the advertising industry in China' (2009). *Chinese Journal of Communication*, Vol. 1 (1): pp.77–90.

Singha, A. and D. Suvi. 'Ad industry to grow 61%' (10 December 2007). *Business Standard*.

Sinha, D. 'Building brands in a youthful country' (April 2009). ESOMAR Asia Pacific (Beijing) Conference paper. Online. Available at: www.warc.com (accessed 4 August 2009).

Sklair, L. *Globalisation, capitalism and its alternatives* (third edition). Oxford: Oxford University Press. 2002.

Smita, G. 'Modern messages told the traditional Indian way' (12 December 2002). Online. Available at: www.brandrepublic.com/news/154228/ANALYSIS-Advertising---Modern-messages-told-traditional-Indianway-Female-advertising-not-the-world-over-reports-GuptaSmita (accessed 14 September 2011).

Srinivas, P. 'Advertising services: India' (1999). New Delhi: U.S. & Foreign Commercial Service and U.S. Department of State. Online. Available at: www.tradeport.org/ts/countries/isa/isar0012.html (accessed 16 October 2002).

St-Maurice, I., C. Süssmuth-Dyckerhoff and H. Tsai. 'What's new with the Chinese consumer?' (2008). *McKinsey Quarterly Online*. Available at: www.mckinseyquarterley.com/Whats_new_with_the_Chinese_consumer_2218 (accessed 29 October 2008).

State Administration of Foreign Exchange of the People's Republic of China. *China's current account balance 1982–2011*. Online. Available at: www.chinability.com/CurrentAccount.htm (accessed 11 September 2011).

Stengel, R. 'For American consumers, a responsibility revolution' (10 September 2009). *Time Magazine*.

Stern, N. 'The Economics of Climate Change'. Cambridge: Cambridge University Press. 2006.

Stern, N. 'Managing climate change and promoting development: risks, scale and values' (8 September 2010). Sir Douglas Robb Lectures (Lecture 1), The University of Auckland.

Stern, N. 'U.S. Trade Boycott Could Result If It Doesn't Address Climate Change And Reduce Carbon Emissions' (19 November 2010). *The Huffington Post*. Online. Available at: www.huffingtonpost.com/2010/11/19/nicholas-stern-us-faces-t_n_786285.html (accessed 5 May 2011).

Stern, N. *Stern Review on the Economics of Climate Change*. Online. Available at: www.hm-treasury.gov.uk/independent_reviews/stern_review_economics_climate_change/sternreview_index.cfm (accessed November 2006).

Stewart, S. and N. Campbell, 'Advertising in China: a preliminary study' (1986). *International Journal of Advertising*, Vol. 5: pp. 317–23.

Stiglitz, J. E. 'Wall Street's toxic message' (17 July 2009) *Global Policy Forum*. Online. Available at: www.globalpolicy.org/social-and-economic-policy/the-world-economic-crisis/47930.htm (accessed 9 May 2011).

Stiglitz, J. E. *Globalization and its Discontents*, London: Penguin. 2002.

Stiglitz, J. E. *Making Globalization Work*, London: Penguin. 2006.

Swanson, L. 'Advertising in China: viability and structure' (1990). *European Journal of Advertising*, Vol. 24 (10): pp. 19–31.

Swanson, L. A. 'People's advertising in China: a longitudinal content analysis of the People's Daily since 1949' (1996). *International Journal of Advertising*, Vol. 15: pp. 222–49.

Synovate. 'Consumer habits converging in China' (6 September 2010). Original material sourced by WARC. Online. Available at: www.warc.com/News/PrintNewsItem. asp?NID=27585 (accessed 6 December 2010).

Synovate. 'Word of mouth most trusted medium in India' (7 September 2010). Original material sourced by WARC. Online. Available at: www.warc.com/News/PrintNews-Item.asp?NID=27207 (accessed 10 September 2010).

Synovate/Reuters. 'TV, radio, key for automakers in China' (20 October 2010). Original material sourced by WARC. Online. Available at: www.warc.com/News/PrintNews-Item.asp?NID=27389 (accessed 21 October 2010).

Tai, S. H. 'Advertising in Asia: localise or regionalise?' (1997). *International Journal of Advertising*, Vol. 16: pp. 48–61.

Tam Media Research. 'Adspend evades Indian broadcast giant' (1 September 2009). Original material sourced by WARC. Online. Available at: www.warc.com/News/PrintNewsItem.asp?NID=25612 (accessed 17 August 2010).

Tantsura, G. 'IMI: Developments in Advertising in Russia' (18 April 1995). St Petersburg. Published by US and Foreign and Commerical Service.

Taylor, P. (ed.). 'Economic Report', (September 2006). World Advertising Research Center (WARC). Online. Available at: ww.warc.com (accessed 16 December 2009).

Telecom Yatra. 'Mobile advertising set to grow in India' (February 2010). Original material sourced by WARC. Online. Available at: www.warc.com/News/PrintNewsItem. asp?NID=26265 (accessed 18 March 2010).

Televisionpoint. 'Indian newspapers receive further support' (18 July 2009). Original material sourced by WARC. Online. Available at: www.warc.com/News/PrintNews-Item.asp?NID=25375 (accessed 11 August 2010).

Terzi, A. 'BRIC beauty brands looking good' (2009). Online. Available at: www.brand-channel.com/print_page.asp?ar_id=467&section=main. (accessed 13 January 2011).

Tharpe, Marye. *Advertising agencies in Brazil* (no date). Compiled by Marye Tharpe. Online. Available at: www.bbbbgsu.edu/departments/tcom/faculty/ha/brazil (accessed 31 July 2009).

Tharpe, Marye. *Advertising Agencies in China* (no date). Compiled by Marye Tharpe. Online. Available at: www.ou.edu/class/jmc3333/chinaag.htm (accessed 13 May 2011).

Tharpe, Marye. *Advertising Agencies in India* (no date). Compiled by Marye Tharpe. Online. Available at: www.ou.edu/class/jmc3333/india.htm (accessed 13 May 2011).

Tharpe, Marye. *Advertising Agencies in Russia* (no date). Compiled by Marye Tharpe. Online. Available at: www.bgsu.edu/departments/tcom/faculty/ha/russia.htm (accessed 13 May 2011).

The Coca-Cola Company (2011) cited on www.adbrands.net/us/cocacola_us.htm, (accessed 16 January 2011).

The Hindu Business Line (internet edition). 'Internet a big contender for ad space' (18 March 2009). Online. Available at: www. Blonnet.com/2008/03/19/stories/2008031951760500. htm (accessed 28 September 2009).

The Hindu Business Line (internet edition). 'Print media outpaces TV in advertising: Adex study' (5 January 2005). Hindu Group of Publications. Online. Available at: www.thehindubusinessline.com (accessed 12 December 2005).

The Times. 'Fire recall dents Toyota's Chinese plans' (25 August 2009). Original material sourced by WARC. Online. Available at: www.warc.com/News/PrintNewsItem. asp?NID=25579 (accessed 17 August 2010).

The United States–China Business Council. 'Understanding the US–China, Balance of Trade' (1998). Washington DC.

The Worldwatch Institute. *The State of the World 2004: Special Focus the Consumer Society*, New York: W.W. Norton and Company. 2004.

Thomas, A. *Transnational Media and Contoured Markets*, Sage: New Delhi. 2006.

Tickle, L. 'Recycling electrical waste can be made safer, researchers say. Dealing with our electronic waste is hazardous – but a new course hopes to make it safer for the 'dismantlers"' (12 October 2010). *The Guardian*. Online. Available at: www.guardian.co. uk (accessed 16 January 2011).

Timmons, H. 'In India, magazines that translate well' (2008). *New York Times*. Online. Available at: www.nytimes.com/2008/07/14/business/media/14mag.html (accessed 22 October 2008).

Tobacco Free Center. 'Tobacco Industry Profile: Russia' (2010). Online. Available at: www.tobaccofreecenter.org/files/pdfs/en/IW_facts_countries_Russia.pdf (accessed December 2010).

Tobacco Free Center. 'Women and Tobacco: Essential Facts' (April, 2010). http://tobac-cofreecenter.org (accessed 11 January 2011).

Tungate, M. '*Adland: A Global History of Advertising*', London: Kogan Page Ltd. 2007.

United Nations Development Programme. Human Development Report Brazil: Country profile of human development indicators (2011a). Online. Available at: http://hdrstats. undp.org/en/countries/profiles/BRA.html (accessed 21 March 2011).

United Nations Development Programme. Human Development Report China: Country Profile of Human Development indicators (2011d). Online. Available at: http://hdrstats. undp.org/en/countries/profiles/CHN.html (accessed 21 March 2011).

United Nations Development Programme. Human Development Report India: Country Profile of Human Development indicators (2011c). Online. Available at: http://hdrstats. undp.org/en/countries/profiles/IND.html (accessed 21 March 2011).

United Nations Development Programme. Human Development Report Russia: Country Profile of Human Development indicators (2011b). Online. Available at: http://hdrstats. undp.org/en/countries/profiles/RUS.html (accessed 21 March 2011).

United Nations Environmental Programme. 'UNEP international expert meeting: advertising and sustainable consumption, Paris' (January 1999). United Nations Environmental Programme: Division of Technology, Industry and Economics.

United Nations Statistics Division. Environmental Statistics. Country snapshot: Brazil (2008a). Online. Available at: http://unstats.un.org/unsd/environment/default.htm (accessed 8 October 2008).

United Nations Statistics Division. Environmental Statistics. Country snapshot: Russia

(2008b). Online. Available at: http://unstats.un.org/unsd/environment/default.htm (accessed 8 October 2008).

United Nations Statistics Division. Environmental Statistics. Country snapshot: India (2008c). Online. Available at: http://unstats.un.org/unsd/environment/default.htm (accessed 8 October 2008).

United Nations Statistics Division. Environmental Statistics. Country snapshot: China (2008d). Online. Available http://unstats.un.org/unsd/environment/default.htm (accessed 8 October 2008).

United States Bureau of the Census. International Database: Brazil. (2011a). Online. Available at www.census.gov/ipc/www/idb/country.php (accessed 21 March 2011).

United States Bureau of the Census. International Database: China. (2011d). Online. Available at www.census.gov/ipc/www/idb/country.php (accessed 21 March 2011).

United States Bureau of the Census. International Database: India (2011c). Online. Available at www.census.gov/ipc/www/idb/country.php (accessed 21 March 2011).

United States Bureau of the Census. International Database: Russia (2011b). Online. Available at www.census.gov/ipc/www/idb/country.php (accessed 21 March 2011).

United States Commercial Service. *India Country Commercial Guide 2008*.

United States Information Administration (EIA). (2010). Online. Available at: www.eia.doe.gov/countries/ (accessed 5 May 2011).

United States Library of Congress. *Brazil: The environment* (2011a). Online. Available at http://countrystudies.us/brazil/25.htm (accessed 6 February 2011).

United States Library of Congress. *Russia: The environment* (2011b). Online. Available at http://countrystudies.us/russia/25.htm (accessed 6 February 2011).

Vascotto, C. 'Femininity in the 21st century' (September 2004). *Admap Magazine*, Vol. 453.

Venkateswaran, S. & J. Philip. 'Nokia loses its India plot, market share tanks 20%' (29 September 2010). *Economic Times India*. Online. Available at: http://economictimes.indiatimes.com (accessed 26 January 2011).

Vertinsky, I., W. Zhang and D. Zhou. 'Advertising trends in urban China' (2002) *Journal of Advertising Research*, Vol. 42 (3).

Vidal, J. and D. Adam. 'China overtakes US as world 's biggest CO2 emitter'. *The Guardian*. Online. Available at: www.guardian.co.uk/environment/2007/jun/19/china.usnews/print (accessed 25 November 2010).

Vilanilam, J. (1989) 'Television advertising and the Indian poor', *Media, Culture and Society*, 11(4): 485–97.

Wal-Mart. 'Brands must adapt to the "new normal"' (17 August 2009). Original material sourced by WARC. Online. Available at: www.warc.com/News/PrintNewsItem.asp?NID=25543 (accessed 18 August 2009).

Wall Street Journal. 'E-commerce sales to surge in China' (21 October 2010) Original material sourced by WARC. Online. Available at: www.warc.com/News/PrintNewsItem.asp?NID=27395 (accessed 22 October 2010).

Wall Street Journal. 'Most advertising expenditure is at provincial and city levels according to Nielsen Media Research' (22–24 August 2008). Online. Available at: wsj.com (accessed 24 August 2008).

Wall Street Journal. 'Product placement growing in China' (17 June 2009. Original material sourced by WARC. Online. Available at: www.warc.com/News/PrintNewsItem.asp?NID=25281 (accessed 18 June 2009).

Wall Street Journal/Time Magazine. 'Wal-Mart to open Indian arm' (29 May 2009). Original material sourced by WARC. Online. Available at: www.warc.com/News/PrintNewsItem.asp?NID= 25201 (accessed 3 June 2009).

Wallace, S.) 'The last of the Amazon' (January 2007). *National Geographic*: pp. 40–71.

Walsh, B. 'Banking on Carbon' (3 December 2010). *Time Magazine* Vol. 40. Online. Available at: www.time.com.

Wang, Jian. *Foreign Advertising in China: Becoming Global, Becoming Local*, Ames: Iowa State University Press. 2000.

Wang, Jing. *Brand New China*, Boston: MIT Press. 2008.

Watts, J. 'China unveils climate change plan' (4 June 2007). *The Guardian*. Online. Available at: www.guardian.co.uk/world/2007/jun/04/china.jonathanwatts (accessed 8 August 2008).

Weber, I. G. 'Challenges facing China's television industry in the age of spiritual civilisation: an industry analysis' (2000). *International Journal of Advertising*, Vol. 19 (2): pp. 259–81. Online. Available at: www.warc.com (accessed December 2009).

Weisert, D. 'Coca Cola in China: quenching the thirst of a billion' (2001). *China Business Review*, Vol. 28 (4): pp. 52–56.

Wells, L. G. 'The Professional Advertising Associations in Russia' (1996). *International Journal of Advertising*, Vol. 15 (2): pp.103–115.

Wentz, L. 'Center stage: a band of passionate, young creatives raises the Latin Nation to the status of global ad superpower' (28 September 1998). *Advertising Age*.

Wentz, L. 'Is Paris Hilton too sexy for Brazil? Self regulatory body investigates her risqué launch campaign for Devassa's "Very Blonde beer"' (25 February 2010). *Advertising Age*. Online. Available at: http://adage.com/print/142291.

Wicken, G. 'Marketing in Russia' (June 1996). *Admap Magazine*. Online. Available at: www.warc.com/admap (accessed December 2009).

Wicken, G.; P. Carter and R. Lobl. 'Building in the BRICS – market understanding and strategic development for international brands' (September 2006). Global Diversity Conference, ESOMAR. Online. Available at: www.warc.com (accessed December 2009).

Wiggins, J. 'Multinationals eat into the Russian market' (18 June 2008). *Financial Times*.

Wilson, D. and R. Dragusanu. 'The expanding middle: the exploding world middle class and falling global inequality' (7 July 2008). *Global Economics Paper No. 170*. Online. Available at: https://360.gs.com (accessed 6 October 2010).

Women and Tobacco: Essential Facts. (April 2010). Online. Available at: http://tobaccofreecenter.org (accessed 11 January 2011).

World Advertising Research Council. 'On the other hand: online advertising' (3 July 2009). Online. Available at: www.warc.com/News/PrintNewsItem.asp?NID=25357 (accessed 18 August 2010).

World Advertising Trends 2001. *International Journal of Advertising* (2002), Vol. 21 (1).

World Advertising Trends. 'Global adspend trends' (2002). *International Journal of Advertising*, Vol. 21: pp. 283–88.

World Association of Newspapers. 'World Press Trends: Advertising Rebounds, Circulation Down Slightly' (2004). Online. Available at: www.wan-press.org/article4473.html (accessed 11 December 2010).

World Association of Newspapers. (2005). Online. Available at: www.wan-press.org/article2825.html (accessed 18 November 2008).

World Association of Newspapers (WAN-IFRA). *World Press Trends 2010* (2010) Darmstadt and Paris.

World Bank. *Country Indicators: China at a glance* (7 September 2005). Online. Available at: www.worldbank.org (accessed December 2005).

World Bank. *Country Indicators: Russia* (2008). Online. Available at: www.worldbank. org (accessed 29 January 2010).

World Bank. *Country Indicators: Russia* (2010). Online. Available at: www.worldbank. org (accessed 29 August 2010).

World Gazetteer. (2010). Online. Available at: www.world-gazetteer.com (accessed 5 December 2010).

World Magazine Trends: India 2001/2002. (2002). Online. Available at: www.magazine-world.org/members (accessed 2002).

Worldwatch Institute. *The State of the World 2004*, London and New York: W.W. Norton and Company. 2004.

Worldwatch Institute. *The State of the World Special Focus India and China: Report on Progress towards a Sustainable Society* (11th edition), London and New York: W.W. Norton and Company. 2007.

Xu, Y. B. '*Marketing to China, One Billion New Customers*, Chicago: NTC United Nations Development Program (UNDP), (20). 1990.

Yang, A. 'China's contribution to solving global climate challenges' (14 April 2010). Public Lecture, Victoria University Wellington New Zealand.

Yin, J. 'International strategies in China: a worldwide survey of foreign advertisers' (November 1999). *Journal of Advertising Research*, Vol. 9 (6): p25.

Young, S. (ed.). *Country Focus: Brazil* (2006). Online. Available www.warc.com (accessed January 2010).

Zaitseva, O. 'An analysis of FMCG advertising effectiveness in Russia' (August 2008). Mediacom. Online. Available at: www.warc.com (accessed December 2009).

Zenith Optimedia. 'India: World Magazine Trends 2001/2002' (no date). Online. Available at: www.magazine.org.tw/events/school/report/wmt/IndiaWMT01.pdf: pp. 90–91.

ZenithOptimedia. 'Asia key global ad growth driver; internet spends skyrocket' (5 December 2005). Online. Available at: www.indiantelevision.com/mam/headlines/y2k5/decmam15.htm (accessed 26 September 2009).

Zhang, Y. 'The shadow over rural China' (10 February 2011). Online. Available at: www.chinadialogue.net, article number 4098 (accessed 15 February 2011).

Zuckerman, L. 'Foreigners see a spending boom: courting China's wealthy consumers' (1992). *International Herald*.

Index

Page references in *italics* denote photographs or illustrations.